Economics as a Political Muse

The International Library of Environmental, Agricultural and Food Ethics

VOLUME 2

ECONOMICS AS A POLITICAL MUSE

Philosophical Reflections on the Relevance of Economics for Ecological Policy

by

Marian Deblonde

KVLV, Leuven, Belgium

KLUWER ACADEMIC PUBLISHERS

DORDRECHT / BOSTON / LONDON

A C.I.P. Catalogue record for this book is available from the Library of Congress.

ISBN 1-4020-0165-7

Published by Kluwer Academic Publishers,
P.O. Box 17, 3300 AA Dordrecht, The Netherlands.

Sold and distributed in North, Central and South America
by Kluwer Academic Publishers,
101 Philip Drive, Norwell, MA 02061, U.S.A.

In all other countries, sold and distributed
by Kluwer Academic Publishers,
P.O. Box 322, 3300 AH Dordrecht, The Netherlands.

Printed on acid-free paper

Printed in the Netherlands.

TABLE OF CONTENTS

CHAPTER 1

ECONOMICS AND ECOLOGICAL POLICY

1 ECONOMICS AND THE PROBLEM OF SUSTAINABILITY

In a certain respect, industrial economies are performing very well nowadays. Economic growth is in many Western countries about 3 %. Despite this (monetary) success story, the ecological performance of our economies is worrisome. Pezzey recapitulated the general ecological (and social) tendencies of ongoing industrialisation as follows:

> a) rapid depletion of renewable natural resources (e.g. forests, fish, land and sea mammals);
>
> b) rapid depletion of known reserves of non-renewable energy and minerals, although new discoveries and new extraction techniques have *so far* avoided any decline in availability;
>
> c) rapid depletion of non-renewable stocks of genetic diversity (see Wilson 1988) and soil;
>
> d) severe problems of local, transient pollution in industrialising countries;
>
> e) steadily growing problems of cumulative pollution, both regional and global, principally acid rain, ozone depletion, and the
>
> f) accumulation of greenhouse gases such as CO_2 which are likely to cause global warming (Cline 1991);
>
> g) wide, and recently growing, inequalities between rich and poor nations (UNDP 1992); and greatly increased rates of change in most areas of life [...] (Pezzey 1992, 330-331).

A growing concern about these ecological tendencies found expression in the concept "sustainability". The concept came into existence in the eighties. It cropped up for the first time in the document *World Conservation Strategy; Living Resource Conservation for Sustainable Development* that was published by a group of private environmental organisations, the International Union for Conservation of Nature and Natural Resources (Nelissen *et al.* 1997, 261-263). It got great political power of expression on a national and global level since its incorporation in the Brundtland report *Our Common Future* (1987). In this report the concept "sustainable development" is defined as development that

> meets the needs of the present without compromising the ability of future generations to meet their own needs.

Since its introduction in the Brundtland report, many discussions have taken place concerning the precise meaning of sustainable development. In the report itself development is understood as a linear process of economic growth.

> We see [...] the possibility for a new era of economic growth, one that must be based on policies that sustain and expand the environmental resource base. And we believe such growth to be absolutely essential to relieve the great poverty that is deepening in much of the developing world (WCED 1987, 1).

This interpretation dominates prevailing discourse. Critics have labelled this interpretation as an illustration that the Western world succeeded once again in presenting its cultural paradigm as a model for the whole world (Peeters 1997, 53). In this book, I start from an interpretation of sustainability that is more abstract than the Brundtland interpretation. I interpret sustainability as a "guiding idea" reflecting our striving for intergenerational justice in the way we go about with the ecological dimensions of earthly life. The concept "guiding idea" refers to an ideal that guides our political actions, but that remains without concrete, static content. Its ever provisional, concrete meaning takes shape in historical, political processes. The concept of intergenerational justice refers to our responsibility with regard to future generations. We are responsible for the ecological impacts of our present economic activities on the lives of future generations. We should make sure that these ecological impacts are compatible with the idea of intergenerational justice[1].

Sustainability as responsibility towards future generations presumes that we are able to manage the ecological performance of our economies. This interpretation of sustainability as "responsibility presupposing manageability" offers those who prefer to forget about sustainability as soon as possible an easy shot. They can argue that if the ecological performance of our economies shows to be unmanageable, there is no further reason to feel responsible about it. I consider this as too easy a way of reasoning. Present-day ecological problems are no natural problems, as are (some) earthquakes or impacts of meteorites. Present-day ecological problems are caused by humans. This human origin suffices for justifying human responsibility. And if we experience the ecological performance of our economies as unmanageable, our first task as responsible humans then consists of trying to make it manageable again.

The list of general ecological tendencies mentioned above does not show much evidence of the ecological manageability of our economies. On the contrary, the tension between these general tendencies and the idea of sustainability is growing, despite increasing political and technological efforts to avert these tendencies. This latter conclusion gets reaffirmed again and again. Consider, for instance, the results of the Earth Summit in Rio (1992) and of the Kyoto Summit (1997)

---

[1] This more abstract interpretation resembles the concept "sustainable future" proposed by the Dutch Committee for Long-Term Environmental Policy in its publication The environment. Towards a Sustainable Future. Consider the following quotation: ' [...] a sustainable future is a basic principle; a guiding idea concerning a desirable future; a notion to describe the will of existing people to take care for the future of new generations. The concept of sustainable future has ethic aspects; it emphasizes the need for responsibility of the present generation for the world of future generations' (DCLTEP 1994).

(www.oneworld.org/guides/kyoto/front.html). In Rio, rich industrial countries agreed in principle to stabilise emissions of greenhouse gases at 1990 levels by the year 2010. This agreement – though insufficient according to the best scientific understanding – was, however, non-binding. In the period between the Earth Summit and the Kyoto Summit the level of greenhouse gas emissions has actually risen in most of the rich nations. In Kyoto, a division emerged between the US and the EU. The US stated that it would be more effective for rich nations to invest in new technology in developing countries in order to cut overall global emission. The Europeans accused the US of trying to wriggle out of its responsibility to put its own house in order. Finally, the North has committed itself to *some real* reductions. If we compare this commitment to the results mentioned in the Environmental Balance Sheet 1998 of the Netherlands' National Institute of Public Health and the Environment, possible hope soon gets lost (www.milieubalans.rivm.nl/inl_samen/sheet.html).

> Growth in production and consumption has led to higher energy use, greater mobility and more waste.[...] CO_2 emissions increased by about 2% in 1997. [...] The reduction targets for greenhouse gas emissions, acidification and eutrophication will not be met even after implementation of the measures contained in the National Environmental Policy Plan 3 (NEPP3). These measures cannot fully compensate for the increasing environmental burden of the growing economy. [...]

This conclusion, namely that we turn out not to be able to manage the ecological performance of our economies so far, burdens economic science with a special task. Economics, as the science that has economies as its domain of research, should investigate *reasons for the unmanageability* of the ecological performance of present economies. A science that is not able to provide *reasons*, cannot be expected to inspire fundamental solutions. It can at most contribute to solutions by accident.

We can recapitulate the ecological performance of our economies as showing a growing use of energy, a decrease in bio-diversity and a growing appeal on the assimilative capacity of ecological systems. Such performance causes problems that are often global in space, long-term in time and characterised by many uncertainties and possible irreversibilities. This performance turns out to be characteristic of our industrial era. Ongoing industrialisation involves an ever more roundabout production structure and an ever growing circulation velocity of commodities. The former implies that the means by which final demand requirements are met become more indirect, that the scale of the production chain of all kinds of commodities increases (Common 1988, 25). It also implies that through the expansion of intercontinental trade (and developments in information technology; MD) production chains combine (resource, knowledge and capital) inputs of all over the world (Pezzey 1992, 328-329). Economic activities represent global rather than local dimensions. The latter implies that the lifetime of many commodities becomes ever shorter. Both tendencies of ongoing industrialisation ask for ever increasing inputs of material and energetic resources and for continuous technological innovation in order to overcome problems of exhaustion and pollution (as, for example, the replacement of coal for wood, of gas for oil, and of nuclear energy for gas, oil or coal). Given this statement, namely that typical characteristics of present-day ecological problems relate to industrial (and industrialising) economies, the conclusion of the previous paragraph can be made more concrete. Economics should investigate reasons for the unmanageability of the ecological performance of our *industrial* economies.

To conclude, present-day general ecological tendencies incite the concept "sustainability" as a guiding idea for economic policy. In this book, I propose to consider of the concept in a way that is more abstract than the Brundtland interpretation. I propose to interpret "sustainability" as responsibility towards future generations with regard to the ecological performance of our present day industrial economies. This responsibility presupposes manageability. The general ecological tendencies mentioned show that it is far from evident that we are able to manage the ecological performance of our economies. Therefore, I consider it as a primary task of economics to investigate reasons for this unmanageability.

2 WHICH COURSE TO TAKE?

In economic literature one can roughly discern two reactions to the growing tension between our striving for sustainability on the one hand and the continuing ecological evolution of our economies on the other. The first reaction originated from economists' common complaints that the failing ecological performance of present-day economies is due to – a kind of – "government failure". Economists blame public authorities for neglecting too often their recommendations with respect to ecological policy. This first reaction consists of a trial to ameliorate economists' political impact. The second reaction emerged as a critique on conventional, neo-classically inspired economics. According to its critics, conventional "environmental economics" is not equipped to tackle problems of sustainability adequately. These critics, therefore, propose "ecological economics" as a generic term for a set of alternative economic approaches.

I consider both reactions as worthy trials to cope with the problem of sustainability. In this book, however, I will examine a third possible course. I will investigate the norms to which *economics* should respond in order to contribute in a successful way to political solutions for the problem of sustainability. In this section, I will present (in subsection 2.1 and 2.2) the two former reactions. This presentation will help me to clarify, in section 3, the special issue of the third course that I propose.

2.1 Economists' Political Role

One can find plenty illustrations of economists' discomfort about their meagre political impact in the field of ecological policy[2]. I will restrict myself to two

[2] Ecological policy does not necessarily happen from a sustainability perspective. Some ecological problems can be solved in a way that is acceptable to present generations, but not acceptable – according to present values – to future generations. Other ecological problems can be so local in time (and in place), that they lack an intergenerational dimension. They are ecological problems, but not problems of sustainability. In this book, the problem of sustainability is the structuring problem. For that reason, when

illustrations. Robert Nelson, for instance, records that, despite wide agreement among (American) economists in the 1970s that pollution taxes or fees were the most efficient way to achieve protection of air and water quality, this advice has been almost entirely ignored (Nelson 1987, 68-69). Command and Control regulation proved to be politically more acceptable. Frank Dietz and Jan van der Straaten agree with this general consideration (Dietz *et al.* 1992, 27). They state that economists' recommendations to impose charges on polluting and natural resources-depleting activities are almost fully neglected, as in almost all OECD countries only physical regulations – rates for emission reduction, standards regarding emissions and discharges, product and process requirements - are used to decrease pollution and depletion of natural resources. This experience urged some authors to investigate possible reasons for this discrepancy between economists' recommendations and ecological policy.

Hanley, Hallett and Moffatt consider three possible explanations: a) ignorance of lawmakers and/or administrators, b) theoretical and/or practical problems with incentive-based schemes, and c) institutional or cultural barriers, including the attitudes and behaviours of economists (Hanley *et al.* 1990). With respect to the latter kind of explanation, they point to economists' *focus on efficiency*. Efficiency is not necessarily legislators' and pressure groups' main or only measuring stick for ecological control policy (Hanley *et al.* 1990, 1421; 1426). Both Nelson and Hanley suggest that *lack of consensus* between economists can partly explain why success over ecological legislation was not forthcoming (Nelson 1987, 67; Hanley *et al.* 1990, 1422). Dietz and Van der Straaten stress the *role of vested economic interests* in the political arena (Dietz *et al.* 1992, 34-39). The existing imbalance of power in society causes that political objectives are heavily influenced by the individual and short-term interests of vested economic interests. These interests are at odds with environmental economists' interest in a sustainable society. Nelson further notes the *ideological content of alternative economic instruments* to achieve economic efficiency as a possible reason for the discrepancy between economists' recommendations and environmental legislation (Nelson 1987, 68-71). In the years before 1970, economists, in their effort to encourage the use of market mechanisms, put by far the greatest part of their support behind proposals for pollution emissions fees. By comparison, they almost fully neglected the competing idea of creating a system of marketable pollution permits. This latter idea was a similarly efficient but politically more promising means of manipulating market incentives to achieve environmental protection. According to Nelson, it is likely that professional economists did not simply pick the wrong horse. Many of them were aware of at least some of the practical advantages of a market permit system, but could not accept its ideological implications (e.g. distributional effects, public versus private ownership of pollution rights, future flexibility to alter pollution levels). Finally, Dietz and Van der Straaten point to complications related to the *paradigm used* in mainstream (environmental) economics (Dietz *et al.* 1992, 29-34). I will deal

I refer to ecological policy, I refer to ecological problems that have an intergenerational dimension and that should be considered from a perspective of intergenerational justice.

separately with this latter explanation of Dietz and Van der Straaten in the following paragraph.

Environmental economics can be roughly characterised as an extension and application of neo-classical economic theory to ecological problems. This implies that the use of natural resources available is described as an optimisation problem. Ecological quality is considered the result of the aggregated decisions of all individual economic agents, weighing the benefits derived from increasing production and consumption against the benefits enjoyed when the ecological quality is improved. The first complicating factor is that ecological quality can only partly be expressed in exchange relations on the market. Ecological problems are problems of externalities. In order to correct markets for these externalities, economists have to define shadow prices. A second complicating factor then arises: monetary assessment of the benefits of avoided ecological damage poses considerable problems. A third complicating factor is the problem of how to aggregate individual preferences into a collective statement on the value of specific natural resources. A fourth complicating (and unsolvable) problem is that the preferences of future generations are simply unknown. Further complications relate to the nature of ecological problems. Ecological problems are so complex that we often lack necessary insights into ecological relations. Thresholds, synergetic effects and delayed reactions prevent an "optimal" use of natural resources.

The observation of the discrepancy between economists' recommendations and ecological policy gave rise to a renewed reflection on *economists'* role in public policy. Nelson's article 'The Economics Profession and the Making of Public Policy' is exemplary in this respect (Nelson 1987). In this article Nelson analyses on a theoretical level – and from an American perspective - how the discrepancy came about. In the history of the twentieth century, he discerns three different interpretations of economists' role in government. Each interpretation implies a particular political theory and a particular conception of the nature of economics.

The first role (typical for the period between 1885 and 1920) is that of the Progressive Neutral Expert (Nelson 1987, 52-54). Progressive Neutral Experts sought to make (American) government serve "the public interest". They were representatives of the public confidence in human progress through science. They defended the introduction of scientific methods and techniques into government. The political theory underlying this first role distinguished between two government functions, those that involve questions of basic policy and social value and those that are administrative or instrumental in nature. Decisions of the former type belong to the realm of politics, decisions of the latter to the separate realm of administration. Administration was the domain reserved for the appropriate experts. Experts were expected to provide government with efficient means, not with political ends. These experts' stress on efficiency gave rise to an interpretation of (economic) science as empirical, verified by the facts. Extensive gathering of data and measurement of social phenomena became crucial.

The second role is that of the Entrepreneur for Efficiency. Experiences of the twentieth century – a series of wars, mass murders, threats of nuclear destruction, and so on – challenged the progressive vision fundamentally. On the one hand, the political theory underlying this second role was more realistic. Government was considered to be actually driven by continual competition among interest groups, rather than by "the public interest". Public policies were determined by the political bargaining among the affected interests. Political leaders and interest groups did not respect progressive boundaries between the properly political and the properly expert. Instead, interest group bargaining often figured prominently in administrative and other technical decisions. The simple division of labour between politicians who achieve consensus on a set of objectives and experts who design and evaluate from efficiency and effectiveness criteria alternative means of achieving those objectives turned out not to exist. This political theory gave rise to an interpretation of economists' role as active advocates of efficiency. Only as advocates of efficiency could they continue to regard themselves as spokesmen for the diffuse and weakly represented interests of the general citizenry, acting as a counterweight to special interests pressures. This new role as entrepreneurs of efficiency was considered to demand some skills in political tactics. A politically successful economist was deemed to have a thorough command of both his scientific and technical knowledge and his political and tactical skills.

The third role is that of the Ideological Combatant. Progressive Neutral Experts still believed that an increase in – neutral – scientific knowledge concerning ever-wider areas of social concern would result in a decrease of the (typically political rather than administrative) domain of social conflict. The experiences of the twentieth century, however, challenged the idea of a declining strength of ideology and of a declining degree of concomitant destructive conflict. Finally, scientific rationality turned out to be itself an ideology. The recognition of the ideological dimension of scientific theories compelled political theorists not only to take the importance of interest-group power in political processes into consideration, but also of ideology. Compatible with this third political theory, economists' role is that of proponents of their particular framework of thinking. According to Nelson, economists indeed have had the greatest success in government as proponents for markets, for efficiency-related values, and generally for their framework for viewing the world, rather than as technical analysts of particular policy details. This role as ideological combatant calls in its turn for particular types of skills, especially for the ability to penetrate and criticise the philosophical underpinnings of social and political values and theories.

According to Nelson, most members of the economics profession today still see their policy-making role fundamentally in the progressive vein. They consider themselves as professionals who advise government in technical and scientific matters and take social values and political preferences as given. Once politicians have expressed these values and preferences, economic expertise can be brought into action to help realise them as efficiently and as effectively as possible. Nelson adds, however, that the original progressive dichotomy of politics and administration is replaced by a trichotomy. Democratic politics is seen as sandwiched between professional experts. First, economists define options and lay out the technically feasible menu for political choice. Then, the political process is considered to weigh social values against these options and to make the socially preferred choice. After this, it is again professional experts who are responsible for carrying out the implementation of the political decisions reached. In this trichotomy the central thrust of the progressive vision, namely that the arenas of politics and technical expertise can and should be kept separate, remains preserved. Mainstream economists are uncomfortable with or simply reject outright the notion that at bottom their scientific views constitute an ideology.

From Nelson's theoretical analysis we can derive some conclusions that are helpful to position my own research project. To start with, his analysis shows that some internal connections exist between interpretations of politics, of economists' political role and of the nature of economic science. An interpretation of economics as neutral conforms to an interpretation of politics as separated in "subjective" decision-making concerning political objectives and "objective" scientific administration. An interpretation of politics as a bargaining process between more or less powerful interests urges economists to become advocates of the "general interest" through their pleading for economic efficiency. An interpretation of economics as a kind of ideology transforms economists' political task into that of active proponents of a typically economic worldview.

My own research project takes this idea of internal connections between interpretations of politics and interpretations of the nature of economic theory as a thread. In chapter 2, I will argue for a particular interpretation of politics, namely deliberative democracy. In chapter 4, I will propose four norms for the nature of a politically relevant economics. Some of these norms relate directly to this interpretation of politics as deliberative democracy.

Nelson's theoretical analysis leads him, further, to provide *economists* with recommendations to ameliorate their political impact. Economists' participation in public policy will be more successful in case they have a realistic interpretation of politics and, hence, are able to develop the skills required to successfully participate in it. They should regard themselves as entrepreneurs and advocates for specific economic policies, rather than as neutral technical analysts. The skills needed – political awareness, knowledge of legal processes and reasoning, writing skills, facility in reasoning by analogy, ideological sensitivity, philosophical knowledge, the ability to "tell a story" that makes sense and that succeeds in organising an overwhelming amount of information and data in some meaningful way – are the skills of a craftsman rather than of a scientist. These skills are, according to Nelson, most in demand in professional roles in government (Nelson 1987, 86). In my research project, on the contrary, stress is on the characteristics of a politically successful *economics*, rather than *economists* (though I feel no need to deny the relevance of Nelson's recommendations).

Nelson's theoretical analysis of the political sphere is, finally, intended descriptively. His recommendations for policy economists mainly arise from a particular description of real-world politics. My analysis is, on the contrary, intended normatively. Accepting "sustainability" – possibly in opposition with vested economic interests - as a guiding idea in economic policy, starting from "deliberative democracy" as a guiding idea for politics and taking philosophical considerations concerning the nature of economic science seriously, my research question sounds: which economics do we need in order to contribute successfully to ecological policy.

2.2 Economic Practice within a Political Context

The second reaction to the discrepancy noticed between general ecological tendencies and the aim of sustainability stems from dissatisfaction with the conventional, i.e., neo-classical paradigmatic approach. "Ecological economics" is a generic term for a variety of endeavours to deal more adequately with environmental problems on a scientific level. Giuseppe Munda characterises "ecological economics" in opposition to "environmental economics" (Munda 1997). He describes environmental economics as a particular specialisation of neo-classical economics. This neo-classical origin explains its ethical commitments and epistemological self-understanding. Environmental economics is devoted to "sustainable development". Here "development" means

> the set of changes in the economic, social, institutional and political structure needed to implement the transition from a pre-capitalistic economy based on agriculture, to an industrial capitalistic economy (Bresso, cited in Munda 1997, 215).

This interpretation of development implies a) that the changes needed are not only quantitative, but also qualitative (social, institutional and political), and b) that the development of western industrialised countries is considered the only possible model, the model with the best knowledge, the best set of values, the best organisation and the best set of technologies. "Sustainability" in its turn means "weak sustainability": an economy is weakly sustainable if it saves more than the combined depreciation of natural and man-made capital, expressed in monetary terms. This concept of weak sustainability is based on the assumption of perfect substitutability between these different forms of capital. Intergenerational justice is interpreted as leaving future generations with a total stock of capital not smaller than the one enjoyed by the present generation. Correct, i.e., "rational" management of natural resources means "optimal inter-generational allocation". Environmental economists further regard, according to Munda, their recommendations as a matter of "scientific" arguments: value neutral and objective.

Ecological economics, on the contrary, has different epistemological foundations and ethical commitments. It adopts, to start with, a co-evolutionary paradigm. Economic development is considered a process of adaptation to a changing environment while itself being a source of environmental change. There is, however, neither unique nor predictable direction of change. Ecological economics has some points in common with institutional economics: its recognition of the impossibility of a value free science, emphasis on the importance of the distribution of property rights, and strong criticism of monetary reductionism. It takes, further, "strong sustainability" as its guiding idea. It is based on the assumption that certain sorts of natural capital are deemed critical and not readily substitutable by man-made capital. This "strong sustainability" criterion of non-negative change over time in stocks of specified natural capital asks for non-monetary, biophysical indicators. It originates from the idea – especially tackled by Herman Daly - of an "optimal scale", i.e. a maximum physical scale of human presence in the ecosystem defined either by the regenerative or absorptive capacity of the ecosystem. Finally, ecological economics takes Funtowicz' and Ravetz' "post-normal science" as its epistemological framework. This framework is developed to tackle policy issues where

> facts are uncertain, values in dispute, stakes high and decisions urgent (Funtowicz and Ravetz cited in Munda 1997, 221).

Ecological economics understands present-day ecological problems as such typical issues.

Especially the concept of "post-normal science" is helpful to make me clarify the issue of my research project. For that reason, I will examine this concept a bit further. The concept is developed as a framework for dealing with contradictions in "emergent complex systems" (Funtowicz and Ravetz 1994a; 1994b). The concept "emergent complex system" is used as a heuristic term to indicate systems that cannot be fully explained mechanistically and functionally, because, in them some at least of the elements of the system possess individuality, along with some degree of intentionality, consciousness, foresight, purpose, symbolic representations and morality (Funtowicz & Ravetz 1994b, 569-570). Continuous novelty thus is a characteristic property of emergent complexity. Human societies are typical examples of such systems. The contradictions in emergent complex systems can be contradictions of destructive conflict or – to use a concept borrowed from Schumpeter - of "creative destruction" (Funtowicz & Ravetz 1994b, 573; 581 note 3). (The concepts are, again, meant heuristically.) Fisheries offer one example of the former: the livelihood of fishermen and their communities from week to week depends on an exploitation of the resource that regularly leads to damage or even destruction of the stock of fish. The concept of "sustainable development" offers, according to the authors, a second example: development as achievement of a (global) consumer society - justified on the humanitarian ideal of equality for all humankind – is ecologically impossible. For that reason an enriched interpretation of "sustainability" is needed: an interpretation implying a qualitative transformation of economic and political structures, a creative destruction of existing non-sustainable structures. Nobody further knows what kind of economic and political structures should emerge out of this creative destruction, but Funtowicz' and Ravetz' ethical starting points are that sustainability is not a matter of mere human survival, but a matter of human lives worth living, and that ongoing industrial process as an "accident-generating system" is something rather to be avoided than to be managed (Funtowicz & Ravetz 1994b, 576; 581).

This latter ethical intuition of Funtowicz and Ravetz – that probably gets a stronger stress in my representation than the authors themselves have in mind – is to some extent at odds with Munda's interpretation of sustainability. Munda interprets (strong) sustainability in terms of "managing" – i.e. monitoring, controlling - critical natural resources so that they remain within an optimal scale. I doubt the feasibility of this endeavour if it remains devoid of an active search for qualitatively different economic and political structures. Funtowicz and Ravetz understand sustainability as an idea guiding our search for economic and political structures in which environmental problems remain "manageable". This interpretation is closer to mine. In the previous section, I proposed to interpret sustainability as responsibility towards future generations and such responsibility implies manageability indeed.

Funtowicz and Ravetz consider post-normal science as an intellectual tool for policy-making (Funtowicz & Ravetz 1994a, 206). They defend "quality" rather than "truth" as its organising principle. This defence partly results from the adventures of science in our past century: scientific "truth" proved to be relative and fragmented. At the same time it is meant as an answer to the kind of 'irreducible uncertainty' related to emergent complexity (Funtowicz & Ravetz 1994b, 578). "Quality" entails both a democratisation of knowledge by an extension of the peer-community (not only experts, but also laypersons) and recognition of diversity in commitments and perspectives. The former expresses a positive evaluation of stakeholders' - non-expert – knowledge. The latter expresses recognition of conflicting interests and of power relationships (often reflected in scientific paradigms). "Quality" is meant as a non-relativistic answer to the fragmentation in scientific knowledge. It is meant to deal as good as can be hoped for with scientific uncertainties and ethical complexities in emergent complex systems.

To recapitulate the idea of post-normal science in my own words, it is first and foremost an interpretation of a desirable *use of science in politics* (or, better perhaps, an interpretation of a desirable *scientific practice within a political context* (Gremmen 1999). This scientific practice should – as science itself should - respond to criteria of quality that presuppose specific ethical principles. The idea thus presents norms for acting scientifically in a political context, rather than for science itself. The remarkable thing about these norms is that they reflect an interpretation of scientific practice as a kind of politics (knowledge resulting from a democratic dialogue between various value-laden perspectives). This interpretation contrasts with a (rather common, positivistic – or, what Nelson called, Progressive -) interpretation of politics as a kind of science (politics as resolving or avoiding value-laden conflicts through objective science). To conclude, Funtowicz and Ravetz present post-normal science as a new interpretation of scientific *practice* (Funtowicz & Ravetz 1994b, 577). Consequently, post-normal science does not fully respond to ecological economists' original intent to look for a *substantive* alternative for neo-classically inspired environmental economics.

The issue of my research project relates to the previous conclusion. My hypothesis is that, if we really aim for a "creative destruction" leading to economic and political structures compatible with the idea of sustainability as presented by Funtowicz and Ravetz (rather than by Munda), it does not suffice to present norms for scientific *practice* within a political context. We also need norms for *science itself* in order to let it be *politically useful.* For, taking Dietz' and Van der Straaten's conclusion serious that the conventional, neo-classical economic paradigm is not straightforwardly applicable to problems of sustainability (see section 2.1), it is conceivable that an extension of the peer community, a plurality of existing disciplinary methodologies and trans-disciplinarity are not sufficient to allow for an acceptable – in terms of sustainability – "creative destruction". My research project is, therefore, meant as an initial impetus to define norms for a politically useful *economic science.* Or to express my intention in a rather slogan-like way (inspired by the title of Funtowicz' and Ravetz' paper (1994a)): rather than looking for a qualitatively satisfactory political definition of the worth of a songbird with the help of post-normal science, I am looking for a qualitatively satisfactory economic theory that can help us to organise our economies so that the need to politically define the worth of a songbird disappears (because the bird's life is not threatened any longer).

3 AN ECOLOGICALLY SUCCESSFUL ECONOMICS

My research project is meant to develop norms not for economists as political actors (see Nelson), nor for economic practice within a political context (see Funtowicz and Ravetz), but for an ecologically successful economics. What does an ecologically successful economics mean, however? And what are the sources from which I will develop these norms? In the following subsections, I will briefly answer these two questions.

3.1 Two Standards for an Ecologically Successful Economics

I propose two standards to evaluate economic contributions to ecological policy. The first standard is the one noticed by Nelson, namely the impact of economic knowledge on final policy results. (Whether this "impact" should be understood in a direct way – economics as a political toolbox – or not is another topic to be dealt with in chapter 4.) This standard is a measure from which to develop norms – in chapter 4 – for the *nature* of a politically relevant economics. Given the growing tension between general ecological tendencies and the ideal of sustainability, this standard can at most be necessary, but not sufficient. A second standard, therefore, relates to the capacity of economic knowledge to offer insights into possible ways to reduce this tension or, to express the same in terms of Funtowicz' and Ravetz' concepts, to allow for transformations of economic structures that make ecological problems manageable again. This second standard is a measure to evaluate the *content* – or *subject matter* – of economics. I will sketch the contours of this content in chapter 3.

3.2 *A Confrontation between David Pearce and Daniel Bromley*

A confrontation between two exemplary economic theories will be the initial source for my investigation. These economic theories are David Pearce's on the one hand and Daniel Bromley's on the other. Both authors have done pioneering work. Pearce was among the first economists – consider the Blueprint books of which he was one of the authors - to warn that the problem of sustainability cannot be reduced to the conventional economic problem of optimal allocation. He stressed, at an early stage, the need to keep the level of some critical natural resources intact, independent of considerations of economic efficiency. Bromley's fame especially relates to his questioning of Hardin's article *The Tragedy of the Commons*. He points out that Hardin's critique does not regard so much common property regimes, but open access regimes. This correction gave a new shot to the discussion between advocates and opponents of private property as a solution to all kinds of ecological problems.

The positions of both authors are so divergent – Pearce's economics is neo-classically inspired, while Bromley's is in the tradition of institutional economics - that they allow for a fruitful confrontation. Since both Pearce and Bromley are, in the first instance, economists, I will enlist the help of both Weber's and Neurath's (contrasting) ideas to clarify Both Pearce's and Bromley's aims and assumptions. Both Neurath's and Weber's professional activities date from the beginning of the twentieth century. Both Neurath and Weber are economists who reflect on the philosophical aspects of the methodology of the social sciences. Within the community of ecological economists they are, moreover, deemed precursors (Martinez-Alier 1990). Weber is a precursor in the sense that he rejects the idea that "pure" economics, i.e., an economics based on the theory of marginal utility, can contribute to ecological problems. Neurath, on the contrary, is a precursor in the sense that he pleads for a kind of economics suitable to contribute to this topic.

4 OUTLINE OF THE BOOK

The first part of this book – consisting of chapters 2, 3 and 4 – is a philosophical exploration of the characteristics of an economics that intends to be relevant for the problem of sustainability. In chapter 2, I will analyse economic and political theories as conceptual constructs referring to the economic and political sphere respectively. I will argue that such conceptual constructs inevitably are value-laden and that, hence, different conceptual constructs of the same sphere can exist. I will argue, moreover, that and why it is important to distinguish between the economic and the political sphere. I will derive the latter arguments from a confrontation between Buchanan's and Arendt's political theory.

In chapter 3, I will discuss an economy as consisting of two dimensions, a symbolic or institutional one and an ecological one. Such interpretation will allow us to understand the ecological performance of an economy as the counterpart of its institutional organisation. I will further argue that, in order to get insights into the internal relationships between an economy and its ecological performance, we need insights into the institutional whole of an economy. And I will elaborate on what I mean by "an institutional whole". I will suggest that it is a matter of conceptually analysing different types of economic institutions and different hierarchies of institutions. Chapter 3 will thus offer us some *substantive* norms for an economics that aims at contributing successfully to the political objective of "sustainability".

In chapter 4, I will derive four norms for the *nature*, rather than the *content*, of a politically successful economics. I will suggest that a politically successful economics should, to start with, be objective in the sense that it should aim at intersubjective consensus among economists. Objectivity as intersubjective consensus does, however, not imply neutrality. I will suggest, further, that economics should provide economic policy with insights, rather than instruments. This means that economics should aim at (non-neutral) description and explanation, not at (non-neutral) prescription and prediction. I will assert, finally, that economics should be rather impartial than partial. It should explain economic sources of political inequality and contribute to political freedom. Both Arendt's interpretation of politics as a deliberative democracy and Weber's and Neurath's philosophical reflections on the nature of the social sciences will function as the breeding ground for these norms.

In the second part of this book, i.e., chapters 5, 6, 7 and 8, I will confront the norms developed concerning both the content and the nature of an ecologically successful economics with the writings of David Pearce and Daniel Bromley. Chapters 5 and 7 are a substantive reconstruction of Pearce's and Bromley's theoretical work respectively. Chapters 6 and 8 are an analysis of the nature of their economics. Chapters 5 and 7 will make clear to what extent their writings comply with the substantive norm I propose in chapter 3. Chapters 6 and 8 will illuminate to what extent their writings meet the four norms suggested, in chapter 4, for the nature of an ecologically successful economics.

Part I and II will be closed by chapter 9, in which I will give an overview of the main conclusions of this research project.

5 CONCLUSION

For the sake of sustainability, economists should improve their political influence. I assume that many ecological activists would greet the former provocative statement with disdain. For economists' impact in ecological policy is commonly believed to be already too much of a good thing. Ecological activists (and many other citizens) suspect political translations of problems of sustainability into economic terms – i.e. into terms of (monetary) costs and benefits – because these translations do not respect and overrule people's value-laden interpretation of these problems. I support their objections. Nevertheless, I am convinced that economists should improve their political impact in order to help us to face up to present-day intergenerational ecological problems more adequately than we used to do in the past. The key question is, however, what *kind of economics* is needed to allow for successful contributions to ecological policy.

This book will not offer its readers a finished and well-designed new economic paradigm (for developing a new paradigm is a historical event emerging from the collaboration between many economic scientists). My research project is meant as a first step, an initial impetus to discuss the need for and the outlook of an economics that contributes to politically defined solutions for the problem of sustainability. In the first part, I will develop the contours of such an economics from philosophical considerations (concerning the nature of the problem of sustainability, the nature of the economic and political sphere, deliberative democracy as a normative ideal of politics, and the nature of economic theories). In the second part, I will confront the writings of two exemplary economic scientists with these philosophical contours. This confrontation will help us, to begin with, to make these contours more concrete. It will learn us, moreover, in which direction further research should be done in order to fill remaining gaps.

CHAPTER 2

THE ECONOMIC AND THE POLITICAL SPHERE

In this book I intend to develop norms for an ecologically successful economics. By an ecologically successful economics I mean a theory that has our economies as its domain of research and that is influential in the political arena in the sense that it helps political actors to find effective solutions for the problem of sustainability. My research project thus implicitly makes a distinction between the economic and the political sphere. The economic sphere is the domain *about which* economics is meant to provide us with knowledge. The political sphere is the domain *in which* economics is meant to be an influential factor. In the course of my research project I noticed that, within the community of economists, there is some disagreement about whether it is useful to distinguish between the political and the economic sphere or, in other words, to distinguish between economic and political (aspects of) human actions. In this chapter I will argue that this distinction can and should be made.

In order to explain that this distinction *can* be made, I will reflect, in section 1, on economic and political theories as conceptual constructs. Considering economic and political theories as conceptual constructs implies that they are perspectivistic (i.e., value-laden) descriptions of human reality, a multiplicity of theories is possible, and it depends on the conceptual construct used whether the distinction between the economic and the political sphere is deemed significant. In section 2, I will present four possible conceptual constructs of the economic sphere. These conceptual constructs can be discerned in the history of economic theory. (I count both Weber's and Neurath's economic writings as being part of this history.)

In order to defend that this distinction *should* be made, I will start with a presentation of Buchanan's Public Choice theory (section 3). Public Choice theory is a political theory originating from an extension of economics to the political sphere. This implies that Buchanan recognises the existence of both a political and an economic sphere, but considers the rationality of actions occurring in both spheres as similar. In other words, Buchanan's conceptual construct of the political sphere is based on the opinion that it is not very significant to make a distinction between the rationality of human interactions within the political and the economic sphere. This opinion gives, however, rise to a redefinition of typically economic and typically political phenomena. The former are, henceforth, interpreted as voluntary and the latter as involuntary interactions. In section 4, I will present deliberative democracy as an alternative political theory. In section 5, I will argue that an interpretation of the political sphere in terms of a deliberative democracy is better equipped to deal with the political objective of "sustainability" than is Buchanan's Public Choice theory.

1 ECONOMIC AND POLITICAL THEORIES AS CONCEPTUAL CONSTRUCTS

In this section, I will argue that economic and political theories are conceptual constructs. This statement implies that we cannot conceptually circumvent the gap between spheres in reality on the one hand and economic or political theories on the other, economic and political theories are not and cannot be neutral, and different economic or political theories referring to the same economic or political sphere are possible. Max Weber and Otto Neurath inspired my thinking over the nature of economic and political theories as social constructs. They both provided us with a thorough analysis of the methodologies of the (social) sciences[1]. Despite the differences with respect to their position in the philosophy of science tradition (and their political temper), they agree that social theories cannot be but conceptual constructs.

1.1 Weber: Social Sciences as Ideal-Typical Conceptual Constructs

Weber is both a social scientist and a methodologist of the social sciences. As a methodologist, he strongly objects to Comte's positivist idea that the social sciences do not differ fundamentally from the natural sciences. In his view, the fact that the domain of the social sciences consists of cultural phenomena urges the social scientist to fall back on a different methodology. The term "ideal type" is an essential concept for this methodology. In the following paragraphs, I will briefly explain Weber's basic ideas.

To start with, Weber states that it is the specificity of the domain of investigation of the social sciences that urges us to understand social sciences as social constructs. According to Weber, the subject matter of the social sciences is always part of a *cultural* reality (MSS 76). Cultural reality consists of cultural phenomena, i.e. meaningful phenomena or phenomena that are related to value ideas. Following Rickert, Weber understands this cultural reality as endlessly complex[2]. It

> presents an infinite multiplicity of successively and coexistently emerging and disappearing events, both "within" and "outside" ourselves. The absolute infinitude of this multiplicity is seen to remain undiminished even when our attention is focused on a single "object", for instance, a concrete act of exchange, as soon as we seriously attempt an exhaustive description of *all* the individual components of this "individual phenomenon", to say nothing of explaining it causally (MSS 72).

---

1 Within the community of economists, there turns out to exist some disagreement about whether economics is a social science or not. I consider economics as one of the social sciences.

2 For a more extensive comparison between the thoughts of Rickert and Weber, see Rein de Wilde (1989, 114-124).

The finite human mind cannot tackle this infinite reality without carving a finite portion out of it. The criterion which is used in the social sciences to select this segment is a particular value idea. Whether a phenomenon is of a certain social science type does not depend so much on its objective characteristics, but on its value-relevance. This implies that the meaningfulness of certain empirical data is always presupposed.

> We cannot discover, however, what is meaningful to us by means of a "presuppositionless" investigation of empirical data. Rather perception of its meaningfulness to us is the presupposition of its becoming an *object* of investigation (MSS 76).

To recapitulate, a specific value idea makes us perceive some phenomena as meaningful. The set of phenomena that take their meaning from this particular value makes up the subject matter of a social science. Our value ideas thus construct the domain of a social science. Social-sciences are value-laden perspectives on human reality. Whether we distinguish economic from political science depends on whether distinct value ideas are deemed significant to constitute a political and an economic sphere respectively.

Values do, further, not only define the subject matter of the social sciences, but also the concepts and laws that become the instruments of scientific research, and of whole theories. To express the value-relatedness of these theoretical instruments, Weber introduces the term "ideal type".

> An ideal type is formed by the one-sided *accentuation* of one or more points of view and by the synthesis of a great many diffuse, discrete, more or less present and occasionally absent *concrete individual* phenomena, which are arranged according to those one-sidedly emphasized viewpoints into a unified *analytical* construct (*Gedankenbild*) (MSS 90).

Since ideal-types are arrived at by the accentuation of certain elements of reality which seem important with respect to a specific point of view, they cannot be understood as a reflection of reality (MSS 90-93). They are not *true*: they do not simply correspond to particular empirical phenomena. They are a *logical* ideal, i.e., a well defined analytical construct, a limiting concept which allows us to compare reality with it. Ideal-types have a heuristic and expository function. Comparison between the ideal-type and reality, the estimation of similarities and discrepancies, can make the characteristic features of empirical phenomena clear and understandable. An ideal-type is not a description of reality but

> aims to give unambiguous means of expression to such a description. [...] It is no hypothesis but it offers guidance to the construction of hypotheses (MSS 90).

To recapitulate, social-scientific concepts and laws or, in short, social-scientific theories are ideal-typical. This implies that they are not neutral. Not only *science* – in the sense of a particular, for instance, economic or political discipline -, but particular scientific *theories* – in the sense of particular disciplinary paradigms (to use Kuhn's terminology) - are non-neutral social constructs. Economic and political theories result from particular points of view. For that reason, they cannot simply be understood in terms of truth, i.e., correspondence with reality.

Since ideal types depend on the perspective of their constructor, Weber admits, moreover, that a multiplicity of ideal-types, of which none resembles another, none of which can be observed in reality as actually existing, but each of which pretends to be a useful theoretical construct, is possible.

> For those phenomena which interest us as cultural phenomena are interesting to us with respect to very different kinds of evaluative ideas to which we relate them. Inasmuch as the "points of view" from which they can become significant for us are very diverse, the most varied criteria can be applied to the selection of the traits which are to enter into the construction of an ideal-typical view of a particular culture (MSS 91).

Ideal types can thus take different forms. They are not necessarily "rational", i.e., empirically and logically correct and consistent constructs (MSS 42-43). In many cases people do not act rational:

> there are whole spheres of action (the sphere of the "irrational") where the simplicity offered by isolating abstraction is more convenient than an ideal-type of optimal logical rationality.

Ideal-types do not have to be normatively correctly constructed either.

> It is true that, in practice, the investigator frequently uses normatively "correctly" constructed "ideal-types". From the logical point of view, however, the normative "correctness" of these types is not essential. For the purpose of characterizing a specific type of attitude, the investigator may construct either an ideal type which is identical with his own personal ethical norms, and in this sense objectively "correct", or one which ethically is thoroughly in conflict with his own normative attitudes; and he may then compare the behavior of the people being investigated with it. Or else he may construct an ideal-typical attitude of which he has neither positive nor negative evaluations (MSS 43).

Weber's view that ideal types can take many forms implies, among other things, that a multiplicity of economic and political theories is possible.

Finally, which values must underlie a scientific investigation is, according to Weber, a question that cannot be answered scientifically. The values which consciously or unconsciously direct scientific endeavours are the result of ultimate decisions through which the scientist's '[soul] chooses its own fate' (MSS 18). Weber, however, stresses that a lot of scientists are mistaken concerning the kind of values they deem acceptable as a starting point of scientific research. Firstly, he opposes the view that scientific validity is achieved by weighing the various evaluations against one another and making a compromise among them. In his view, the "middle way" is just as undemonstrable scientifically (with the means of the empirical sciences) as the "most extreme" evaluations (MSS 10).

> *Scientifically the "middle course" is not truer even by a hair's breadth*, than the most extreme party ideals of the right or left (MSS 57).

Secondly, Weber strongly contests the conviction that a scientist may be contented with the

> conventional self-evidentness of very widely accepted value-judgments (MSS 13).

On the contrary, he considers the questioning of those things which convention makes self-evident as a specific function of science. To recapitulate, in Weber's opinion, we have no *scientific* reasons to prefer one economic or political theory to another.

1.2 Neurath: Sciences as Historically Contingent Conceptual Constructs

Neurath was a remarkable member of the Vienna Circle, a group of mainly natural scientists with a philosophical interest in scientific methodology. As a member of this group, Neurath is a defender of logical empiricism (Neurath 1929, 305-310). Logical empiricists reject the idea that the methodologies of the natural and the social sciences differ. They only discern practical differences – due to greater complexity of social reality - between both kinds of sciences. Contrary to the received view of logical empiricism (a view that is heavily influenced by Hempel's work), Neurath does not state that either social-scientific or natural-scientific theories can be considered true. On the contrary, in his view, not only social-scientific, but also natural-scientific theories are conceptually constructed. They are conceptual constructs because they both originate from historical human language and because they are the result of many decisions. In the following paragraphs, I will deal more extensively with Neurath's explanation of the meaning and implications of conceptually constructed theories.

Logical empiricism is, as the term indicates, a combination of logic and empiricism. Empiricism comprises three elements: empirical theories consist of 1) spatio-temporal statements that are 2) expressed in purified language and 3) testable. According to Neurath, scientific theories should be built upon positive - or observation or protocol - statements (Neurath 1931a, 48; 1931b, 53; 1932, 93; 1934, 101; 1936c, 151-153; 1941, 220-221)[3]. These statements are always spatio-temporal formulations (Neurath 1931b, 53-54). They are expressed in a unified language (Neurath 1931d, 59, 62; 1932, 96-97; 1934, 101; 1936a, 133; 1936b, 139; 1937a, 173; 1937e, 202-203; 1938, 837; 1941, 214, 221). This unified language can, with slight alterations, be derived from everyday language. Everyday language has to be purified from metaphysics and it has to be made intersubjective and intersensual.

> It connects the statements of a man talking to himself today with his statements of yesterday; the statements he makes with his ears closed, with those he makes with his ear open (Neurath 1931d, 62).

Neurath calls this purified everyday language a physicalist language[4].

---

[3] Neurath wrote more than 400 articles, pamphlets and monographs, which, according to Cartwright c.s., are discursively and repetitively written and loosely structured (Cartwright *et al.* 1996, 4). That is why I should; with respect to a single topic, refer to many places in Neurath's work in order to be more or less complete.

[4] Neurath describes this purified everyday language as a physicalist language. The meaning of the term "physicalism" shifts from "the language of physics" (Neurath 1931c, 62) to "universal jargon" or "universal slang" (Neurath 1936c, 155; 1937a, 180). See also Reisch (1994, 160).

By induction of these statements, scientists formulate laws - laws are a kind of non-protocol statements -, which are directives for finding predictions - expressed in protocol statements - of individual courses of events (Neurath 1931b, 53; 1932, 94). Protocol statements can be controlled. They are, therefore, meaningful sentences which make the testing of those predictions possible (Neurath 1931a, 48; 1931b, 53). Testing means comparing one protocol statement with another. Testing does certainly not mean comparing it with "reality" or with "things" (Neurath 1931b, 53; 1931d, 61, 67; 1934, 102, 107-110). According to Neurath, logical empiricism leaves no room for comparing statements with things or reality. "Das Ding an sich" – to speak with Kant- or "reality" are metaphysical concepts. Empirical scientists can only compare statements with other statements. Oppositions such as statement/reality, language/reality, thinking/being, knowledge/reality, subject/object, logical form/experience all lead to pseudo-problems (Neurath 1936d, 754). Scientific "truth" cannot be a sake of correspondence between a statement and reality. The only possible concept of "truth" is one of coherence or consistency between a statement and the totality of existing scientific statements (Neurath 1913a, 3; 1931b, 53; 1931d, 61, 66; 1934, 102). 'If it agrees with them, it is joined to them; if it does not agree, it is called "untrue" and rejected; or the existing complex of statements of science is modified so that the new statement can be incorporated; the latter decision is mostly taken with hesitation' (Neurath 1931b, 53). Neurath thus explicitly states that the gap between the reality that humans experience and the statements about this reality cannot be bridged conceptually.

In Neurath's view, coherence or consistency is a necessary, not a sufficient condition for scientific "truth". The physicalist program lacks an unambiguous criterion of truth (Neurath 1934, 105-107). The history of optics, for instance, demonstrates that several groups of statements that are without contradictions in themselves but exclude each other still remain. One cannot distinguish logically between these groups. Only the practice of living - the restricted views of our environment, the limited powers of individual scientists - reduces the multiplicity. For that reason one cannot speak of a true system of statements, not even as a conceptual boundary (Neurath 1931d, 61). Finally, Neurath proposes to drop the concepts "true" and "false" statements or theories altogether and to replace them with "accepted" and "unaccepted" or more or less "plausible" ones (Neurath 1941, 221-222). To conclude, Neurath's refusal to interpret theories in terms of truth, i.e. correspondence between theory and reality, opens room for a multiplicity of coherent theories about reality.

In addition to empiricism, Neurath's conception of science is characterised by logical analysis, based on modern symbolic logic (Neurath 1929, 306-309; 1937a, 175). Logical analysis is used to reduce random statements and concepts to precise statements and concepts about the given and to formalise the intuitive process of inference of ordinary thought. Moreover, logical analysis is needed to avoid metaphysical aberration. Metaphysics results from two basic logical mistakes: mistakes related to the use of unpurified traditional language and to confusions about the logical achievements of thought (pseudo-rationalism, see chapter 4).

Unfortunately, Neurath is not clear about the criterion with which to decide whether language is purified from metaphysical terms or not[5]. Anyhow, his falling back on logic to purify language suggests that he considers scientific language as a neutral language. This conviction is, however, at odds with his analysis – see the following paragraphs - of everyday language as consisting of a more or less coherent set of historically contingent concepts and of purified scientific concepts as originating from everyday language as a result of (ever preliminary) decisions.

In 'The lost wanderers of Descartes and the auxiliary motive' Neurath describes theoretical thinking as a kind of action (Neurath 1913a). A characteristic of "action" (and of "non-action"), whether practical or theoretical, is that, since the agent lacks complete insight, it is unavoidably based on a decision. Science, as a kind of action, is itself the result of many decisions. The limits of scientific insight crop up each time a scientific concept, law or system of hypotheses is accepted. First, the acceptance of scientific concepts is the result of a decision, since the unified language of physicalism is obtained from a purification of a historically given ordinary language. This purification results in a 'physicalist ordinary language' which is at most unequivocal, but never completely determinate (Neurath 1932, 91; 1936c, 147; 1941, 215; 1944, 931-933). Their indefiniteness is inevitable, since each concept is linked with other ones. 'Even if we wish to free ourselves as far as we can from assumptions and interpretations we cannot start from a *tabula rasa* as Descartes thought we could. We have to make do with words and concepts that we find when our reflections begin. Indeed all changes of concepts and names again require the help of concepts, names, definitions and connections that determine our thinking' (Neurath 1921, 198). The historical contingency of language hampers the existence of evidences, of "primitive" or "atomic" statements which need no verification (Neurath 1932). It hampers, moreover, a methodological solipsism: the use of a private (phenomenal) language. Every language is necessarily inter-subjective. It impedes, finally, a definitely finished unified language. Unified language will always be in the making 'just as our life and our sciences' (Neurath 1941, 214). It will be achieved by successive adaptations and compromises, not mainly by deliberate conventions, nor by a test. Unified language results, *dixit* Neurath, from a decision (Neurath 1946a, 235).

Second, the acceptance of a scientific law cannot happen without a decision. Laws are derived from observation statements through induction. Induction cannot be logically obtained. One can at most test the induced law by comparing its predictions with protocol statements. No general method of induction exists. And what is more, even a general method of testing is lacking, since definitely established protocol statements are missing (Neurath 1935b, 122-123). An "experimentum crucis", which can definitely falsify a particular hypothesis, does not exist (Neurath 1944, 954). For that reason, Neurath does not agree with Popper, who

[5] For another critique on Neurath's unified language project, see O'Neill (1995, 33). O'Neill argues that Neurath's programme to eliminate all intentional, ethical and metaphysical terms from the (social) sciences – which is clearly the most positivistic element in his work - is at odds with the "non-purified" vocabulary Neurath himself uses in his papers.

presents falsification as a logical method (Neurath 1935b, 123-124). Just as Popper replaces "verification" by "confirmation" of a theory, Neurath replaces "falsification" by "shaking". 'Negative results can *shake* [a scientist's] *confidence* in an encyclopedia, but not reduce it automatically to zero so to speak through the application of certain rules' (Neurath 1935b, 124).

Finally, the acceptance of a system of hypotheses results from a decision. The choice for a particular system of hypotheses depends on a specific selection of facts, on the use of specific analogies and on certain driving ideas which reflect a scientist's world view (Neurath 1916, 23-28). Different systems of hypotheses that are free from contradictions can exist. Among these systems, one can only make a selection on the basis of extra-logical factors (Neurath 1934, 106). Moreover, a completely axiomatised system that reveals possible remaining contradictions hardly occurs in practice. In practice

> one proceeds much more clumsily and is mostly glad to have some contradiction pointed out or a greater number of conformities. It is precisely the history of physics that shows that our procedures are often quite consciously defective. It happens that occasionally two contradictory hypotheses about the same subject are used at two places with some degree of success. And still, one knows that in a more complete system only *one* hypothesis should be used throughout. We just resign ourselves to a moderate clarification in order to delete or accept statements later (Neurath 1934, 109).

To recapitulate, according to Neurath science cannot be founded on something "absolute", "evident" or "a priori", be it primitive or atomic statements, absolute laws or systems of hypotheses, an indubitable method for inducting or testing or certain auxiliary tools such as logic, mathematics and an adequate unified language. It is the many decisions involved in scientific practice that urge us to see scientific theories as conceptual constructs. In Neurath's work, however, a tension exists between the positivistic idea that the concepts used are neutral (since purified from metaphysics) on the one hand and the idea that they are historically contingent and based on many decisions on the other. In this respect, Weber's analysis of the (social) sciences as ideal-typical and thus non-neutral is much more explicit and convincing. Since Neurath explains, moreover, that scientific "truth" cannot be a matter of correspondence, but at most a matter of coherence or consistency, we lack a *scientific* criterion to prefer one theory to another. The gap between conceptual constructs on the one hand and human reality on the other cannot (conceptually) be circumvented. Consequently, Neurath pleads for tolerance and pluralism within the community of scientists and for a multiplicity of scientific communities and, hence, theories.

1.3 Conclusion

Despite their different philosophical position, both Weber and Neurath agree that economic and political theories are conceptual constructs. According to Weber it is a value idea that defines the subject matter of a social science. Whether the economic and political sphere can be indicated as different domains of investigation thus depends on whether we can define different value ideas that make some phenomena economic ones and some (other) political ones. Weber's analysis of social-scientific methodology as ideal-typical convinces us that economic and political theories are conceptual constructs that arise from particular value-laden perspectives. Economic and political theories cannot be neutral. Since a variety of values can constitute a particular perspective, a multiplicity of economic and political theories is, in principle, possible. Weber argues, moreover, that no scientific criteria exist to prefer one value-laden perspective (i.e., one non-neutral theory) to another. Neurath's analysis of scientific theories confirms Weber's interpretation of them as conceptually constructed. In Neurath's view, they are conceptually constructed because they result from threefold decisions. First, scientists have to decide on the language used: how far should historical ordinary language be purified in order to be fit for scientific use? Second, both inducting from and testing protocol statements ask for decisions. Third, the acceptance of whole systems of hypotheses, i.e., of a theory, depends on decisions concerning the particular selection of data, the analogies used and the driving ideas constituting ones world view. Neurath's recognition of the various decisions needed to construct a theory confirms Weber's statement that theories are value-laden descriptions. Neurath further agrees with Weber that no scientific criteria exist to choose between theories. Neurath, like Weber, thus acknowledges that a multiplicity of economic and political theories can exist.

2 FOUR CONCEPTUAL CONSTRUCTS OF THE ECONOMIC SPHERE

In the history of economics we can find various perspectivistic descriptions of the economic sphere. In this section I will sketch four of them. Each description can be reconstructed as constituted by a different entry. The first entry consists of the products of economic actions, the second of their rationality, the third of the decision units within which economic actions occur, and the fourth of the institutions defining both products as well as rationality and decision units.

Economists use to consider Robbins' definition of economics as a good presentation of present-day orthodox economic theory (Dietz *et al.* 1994, 15; Mulberg 1995, 64). Lord Robbins exposes his paradigmatic framework in his Essay *on The Nature & Significance of Economic Science*, which he first published in 1932 [6]. Here, he defines orthodox, i.e., neo-classical theory as an analytical science. He contrasts this analytical conception with the older, classical definition that he calls classificatory (Robbins 1984, 16-31)[7]. The classical, classificatory conception delimits certain kinds of activities, namely those directed at the procuring of material welfare. The analytical conception, on the contrary, focuses on a particular aspect of behaviour, namely the form imposed by the influence of scarcity. Analytical

[6] Here, I will refer to the third edition of 1984.

[7] Dietz *et al.* use the terms "material" instead of "classificatory" and "formal" instead of "analytical" (Dietz *et al.* 1994, 15).

> economics is the science which studies human behaviour as a relationship between ends and scarce means which have alternative uses (Robbins 1984, 16).

It investigates human behaviour that occurs when four conditions of human existence are met at the same time. The first (and "evident") condition is that humans have a multiplicity of ends. The second one consists of the fact that the means needed to satisfy these ends are limited. Robbins calls this condition the condition of relative scarcity (a condition that is 'almost ubiquitous' (Robbins 1984, 15)). The third one occurs when those scarce means are capable of alternative application. The fourth and last condition is that those different ends have a different importance. When these four conditions are satisfied at the same time, human behaviour 'necessarily assumes the form of choice' (Robbins 1984, 14). Orthodox economics is meant to study this aspect of economic behaviour.

To recapitulate the two perspectives sketched by Robbins, we could state that it are the "products" made within an economy that constitute the subject matter of the classificatory conception of economics, while it is the "rationality" of actions within an economy that constitutes the subject matter of the analytical conception.

Robbins' analytical conception of economics conforms to Weber's interpretation of what he calls "pure" or "exact" economics. These terms point more particularly to the theory of marginal utility. According to Weber, economics originally questioned reality from the practical interest in the increase of the "wealth" of the population (MSS 85). Socialist criticism and the work of the historians caused a transformation of the original evaluative standpoints at the end of the nineteenth century (MSS 86). Since then the task of economics has been consisting of investigating human action which takes place under specific conditions:

> 1) as a consequence of the competition between different desires which long for satisfaction, 2) as a consequence of the limitation not only of the capacity to desire, but in the first place of the actual "goods" and "labour forces" which are useful for the "satisfaction" of each desire, and finally 3) as a consequence of a specific kind of coexistence of different people afflicted with the same or similar desires, but equipped with different stocks of goods to their satisfaction, and competing with each other for the means of satisfaction (GAW 389).

(Pure) economic theory assumes the existence of

> pure economic interests and precludes the operation of political or other non-economic considerations (MSS 44).

Pure economic interests depend on only one psychic motive: maximisation of the satisfaction of one's own competing desires (GAW 391). The subject-matter of pure economics is *rational* economic behaviour, i.e., human action which is "caused" by the only economic motive *and* which succeeds in satisfying this motive. The theory of marginal utility presupposes, among other things, that people are able to act more or less instrumentally, i.e., that they can choose the correct means for a given end by making use of their experience and their capacity to calculate in advance (GAW 390). Economic theory tries to catch this kind of successful, i.e., rational behaviour in a logically consistent axiomatic system.

As indicated in section 1, Weber acknowledges that "pure economics" is not the only possible perspective on an economy. He distinguishes three kinds of social-economic phenomena: (purely) economic, economically relevant and economically conditioned. Firstly,

> a phenomenon is [purely; MD] "economic" only insofar as and *only* as long as our *interest* is exclusively focused on its constitutive significance in the material struggle for existence (MSS 65).

Such are, for example, the phenomena of the stock exchange and the banking world. These phenomena especially - but not exclusively - occur in institutions which were deliberately created or used for economic ends (MSS 64). Secondly, phenomena that do not primarily interest us with respect to their economic significance, but that influence economic events in a manner that is of interest from an economic point of view are "economically relevant" (MSS 64). Good examples in this respect are the influences of religious beliefs (the Protestant ethic) and of political actions and structures (e.g., the state and its legal system). Those phenomena are the object of economic sociology and economic history (MSS 45). Thirdly, phenomena exist which are more or less strongly influenced by economic factors. The development of the artistic taste of a period for instance depends among other things on the social stratification of the artistically interested public. Weber calls those phenomena "economically conditioned" (MSS 64-65).

To recapitulate Weber's opinion, Weber imagines three possible perspectives on an economy. The first perspective conforms to Robbins' analytical conception of economics. In this case, it is the "rationality" of economic actions that constitutes the subject matter of economics. The second perspective regards the institutional order of an economy. It are the "institutions" influencing economic actions that constitute the subject matter of this second conception of economics. (I will define the concept "institution" more precisely in the next chapter.) The third perspective relates to the impacts of economic actions on other spheres in human reality.

Weber's second conception of economics shows, in its turn, some similarities with Neurath's interpretation of economics. For Neurath, the first task of economics is to compare different possible economies with regard to their economic quality (Neurath 1917, 103-111). An economy is an *order of life* or a *social structure* as far as it conditions human happiness (Neurath 1917, 109; 1931c, 395). An order of life is the totality of measures, institutions and customs and their changing (Neurath 1931c, 392-403). This order of life is always embedded in a certain *terrain of life*, to which belong climate, geographical conditions (such as the presence or absence of rivers and swamps, of populations of plants, animals and humans), and the tools and houses which happen to be at a people's disposal. The order of life is at the same time a reaction on and a stimulus to the terrain of life. On the one hand, this implies that geographical conditions are not decisive for the life of society. The social structure is essential: it can change even when geographical conditions remain constant. On the other hand, it means that a social structure can influence a certain terrain of life, even so profoundly that one recognises less and less what the geographical character was at the start. The order of life together with the terrain of life are responsible for a specific *living standard*, which consists of the provision for people's shelter, food and clothing, but also of their health, the friendliness of their human surroundings, the availability of books and theatres, etc.. Different orders of life may produce very different living standards within the same terrain of life. This living standard becomes itself part of the terrain of life. Consequently, it must be reckoned with thereafter as part of a continuously changing stimulus to a continuously changing order of life and terrain of life. The living standard, understood in its widest sense, conditions people's behaviour, i.e., their style and attitude of life. According to Neurath, it is possible to arrange attitudes in a sequence, depending on the amount of happiness they bring with them. The amount of happiness of a particular order of life is a measure of its economic efficiency (Neurath 1917, 107). Economics is, in Neurath's view, the science that investigates the correlations between orders of life and human happiness. Or, to connect Neurath's conception with previously mentioned ones, Neurath considers "institutions" influencing the "rationality" of economic (inter)actions and the kind of "products" made within an economy as the entities constituting the subject matter of economics.

This overview of Robbins', Weber's and Neurath's perspective on an economy allows me to propose the following four entries to economics. The first entry is the "products" made within an economy, i.e., "goods and services" or "commodities". The second entry is the "rationality" of human actions within an economy. The third entry, inspired by Weber (and Bromley, as we will see in a later chapter) is "decision units" typical for an economy (such as firms, households, banks etc.). The final entry is the "institutions" influencing actions within an economy. This latter entry is in some respect an overarching one, since a) what makes a decision unit an economic one, b) what makes a product a commodity and c) what defines the concrete form of "rational" economic action all depend on particular institutions (I will come back to this topic both in chapter 3 and chapter 7).

These four entries to economics are illustrative for my previous explanation that economic theories are conceptual constructs. Each entry defines in its own manner the set of phenomena that are deemed economic ones. We can, for instance, imagine that some phenomena occurring within economic decision units do not conform to the kind of typically economic "rationality". Such phenomena would be called "economic" according to the third perspective, but they would not according to the second one. Or we can imagine phenomena showing a typically economic "rationality" that, however, occur outside economic decision units. It is no use to ask which entry gives the better picture of an economy, since such question would betray our denying of the nature of an economic theory as a conceptual construct. All that remains is to accept the dissimilarities between various perspectivistic approaches within economics and to look for the entry best suited to solve particular (theoretical or practical) problems.

3 BUCHANAN'S POLITICAL THEORY

Buchanan is one of the originators of Public Choice theory. Public Choice theory is one example of a perspectivistic description of the political sphere. It is, more specifically, a political theory that investigates the conditions for an efficient democracy (De Beus 1989, 218). A democracy is considered to be efficient if it succeeds in correcting market failures through the promulgation of correct private property rights, the provision of desirable public goods, the internalisation of Pareto-relevant externalities and the provision of lacking market information. It is, in other words, a political theory that investigates the conditions for an optimal institutional organisation of the economic sphere. The analytical method of Public Choice theory is borrowed from (neo-classical) economics. Public Choice theory is, in short, an extension of (neo-classical) economics to – economic - policy (De Beus 1989, 214)[8].

Public Choice theory is meant to be a realistic description of political processes in the sense that it

> set[s] aside heroic conceptions of human nature [the "if men were angels" conception] and deal[s] with human behaviour as it is, warts and all (Brennan 1993, 137).

This "realistic" description reflects a particular normative perspective. I will deal more extensively with the normative content of Public Choice theory in order to illustrate the kind of non-neutral political recommendations to which this political theory gives rise.

3.1 *Public Choice Theory as an Extension of Economics*

Public choice theory is a political theory that emphasises the similarities between economic and political actions. It takes the view that political actions show the same rationality as economic actions. In the words of Buchanan,

> [p]ublic choice is a *perspective* on politics that emerges from an extension-application of the tools and methods of the economist to collective or non-market decision-making (Buchanan 1986, 19).

Buchanan adds that this quotation reproduces the public choice perspective accurately only if one has a specific interpretation of economics in mind, namely the interpretation which defines the domain of economics as the set of exchange actions and which accepts the ideal type of *homo oeconomicus* as an adequate description of an individual actor. In short, the economics of Public Choice theory is in the neo-classical vein. This "neo-classical vein" can be recapitulated, in the words of De Beus, as characterised by methodological individualism, subjectivism, and rational (even egoistic) behaviour (De Beus 1989, 240).

[8] I could also present Public Choice theory as a new institutional, rather than a neo-classical, economics (O'Neill 1994, 202). For Public Choice theory criticises (neo-classical) cost-benefit analyses as appropriate instruments to correct (ecological) market failures. The methodology of new institutionalism, however, mainly remains in the tradition of neo-classical economics.

Contrary to the neo-classical approach, Buchanan does not base his definition of economics on its analytical material object (Hemerijck 1994, 231). According to the neo-classical conception, economics investigates the material object constituted by people's striving for formal welfare under conditions of scarcity. Neo-classical economics considers markets, the entity where individuals exchange goods and services with each other, as the institutional domain where economics can be applied. Public choice theory, on the contrary, singles out the co-ordination mechanism deemed typical for an economy, namely exchange, from the neo-classical perspective. In this way, it changes the analytical domain of economics. Public choice theorists do not restrict themselves any longer to the domain of "private" markets. They extend their analysis to the domain of public government. Economics is henceforth the science of exchange actions, or in Buchanan's words, of all processes based on voluntary agreement (Buchanan 1986, 20).

Buchanan's extension of neo-classical economics to the political domain gives rise to a shift in the definition of politics. On the one hand, Buchanan treats political phenomena as if they show, with respect to their rationality, the same characteristics as economic phenomena. On the other hand, this equalisation urges him to introduce a new distinction between the typically political and the typically economic. From now on, actions within the political sphere are deemed to show a typically economic rationality as far as they are characterised by voluntary agreement. They are deemed to show a typically political rationality as far as they are manifestations of non-voluntary agreement. Political theory does henceforth no longer investigate phenomena occurring within a particular sphere, but all kinds of human interactions of which the rationality is a manifestation of coercion (Hemerijck 1994, 231). It investigates phenomena that are manifestations of involuntary relationships, of unequal power relationships (Buchanan 1986, 21). To conclude, the entry that is, according to Public Choice theory, decisive for the distinction between the typically economic and the typically political is the "rationality" of human interaction. It is a particular rationality that makes some phenomena political and other ones economic.

Buchanan acknowledges that both interpretations of economic and political phenomena are *perspectives* on empirical human relationships (Buchanan 1986, 21). He, moreover, stresses that purely economic or political actions hardly exist in reality. All real human interactions show characteristics of both perspectives. Exchange actions on markets are not free from "economic" power relationships, while in government power relationships go hand in hand with "political" cost-benefit considerations. In Buchanan's view

> the public choice perspective on politics [is] analogous to the economic power perspective on markets (Buchanan 1986, 22).

To recapitulate, Public Choice theory is a perspective on the political sphere that originates from an extension of (neo-classical) economics to the institutional domain of politics. This perspective gives rise to a redefinition of both political and economic theory. Political theory has, henceforth, involuntary human interactions as its domain of research. Economics has voluntary actions as its domain of research.

In both the economic and the political sphere, actions can show voluntary as well as involuntary aspects. Buchanan's Public Choice perspective is not so much constituted by a particular distinction between the political and the economic *sphere*. It is constituted by a particular distinction between the *rationality* of human interactions that occur both in the political and the economic sphere.

3.2 Political actors as Homines Oeconomici

According to the Public Choice perspective, the goal of politics consists of creating the institutional context, i.e. the political constitution that allows individuals to realise optimally their private ends. Buchanan, following Elinor Ostrom, distinguishes two levels in a political constitution. The first level, the level of constitutional choice, comprises rules that define political procedures. On the second level, the level of collective choice, political procedures lead to decisions concerning, for instance, economic institutions. The first level thus forms the institutional context of the second level. Buchanan as well as Ostrom interpret "politics" in a restricted sense as the set of decision processes taking place at the level of collective choice (Ostrom 1982, 210).

The task of Public Choice theorists consists of constructing theoretical models of various political constitutions (Buchanan 1986, 28-39). Their theoretical search is meant to track down the political constitution that is Pareto-efficient. A constitution is Pareto-efficient if one cannot find one that is better for one individual without being worse for another. The central question of Public Choice theory sounds: what legal restrictions can we expect individual actors of the type *homo oeconomicus* to acknowledge and to accept as the political constitution that allows them to strive after their private interests without further restrictions – i.e. without having to care about other people's welfare – and with an optimal realisation of the private interests of all economic actors as a result.

According to the Public Choice perspective, politics is initially directed at optimising the institutional organisation of an economy. An optimal institutional organisation of an economy maximises economic productivity and efficiency. Societies, because of their complexity due to the huge amount of democratic actors, need public authorities, a group of professional politicians. Professional politicians, however, are no more saints than are economic actors. Hence, one cannot expect them to act by themselves in service of the "general interest", in service of an optimisation of the institutional organisation of an economy. For that reason professional politicians, in their turn, need an institutional context that legally restricts their political actions (and the actions of those who vote political representatives). Public choice theorists aim at an optimisation of the institutional organisation of the economy as well as the polity. Both are spheres in human reality where actors of the type *homo oeconomicus* can go their own way unimpededly. Optimisation of the institutional organisation of a polity, however, is subordinate to optimisation of the institutional organisation of an economy.

3.3 More Markets, Less Government

Buchanan's Public Choice perspective leads to a normative plea for more "market" and less "government"[9]. His line of reasoning goes as follows:

> To the extent that voluntary exchange among persons is valued positively while coercion is valued negatively, there emerges the implication that substitution of the former for the latter is desired, on the presumption, of course, that such substitution is technologically feasible and is not prohibitively costly in resources. This implication provides the normative thrust for the proclivity of the public choice economist to favour market-like arrangements where these seem feasible, and to favour decentralization of political authority in appropriate situations (Buchanan 1986, 22).

Government has a minimal task to define and protect property rights (Buchanan 1986, 252-256). Property rights define what individuals can do autonomously, i.e. without interference of others. They determine the boundaries between public and private. These boundaries are no natural entities, but result from political processes. Since everybody prefers freedom to coercion, one should aim for maximal freedom. Private properties are, however, mutually exclusive: one person's right is another person's non-right. Consequently, personal freedom has to be limited. Political processes are needed to define these limitations. They are meant to search for fair property rights. Property rights are fair if political actors, acting conform to legal political procedures, can assent to them.

Next to this minimal task of government, Buchanan preserves a minor task related to other political objectives, such as the distribution of income, citizen's health and safety, care for our natural environment, etc. (Buchanan 1986, 256-257). He interprets such political objectives as corrections to be made after "markets" have done their work. He is, moreover, reluctant to leave them to public authorities. In his view, "market failures" more often than not give rise to "government failures", because bureaucrats and politicians – as *homines oeconomici* - aim for a continuous expansion of public expenditures, with irrational and inefficient spending as a result.

3.4 Processes as the Touch Stone of Politics

The public choice perspective interprets political actors as *homines oeconomici.* This interpretation gives rise to an interpretation of political values as strictly subjective. Hence, democratic processes cannot be understood as a means to look for values that receive common consent. Democratic procedures only exist in order to create the institutional environment that allows individuals to realise their private ends in an optimal way. Therefore, public choice theory concentrates on political *processes*, not on political *content.*

> To the extent that political interaction among persons is modelled as a complex exchange process, in which the inputs are individual evaluations or preferences, and the

---

[9] John O'Neill notes that various public-choice-schools exist which disagree with each other in this respect (O'Neill 1994, 203 note 1). The plea for limited government is typical for the Virginian School of Public Policy, where Buchanan belongs to. This school bears a clear Austrian mark: Buchanan's later writings are strongly influenced by Hayek.

> process itself is conceived as the means through which these possibly diverging preferences are somehow combined or amalgamated into a pattern of outcomes, attention is more or less necessarily drawn to the interaction process itself rather than to some transcendental evaluation of the outcomes themselves (Buchanan 1986, 22).

Who aims at ameliorating political decisions, has to improve the rules constituting decision processes.

Buchanan's interest in political constitutions regards the quality of political *processes*. In his view, one cannot argue rationally about the quality of the results of political processes. Whether the result is good, depends on whether the process is good. Political processes are no means subordinate to and derived from a political goal; the goal is rather derived from the process. The quality of the process is the only standard for measuring the quality of the result. But how to measure the quality of the process? Though Buchanan denies that a political constitution aims at a particular "common good", Pareto-efficiency proves to be his standard for measuring the quality of political processes. At the same time, since the values of political actors are strictly private, the concrete meaning of this "efficiency" can only become clear through the political processes themselves[10].

Buchanan's interpretation of political actors as of a *homo oeconomicus* type implies an interpretation of politics as a bargaining process. The public choice perspective assumes that the preferences and interests of political actors are given. The most political actors can do is bargaining with each other till they reach some equilibrium level. Public Choice politics thus results in adding new institutions to the existing set rather than in transforming this set (Faber 1997, 461-463). For to begin with, *homo oeconomicus* is not capable of suspending his short-term interests and imagining his possible interests in a new institutional context. Nor can he estimate whether his long-term interests are more or less acceptable then his immediate ones. Secondly, maximisation of preference satisfaction is his only motive, not one or another "common good" such as a new institutional organisation. In case political actors have to solve some new political problems, all they can do is to define new property rights and to add them to the existing set. Buchanan calls this "The Creation of Rights" (Faber 1997, 461). These new property rights imply an expansion, not a

[10] Stating that "efficiency" is a standard for a good political constitution does not come down to claiming that some persons can judge existing political constitutions on the base of their privileged, concrete insight in the meaning of "efficiency". Consider the following quotation: 'The market is an institutional process within which individuals interact, one with another, in pursuit of their separate individual objectives, whatever these may be. The great discovery of the eighteenth-century philosophers was that, within appropriately designed laws and institutions, separately self-interested individual behaviour in the market generates a spontaneous order, a pattern of allocational-distributional outcomes that is chosen by no one, yet which is properly classified as an order in that it reflects a maximization of the values of the participating persons. What these values are are defined only in the process itself; the individual values, as such, do not exist outside or independently of the process within which they come to be defined. In this sense, and in this sense only, can the order generated in the market process be labelled or classified as "efficient". Economists who presume some inherent ability to define that which is "efficient" independently from the behaviour of persons in the market process itself, a definition that is then utilized to evaluate the performance of the market as an institution, these economists presume an arrogance that simply should not be countenanced' (Buchanan 1986, 88).

transformation of existing political constitution. Paradoxically enough, a Public Choice perspective gives rise to a constitutional democracy that evolves towards a welfare state. According to Faber *c.s.*, Buchanan does not only warn for this – in his view: disastrous – development. He even admits that such development is an inherent dilemma of a Public Choice approach (Faber 1997, 462).

3.5 Conclusion

Buchanan's Public Choice theory originates from an expansion of neo-classical economics to the domain of (economic) policy. This theory does not respect the analytical domain of economics, namely the economic sphere that is the institutional domain of markets. It extends the analytical domain of economics to the political sphere. Buchanan acknowledges that this extension is a particular *perspective* on politics.

This perspective is *not neutral*. To begin with, it considers politics to be, in the last instance, about an optimal institutional organisation of an economy, i.e., an institutional organisation that maximises economic productivity and efficiency. It assumes, further, political actors to be of the *homo oeconomicus* type. Moreover, political processes, rather than their content, are the criterion with which to judge politics. Finally, Public Choice theory leads to political recommendations for more markets and less government.

Curiously enough, the perspective of Public Choice theory gives rise to a *redefinition* of both the typically economic and the typically political. Economic actions are, henceforth, considered to be voluntary, while political actions are deemed to be involuntary. This redefinition stresses a particular rationality as distinctive for economic and political phenomena. "Rationality" is thus the entry that constitutes Public Choice theory as a conceptual construct.

4 DELIBERATIVE DEMOCRACY

Deliberative democracy is an alternative conceptual construct of the political sphere of which Hannah Arendt is an important originator. The main difference between the construct of Public Choice theory and the construct of deliberative democracy regards their respective originator's interpretation of the nature of political rationality. While Buchanan considers typically political interactions as manifestations of coercion, Arendt considers typically political interactions as manifestations of (a particular kind of) freedom. In this section, I will use the four entries mentioned in section 2 to conceptually (re)construct the political theory of deliberative democracy (though I will not introduce these entries in the order previously provided). This reconstruction will show relevant features of the political and the economic sphere respectively and, meanwhile, illustrate that Buchanan's and Arendt's differing perspectives on the political sphere relate especially to the entry of the "rationality" of political interactions.

Some people would call the construct of Public Choice theory an example of a political *theory* and the construct of deliberative democracy an example of a political *philosophy*. According to Goodin *et al.* a possible distinction between political theory and political philosophy could be that the former is rather descriptive, while the latter is rather normative (Goodin *et al.* 1993, 1). Given previous analysis that all conceptual constructs are value-laden, non-neutral, perspectivistic descriptions, this distinction is not accurate enough. Therefore I propose the following reformulation. Both political theories and political philosophies are non-neutral descriptions of a particular domain in human reality. Political philosophies differ, however, from political theories to the extent that they offer good reasons to consider one non-neutral description rather than another as a guiding ideal. In the introductory chapter, I explained (see section 2.1) that my own research project takes "deliberative democracy" as a guiding political ideal. In this section I will explain the features of a deliberative democracy. In section 5, I will offer reasons why we should, from the viewpoint of sustainability, choose deliberative democracy rather than Public Choice theory as a guiding political ideal.

4.1 *Economic* versus *Political Decision Units*

One perspective on the economic and the political sphere takes "decision units" as its entry. In section 2 we mentioned firms, households, banks as examples of economic decision units. As examples of political decision units we can mention parliament, ministries, government, and local councils. The political sphere does, however, not only comprise public authorities. It also comprises citizens that are, in one way or another, politically active. Therefore, we can mention as other examples of political decision units action groups, non-governmental organisations and even unorganised citizens who vote once in a while, who occasionally discuss political themes, or who gather relevant information. The term "decision unit" should thus not be interpreted too literally as a unit in which final decisions are taken, but as a unit in which political themes are at least reflected on and debated. According to this perspective, phenomena taking place in economic decision units are economic phenomena, while phenomena occurring in political decision units are political ones.

4.2 *"Homines Oeconomici" versus "Homines Politici"*

The "rationality" of actions constitutes another perspective. The rationality of economic actions is defined by a specific motive, namely to maximise the satisfaction of the actor's competing desires. This rationality is deemed to be instrumental. It consists of choosing the best means for a particular end. These ends are, further, thought of as given, rather static and hierarchically ordered. The ideal type of *homo oeconomicus* is considered an adequate description of a rational economic actor. I will contrast this ideal type of *homo oeconomicus* with Arendt's explanation of *homo politicus*.

According to Arendt, *homo politicus* cannot be caught in an ideal type. This is because political actors remain, in a certain sense, anonymous, for two reasons (Arendt 1958, 175-181). First, *homines politicos* reveal in acting and speaking *who*, not: *what*, they are. Their uniqueness escapes an unequivocal verbal expression. Whenever we try to explain *who* somebody is, our vocabulary leads us astray into saying *what* he or she is. We cannot but offer a description of qualities that he (or she) necessarily shares with others like him (or her). Such description provides us with a type, with the result that a person's uniqueness – and, hence, the person acting politically - escapes us. A person cannot even dispose of his own uniqueness. Though political actors can, through their words and deeds, show themselves very clearly and unmistakably to others, they remain hidden for themselves. They cannot dispose of who they are; they cannot purposefully aim for the disclosure of their own uniqueness.

Second, *homines politici* do not act alone, but in a "web" of human relationships (Arendt 1958, 181-192). Only in a web of human relationships does political action lead to political events. Political actors are at most a link in, but never the author of a political event. They can begin such an event, but they cannot control or manage it. Every political action falls into an already existing web with innumerable, conflicting wills and intentions. In such a web action almost never achieves its purpose. Every action causes a chain reaction and every process a series of processes. Since action acts upon beings who are capable of their own actions, reaction is not merely a response, but a new action.

The twofold anonymity of political actors explains why political events cannot be understood in terms of means and ends. Political events are not "made". Political events do not conform to instrumental rationality. The "means", i.e. the political action, is at the same time the "end", i.e. a manifestation of *who* people are. This manifestation rests on initiative. To take initiative means to begin something new that cannot be expected from whatever may have happened before. It is an outstanding manifestation of human freedom. Since political events are reflections of human freedom, the political arena is the domain where the 'wholly improbable happens regularly' (Arendt 1958, 300). In this domain it is highly unrealistic not to reckon with the unexpected, that is, not to reckon with something with which nobody can safely reckon.

> To act in the form of making, to reason in the form of "reckoning with consequences", means to leave out the unexpected, the event itself, since it would be unreasonable or irrational to expect what is no more than an "infinite improbability". [...] The political philosophy of the modern age [...] founders on the perplexity that modern rationalism is unreal and modern realism is irrational – which is only another way of saying that reality and human reason have parted company (Arendt 1958, 300).

The boundlessness of the web of human relationships causes the unpredictability of political events. *Homines politicos* never know precisely what they are doing. They always become "guilty" of consequences they never intended or could foresee (Arendt 1958, 233). Political events are at the same time irreversible. No matter how disastrous and unexpected the consequences of political deeds, they can never be undone. The event cannot be consummated unequivocally in one single deed or event.

In the political sphere people should act as equals (Arendt 1958, 180). Only where people act *with* others and neither for nor against them can people reveal *who* they are in speech and action. People who are for or against each other use their words and deeds in order to achieve a goal. They lose sight of the unique identity of political actors. In this case political action is no less a means to an end than making is a means to produce an object. In such instances, speech becomes mere talk, whether it serves to deceive the enemy or to dazzle everybody with propaganda. "Power" is the capacity to act politically, to act as equals (Arendt 1958, 199-203). Freedom, positive and negative, is a condition for political power. Political actors should be free of the day-to-day worries related to the necessities of life. Negative freedom – the absence of immediate necessities – is a requisite for acting as equals in the public sphere. Negative freedom allows persons to postpone their immediate wills and predetermined, short-term interests and to reflect on a desirable societal organisation. Political actors at the same time express their positive freedom. Political events are creative realisations of what it can mean to be human. As such they are more than immediate fulfilment of the necessities of life and the production of useful objects[11].

To recapitulate, according to Arendt it is not possible to construct an ideal type of *homo politicus*. Political speech and action are meant to reveal *who* people are. This unique expression of human freedom cannot be caught in an ideal type. Moreover, political actors always act with each other in a web of human relationships. Consequently, *homo politicus* is never the author of political events. One cannot catch the "rationality" of political events either. Political events are unpredictable and irreversible. Finally, one cannot think of political processes as a means to realise a particular end, since the end, i.e. the realisation of human freedom, is revealed in the processes themselves. This implies that a societal organisation – which is a manifestation of politics - is never "made". This brings us to the third perspective constituted by the "product" of (economic or political) actions.

4.3 "Goods and Services" versus *"Laws"*

Goods and services – including labour power and capital - are the products of economic actions. (Formal) institutions or laws are the "products" – the term is not convenient, as will be clear from the above explanation - of political actions. The analysis of institutions that follows is inspired by, but not a direct reproduction of, Arendt's reflections on "worldly things".

According to Arendt, political *praxis* relates to two in-betweens: the "objective" world of relative stable, physical things on the one hand and the "subjective" web of

[11] Note that Arendt's interpretation of negative and positive freedom is dissimilar to the conventional interpretation that dates back to Berlin's political philosophy. For an explanation of the latter interpretation, see De Beus (1989, 11-21).

human relationships (Arendt 1958, 182-184). The objective world is the world of things that lie between people – and that, therefore, relate and bind them together - and out of which arise their specific, objective, worldly interests. Worldly things are "objective": they are relatively stable, compared to goods and services on the one hand and ever changing natural things on the other. They also provide "objectivity". They supply people with an identity: people can ascribe meaning to various events because they experience them in relation with relative stable worldly things.

Arendt implicitly distinguishes between two kinds of worldly things. First, there are tools and instruments. Instruments are "made" (Arendt 1958, 139-144). The process of making is entirely determined by the categories of means and end. The means is the process of making; the end is the product. A tool or instrument is the realisation of an image or model. This image or model does not only precede the fabrication process, it also survives it. Second, there are works of art (Arendt 1958, 167-174). Works of art have no utility. They are unique and non-exchangeable. Contrary to instruments, they are no realisations of already existing images. They are "thought things": the thought exists together with the reified work of art. Works of art are, according to Arendt, the most worldly things because they go beyond the functionalism of consumption goods and the utility of instruments.

Considering the characteristics that Arendt assigns to "worldly things", institutions can be regarded as worldly entities, though they are not necessarily physical things. Institutions are more or less stable, since they are regularities shown in human actions (I will examine the nature of institutions further in the next chapter). They are the background and interest of political *praxis*. Political (and – indirectly – also other) institutions define political decision units, processes and, hence, their results. Political and other social institutions are the direct interest and "results" of political actions. Some institutions remain implicit. Laws are explicit or formal institutions: as written texts they are made tangible things.

Institutions look more like "works of art" than like "instruments". They are not the realisation of a pre-existing image. They are not "made". Contrary to works of art, institutions are not thought things either. Institutions are no expressions of the thoughts of individual artists, but of the actions of free and equal persons. An institution is an – this is my term - "interaction thing". More than an expression of thinking, it is an expression of acting. More than an expression of acting, it is an expression of acting together from a plurality of positions and perspectives. Institutions reflect what societal organisation we deem dignified. For that reason, the institutional organisation of a society cannot be straightforwardly derived from "objective" science, since it is always a creative answer of people living in a specific historical context and an expression of "new" values.

Arendt calls the typically political "rationality" from which institutions emerge "judging"[12]. Judging is the capacity political actors need in order to form opinions.

[12] These paragraphs are based on Bernstein's reconstruction of Arendt's concept (Bernstein 1983, 207-223). Arendt herself did not find time to work this concept out systematically. "Judgement" was the

The capacity to judge is the capacity to consider a given issue from different viewpoints by making present in one's mind the standpoints of those who are absent.

> The more people's standpoints I have present in my mind while I am pondering a given issue, and the better I can imagine how I would feel and think if I were in their place, the stronger will be my capacity for representative thinking and the more valid my final conclusions, my opinion (Arendt 1961, 241).

The formation of opinions is a typically political activity. It is not a private activity performed by solitary thinkers. In order to form a political opinion, political actors should test and enlarge their personal judgements by confronting them with differing judgements. For that reason, opinions can only be formed within a community of equal political actors that are prepared to submit their judgements to public exposure and debate.

Opinions should be distinguished both from truth and from interests. Truth emerges from cognitive rationality and aims at universal validity. Opinion emerges from judgement and aims at particular validity. Judging is not a matter of subsuming particular states of affairs under general rules, but a matter of ascending from particular interests to public opinions. On the one hand, opinions are not universally valid. They have a restricted validity, for judgement's validity cannot extend further than the others in whose place judging persons have put themselves in the process of forming an opinion. On the other hand, opinions have a wider validity than have private interests. For private interests refer to individual preferences and situations. Opinions, on the contrary, express a *sensus communis*. Opinions emerge from a mode of thinking that is capable of dealing with the particular in its particularity but which nevertheless makes a claim to communal validity.

4.4 Economic versus *Political Institutions*

Institutions (formal or explicit as well as informal or implicit ones) define – as will become more clear in the next chapter - what counts as an economic good or service, give concrete content to rational economic action, and define an economic decision unit. It is also institutions that define political decision units, the rationality of political "processes" and what counts as a law. For that reason I called "institutions" an overarching entry in section 2. Two further remarks related to this institutional perspective on both the economic and the political sphere are on their place here.

To start with, I have to reformulate the remark made in section 2. There, I suggested that some phenomena occurring within economic decision units could show a rationality that is rather political than economic. Think, for instance, of deliberations happening within a firm concerning ecologically benign production processes. Such phenomena would be called economic according to the perspective taking decision units as its entry, but political according to the perspective taking rationality as its entry. We can also imagine the reverse, i.e., phenomena showing a typically

---

topic planned for the third part of her book *The Life of the Mind*, but Arendt died before she could start this project.

economic rationality that, however, occur within political decision units. Think, as an example, of cost-benefit analyses carried out within a particular ministry to provide the citizenry with the most economical public transportation system. Such phenomena would be called political according to the former entry, but economic according to the latter. These examples show that, though it is possible to construct conceptually a distinction between the economic and the political sphere, both spheres cannot simply be separated. Concrete actions often show economic as well as political aspects.

Second, the distinction made with the help of the four entries between the economic and the political sphere – or, in plural, the distinctions made, since the different perspectives do not simply define the same set of phenomena as economic or political respectively – show that institutions are the entities that link both spheres. On the one hand, political actions give rise to implicit and explicit institutions (which does not imply that all institutions are politically defined). On the other hand, it is institutions (politically and non-politically defined ones) that define an economy, i.e., commodities, economic rationality and economic decision units. This link explains the kind of hierarchy that exists between the political and economic sphere. Politically defined institutions are preconditions for economic actions. They enable economic actions and they restrict them at the same time. This kind of hierarchy is a logical one: politically defined institutions are logically prior to economic actions. This logical hierarchy, however, does not exclude another reverse hierarchy between the economic and the political sphere. Since unequal economic power relationships give rise to unequal political power relationships, they prevent citizens and politicians to act in a typically political way as free and equal persons. In other words, they cause a typically political rationality to be suppressed and replaced by a typically economic rationality. If this is the case, predetermined, short-term economic interests of some powerful groups will become dominant political interests. The content of politically defined institutions will then heavily be influenced by the economic institutions that initially gave rise to the unequal economic power relationships in question. This kind of reverse hierarchy is not a logical one. It is a substantive one. It is the concrete content of politically defined economic institutions – economic institutions that allow for particular unequal economic power relationships - that cause a political rationality to shift into an economic one.

4.5 Conclusions

The first three entries mentioned in section 2 – decision units, rationality, products – allowed me to reconstruct, with the help of Arendt's political philosophy, deliberative democracy as an alternative political theory. The features of a deliberative democracy can be recapitulated as follows. To start with, deliberative politics occurs in political decision units that are institutionally defined. Second, deliberative rationality proves to be "irrational" and "communicative". It is irrational in the sense that deliberative politics is unpredictable and irreversible. It is "communicative", not "instrumental" – to use Habermas' terminology – because deliberative politics is a matter of *interacting*, not a matter of *making* nor of *bargaining*[13]. It is a matter of interacting as free and equal persons, i.e., acting with each other, not for or against each other. It is not a matter of making, because deliberative politics cannot be separated into means (i.e., processes) on the one hand and previously defined ends (i.e., institutions) on the other. The ends (or the products, to introduce a third entry) emerge in the course of politics as ever-provisional interpretations of a dignified human society. They are provisional because political interaction is never finished (there is no definite end to realise), because they depend on political actors' creative initiatives, and because they can shift depending on the extent of political equality. It is not a matter of bargaining, because it is not a matter of balancing predetermined interests or values. Political values, objectives or institutions emerge, as "interaction-things", in the course of politics.

In the words of Gutmann, the ideal of deliberative democracy conceives of politics as the set of "processes" where autonomous people relate to one another not merely by asserting their wills or fighting for their predetermined interests, but by influencing each other through the publicly valued use of reasoned argument, evidence, evaluation and persuasion. In a deliberative democracy, people collectively shape their own politics, and hence their societal institutions, through persuasive argument. Reasoned persuasion is considered the most justifiable form of political power because it is the most consistent with respecting the autonomy of equal persons, their capacity for self-government (Gutmann 1993, 417—418).

The fourth entry – institutions – allowed me to understand the relationship between the political and the economic sphere. Between the political and the economic sphere exists a logical hierarchy. Political interaction is logically prior to economic action, because it is politically defined economic institutions that enable and restrict economic autonomy. This logical hierarchy does not necessarily prevent a reverse, substantive hierarchy. The concrete content of economic institutions can give rise to particular unequal (economic and political) power relationships that cause, within the political sphere, a shift from political to economic rationality.

Application of the four entries on both the political and the economic sphere does not only allow me to construct deliberative democracy as an alternative to Public Choice theory. It also allows me to (re)confirm the legitimacy of typically economic action. Within the economic sphere, economic decision units are justified to act rather instrumentally and to organise their means to realise their ends as good as they can. (Though, as will become clear in the next chapter, these ends should not necessarily be interpreted –as Buchanan does - as egoistic.) Economic actors are justified to act autonomously, without caring about others' ends, within the

[13] For a clear explanation about Habermas' interpretation of communicative and instrumental rationality, see Erlauterungen zum Begriff des kommunikativen Handelns, in: Habermas, J. (1984). *Vorstudien und Ergänzungen zur Theorie des kommunikativen Handelns*. Frankfurt: Suhrkamp, p. 571-606.

institutionally defined boundaries of their private domain. The ideal of deliberative democracy indeed leaves room for two types of "autonomy": an individual, private or economic one and a collective, public or political one. The former corresponds to the idea of individual freedom, the opportunity of all persons to live under laws of their own individual choosing. The latter takes the social context of individual choice into consideration. This social context influences and constrains the life choices that individuals can make by themselves for themselves, free from interference. Politics has to some extent control over this social context. Public or political autonomy regards the opportunity and capability to shape this social context through political processes (Gutmann 1993, 417-418).

5 POLITICS AND SUSTAINABILITY

In the introductory chapter, I defined sustainability as a "guiding idea" reflecting our striving for intergenerational justice in the way we go about with the ecological dimensions of earthly life. The concept refers to our responsibility for the ecological impacts of our present economic activities on the lives of future generations. We should make sure that these ecological impacts are compatible with the idea of intergenerational justice. The concept assumes, to start with, that we are able to manage the ecological impacts of our economies. For responsibility presupposes manageability. It assumes, moreover, that we are able to provide the concept with concrete content. I consider it to be a task of economics to help us make the ecological impacts of our economies manageable again. Therefore, economics should investigate reasons for the unmanageability of the ecological performance of our present industrial economies. I consider it to be a task of politics to provide the term sustainability with concrete content, provisional though it may be. Formulated more precisely, I consider it a task of politics to look for institutions that reflect our tentative interpretations of an ecologically manageable and intergenerationally just economy.

Arendt's deliberative interpretation of politics is better equipped to deal with the question of sustainability than is Buchanan's Public Choice perspective, for two reasons. First, it leaves room for sustainability as a possible political objective. Public Choice theory, on the contrary, reduces political objectives to the only objective of an *optimal* institutional organisation of an economy. Second, it allows for a typically political interpretation of these objectives.

To begin with the first reason, Arendt strongly disapproves of the (Modern) idea that private wealth is no longer a condition that allows people to act as free and equal political actors, but a reason to act politically in order to gather more and more wealth (Arendt 1958, 69) [14]. In other words, she disapproves of Buchanan's

[14] Arendt strongly rejects the Modern idea that private wealth is not a private matter, but a public affair. She, therefore, introduces a distinction between social and political questions. Social questions relate to the distribution of wealth. Hence, the existence of poverty is the most prominent social question. Political questions regard questions concerning a dignified, creative organisation of our societies. In Arendt's view political questions can only be resolved after the social question of poverty is resolved,

interpretation of politics as being in the service of an optimal, i.e., most productive and efficient, organisation of an economy. In Buchanan's perspective, politics is reduced to an administration of a national household. It is mainly meant to avoid conflicts between wealth-accumulating individuals, rather than to express creative interpretations of a desirable human society.

Public Choice theory considers an optimal, not a sustainable, organisation of an economy as the first and nearly exclusive interest of professional politicians. An interpretation of politics in terms of a deliberative democracy, on the contrary, leaves room for political objectives other than economic optimality as, for instance, a fair distribution of wealth or a safe and healthy (ecological) environment.

Deliberative democracy leaves, moreover, room for a political interpretation of these objectives. In Buchanan's view, political processes are bargaining processes. Bargaining processes are strategic actions. Strategic people act in order to satisfy their predetermined, private interests as good as possible without showing much consideration for others' interests. The concrete content of political objectives will, hence, depend on subjective values, not on ethical dispute. Strategic actors do not act with each other, as free – free from immediate concerns for private wealth – and equal – equal in their capacity to express personal visions on a humanly organised society – individuals. They are simply not capable of dealing with reasoned arguments that threaten to change their preferences and interests. In Arendt's view, on the contrary, political processes are creative processes. They introduce new interpretations of common as well as private interests and values. They thus provide individuals with opportunities to gain new insights and to transform their interpretations of interests and values *and* of institutional organisations that possibly can realise them. Deliberative actors are, in the words of O'Neill, capable of reflecting on the institutional conditions for sustainable economic practices. They can imagine what institutions could foster a wide conception of their interest that encourages sustainable practices (O'Neill 1994, 213-214).

6 CONCLUSIONS

In this chapter, I argue that we can and should distinguish between the political and the economic sphere. From Weber's and Neurath's methodological writings, we learn that economic and political theories are conceptual constructs. This implies, to start with, that they are perspectivistic descriptions of human reality. Weber is more consistent in his interpretation of the meaning thereof than is Neurath. While Neurath understands a perspectivistic description, rather positivistically, as a merely historically contingent description, Weber plainly acknowledges its value-ladenness or non-neutrality. That economic and political theories are conceptual constructs implies, moreover, that a multiplicity of theories is possible and that no scientific

because political questions ask for political actors, i.e., for free and equal individuals. Social liberation is a condition for political freedom. Bernstein notes that this distinction cannot be upheld, for, if – as Arendt states – every person must be given the opportunity to participate in politics, then a primary political question is how to resolve the social question (Bernstein 1986, 120).

criterion exists to prefer one theory to another. It implies, finally, that the economic and the political sphere *can*, in principle, be distinguished.

In the history of economic science we can discern four possible perspectives on the economic sphere. These perspectives allow us to define four entries constituting four possible economic theories, namely decision units, rationality, products and institutions (of which the latter is an overarching one). The harvest of this historical overview does, however, not yet answer the question whether we *should* distinguish between the economic and the political sphere.

To answer this latter question, I contrast Buchanan's Public Choice theory with deliberative democracy. Public Choice theory originates form an extension of (neo-classical) economics to the political domain. It considers political actors as *homines oeconomici*, who bargain with each other to balance their predetermined, short-term interests. It interprets political processes as a means to fulfil political ends. Economic optimality proves to be the main political end. Deliberative democracy, on the contrary, considers political actors as free and equal individuals who interact with each other in order to gain creative, reasoned and shared interpretations of desirable (economic) institutions. It understands political ends as coming into existence in the course of political debates and it interprets institutions as historical reflections of these ever-provisional ends.

Initially, Buchanan stresses the similarities between economic and political phenomena. He treats both political and economic phenomena as if they show the same rationality. Interestingly enough, his approach gives rise to a redefinition of the typically economic and the typically political that is based on a new distinction. Typically economic interactions are, henceforth, deemed voluntary, while typically political interactions are deemed involuntary.

Buchanan's Public Choice theory proves, further, not to be well equipped to deal with the problem of sustainability, for two reasons. First, it subjects the political objective of sustainability to the political objective of economic optimality. Second, it does not stimulate a creative and reasoned public search for economic institutions that contribute to the satisfaction of our (newly defined) private interests and values on the one hand and to shared, though provisional, interpretations of sustainability on the other.

Contrary to Buchanan, Arendt stresses, from the very beginning, the dissimilarities between the economic and the political sphere. The distinctions she makes do not only open political ways to deal with the problem of sustainability. They also reconfirm the legitimacy of economic action. Economic actors are justified to act rather instrumentally in order to satisfy their private interests as good as they can. Justified economic action, however, depends on logically prior political action. It is the task of politics to define the institutional boundaries of the private domain that allow economic actors to act autonomously. To conclude, though we lack a scientific criterion to prefer one political theory to another, we have at least two good reasons to choose deliberative democracy rather than Public Choice theory. It is with the ideal of a deliberative democracy in mind, that, in chapter 4, I will develop norms for the nature of a politically successful economics.

CHAPTER 3

THE INSTITUTIONAL AND ECOLOGICAL DIMENSION OF AN ECONOMY

In the previous chapter, I argued for *deliberative democracy* as a suitable conceptual construct of the *political* sphere in order to deal with the problem of sustainability. The normative ideal of a deliberative democracy embroiders on a distinction between economic and political actions. It presumes a typically economic (i.e., instrumental) and a typically political (i.e., communicative) rationality, typically economic and typically political products (i.e., commodities and institutions respectively), and typically economic and political decision units. In this chapter, on the contrary, I will reflect on a suitable conceptual construct of the *economic* sphere in order to deal with the problem of sustainability.

In the introductory chapter 1, I argued that economics should investigate *reasons* for the present unmanageability of the ecological performance of industrial economies. This statement is still too abstract. For a politically relevant economics should not investigate whatever kind of reasons, but reasons that can be influenced, transformed or removed through political action. Since institutions are the domain of political action, this implies that it should look for *institutional reasons*. In other words, the nature of my research question prompts for an institutional perspective on the economic sphere. Such institutional interpretation accepts the distinctions between (the rationality of) economic and political action underlying the normative ideal of a deliberative democracy, but it concentrates on "economic institutions" as the entities that make economic rationality as well as economic products and economic decision units concrete.

The statement that it is economic institutions that make economic action concrete implies that it is economic institutions that define the ecological performance of economic action. This latter implication expresses the conviction that an internal relationship exists between the ecological performance of an economy and its institutional organisation. In order to found this conviction, I will, in section 1, deal extensively with the concept "institution" in general. I will propose an interpretation of the concept that considers it as one dimension, namely the symbolic dimension, of human action. The other dimension of human action consists of its material (or physical or ecological) *substratum*. This interpretation of institutions allows us to understand (economic and other) actions as phenomena that unavoidably consist of both a symbolic and an ecological dimension. In section 2, I will concentrate on *economic* institutions and I will illustrate the idea that the ecological performance of an economy is internally connected to its institutional organisation. I will, further, argue that, in order to understand this internal connection, we need insights into the institutional whole of an economy. This institutional whole can be interpreted in a classificatory or a hierarchical way.

1 INSTITUTIONS

The term "institution" is a concept with many senses. Economics, political science, history, sociology and philosophy each have their own interpretation of the concept. In this section I will, first, propose a definition of an institution that is in line with its use in the tradition of institutional economics. Veblen and Commons are two important originators of this tradition; Neale is a prominent present-day representative. For that reason, their interpretations of the concept "institution" function as starting points. Since Bromley, whose theoretical work is the subject matter of chapter 7 and 8, also belongs to this same tradition, his interpretation will be another point of reference. The definition I propose is so constructed that it allows us to distinguish between economic and other institutions, and to consider of an economy as a sphere in human reality of which its ecological performance is the counterpart of its institutional organisation. The latter part of this statement will be illustrated in section 2.

Second, I will enlarge on the way institutions come about. This explanation will enforce Arendt's statement (see section 4.2 in chapter 2) that one cannot characterise a particular "rationality" with which to grasp the coming into existence of institutions. Institutions are creative, unpredictable and irreversible events. They have no single author. They are, nevertheless, the (often unintended) result of intentional interaction.

Third, I will deal with the nature of institutions as both enabling and restricting. This nature holds in a double sense: In one sense, institutions that restrict one party enable another party. In another sense, individuals are only able to act thanks to institutions that condition the form of their actions. This is another way to say that absolute freedom does not exist. Freedom is always relative to rules that provide actions with meaning.

Finally, I will reflect on the nature of institutions as "public facts". Institutions are public facts in the sense that they result from political action and in the sense that they are valid for all members of a political community. I introduce the concept "publiç fact" to distinguish institutions from "public goods". (The relevance of this distinction will become more clear in section 2). Institutions as "public facts" are political entities, while "public goods" are economic entities.

1.1 Institutions as the Symbolic Dimension of Action

Veblen defines institutions as

> prevalent habits of thought with respect to particular relations and particular functions of the individual and of the community (Veblen 1965, 190).

According to Commons, an institution is

> collective action in control of individual action (Commons 1934, 1).

Neale's understanding of institutions comes close to a sociological definition. According to Neale, an institution is identified by three characteristics (Neale 1987, 1182-1185). First, there are a number of people doing. The people doing can be seen doing; their actions can be observed empirically. Second, there are rules. From the observation of actions, an analyst can construct testable rules of regularity. By ordering actions into repetitive event sequences, an analyst can state that

> in such-and-such a kind of situation this person will do thus-and-such and another will do thus-and-so, with some variation in the detail and style with which it is done (Neale 1987, 1182).

Third, there are folk views. Neale notes that observing a certain regularity in people's actions does not yet imply understanding their actions. Knowing the rules is insufficient for understanding, i.e. knowing when to participate and being able to explain why one is participating. Knowing the rules is, therefore, insufficient for identifying institutions.

> Consider how easy it would be to confuse dancing for fun at a party, dancing for rain in a religious ceremony, and dancing for money on the evidence of the dancing alone (Neale 1987, 1183).

Folk views provide the information needed to participate intelligently in the activities of society. Folk views justify the activities or explain why they are going on, how they are related, what is thought important and what unimportant in the patterns of regularity. Folk views, Neale adds, can also be discovered by observation, but here the ear is the relevant instrument. The analyst has to ask questions and listen to the answers in order to "observe" folk views. These answers provide us with the ideas of a culture that constitute interpretations of events and explanations of the world.

After this identification of the three characteristics of institutions, Neale defines an institution as a grouping of situations in accordance with the organising ideas of the folk view. A situation is the total relevant context in which a participant in a society finds himself at any moment. It includes the social rules and the cultural folk views as well as the physical or natural environment. The relevant context is this whole environment *as perceived by the participants*. The perception of the total context is defined by the folk view of relevancy, i.e. ideas of cause and effect and of decency and morality.

Bromley's definition of institutions remains close to Commons' interpretation. Bromley distinguishes two classes of institutions: conventions and rules or entitlements (Bromley 1989, 41-43).

> A *convention* is a regularity in human behavior in which everyone prefers to conform to R [i.e., the regularity in question; MD] on the expectation that all others will also

> conform to R. A convention is a structured set of expectations about behavior, and of actual behavior, driven by shared and dominant preferences for the ultimate outcome as opposed to the means by which that outcome is achieved (Bromley 1989, 42).

On the other hand:

> An *entitlement* is a socially recognized and sanctioned set of expectations on the part of everyone in a society with regard to *de jure* or *de facto* legal relations that define the choice sets of individuals with respect to the choice sets of others (Bromley 1989, 42).

Both conventions and entitlements thus refer to regularised behaviour. Conventions, however, depict social institutions that arise to co-ordinate behaviours derived from shared preferences over *outcomes* but indifference over *means*. Entitlements, on the other hand, depict social institutions that arise to regularise behaviours in the face of discordant preferences over either social *ends* and *means*. Conventions (or 'autonomous institutions' (Bromley 1989, 88-96)) are *self-policed* institutions. They emerge in co-ordination situations in which a "co-ordination equilibrium" exists, i.e. a

> combination in which no one would have been better off had *any one* agent alone acted otherwise, either himself or someone else (Lewis cited in Bromley 1989, 41).

Entitlements (or laws, or 'imposed institutions' (Bromley 1989, 96-103)), on the contrary, regularise behaviour that needs to be policed by an external authority. In situations that are not in equilibrium - i.e. in which each has an incentive to deviate from law and order, although all citizens have a general interest in the existence of this very law and order - some external authority must be instituted to enforce entitlements. Entitlements are *legal relations*[1]. To recapitulate , Bromley interprets institutions as the regularising aspect of human action, i.e. as the rules guiding their actions. Contrary to Neale, Bromley overlooks the role of folk views. According to him, institutions interpreted as rules suffice. They offer the members of a polity information about shared values, about the likely actions of others, and about the consequences of certain acts committed by all members of the group (Bromley 1989, 47-48). Institutions as rules are able to create expectations and, hence, cohesion in social groups.

Considering the previously presented interpretations of the concept "institution", I propose the following definition. An institution is a social rule (in singular) guiding people's actions and the folk views justifying and explaining the rule and its relevance in a particular situation. This definition understands institutions as the symbolic dimension of human actions.

---

[1] Bromley distinguishes between a legal system and a legal relation. A legal system is a structured set of rules and sanctions that guarantees the promulgation and enforcement of the institutions that create social order. This legal system does not necessarily have courts, lawyers, and jails. It is sufficient that the members of the collectivity recognise the rules and sanctions constituting the legal system. A legal relation, on the contrary, is a (formal or informal) societal recognition of the institutions that create a specific aspect of the social order, i.e. of a specific set of ordered relations among individuals (Bromley 1989, 44).

I agree with Neale that a rule alone cannot offer meaning to actions. Rules reflect regularities, but they do not offer ideas of relevant contexts. Only a combination of rules and folk views allows people to act with a high degree of confidence in their expectations of how other people will respond to their actions and allows other people to interpret actions and to respond intelligently.

I do not accept Neale's interpretation of an institution as a grouping of situations, for two reasons. First, this definition suddenly jumps over from a characterisation of institutions as the symbolic dimension of human actions to an idea of institutions as a combination of symbolic and physical aspects. I prefer to keep to the idea of an institution as the symbolic dimension of human actions. The physical aspect then is the counterpart of the institutional one. Second, Neale's definition considers an institution as a grouping of rules. I prefer to associate one institution with one rule, since this allows me to distinguish between economic and non-economic institutions[2]. According to Neale, his definition relieves him to identify or assume classes of generalised types of activity such as economic, religious, or political (Neale 1987, 1187-1188). In his view, this is important because, as Veblen said, there is no neatly isolable range of cultural phenomena that can be rigorously set apart under the head of economic institutions. As I argued in the previous chapter, however, it is important to distinguish between the economic and the political sphere, though I agree that is not (always) possible to separate them. Whether we consider actions as economic or political ones does not simply depend on the phenomena, but on the perceived characteristics of the phenomena. The perceived characteristics in their turn are linked with the perspective from which we look at them . An action can show economic as well as political characteristics. According to my interpretation, the economic characteristics refer to economic institutions, while the political characteristics refer to political ones. This interpretation asks for a characterisation of what is typically economic or political, a characterisation to which even Neale cannot escape. Consider the following line of reasoning of him. Neale contends that his definition of institutions relieves the analyst of prejudging which institutions are to be compared. Analysts do not have to ask about "economic institutions", but about economic aspects of institutions. This latter search for economic aspects, however, assumes itself ideas of what makes "aspects" of actions economic ones and others non-economic ones. This illustrates that Neale cannot sidestep the question how to identify the economic *versus* the non-economic.

I propose to preserve the term "institution" for a rule guiding human action and the accompanying folk views that provide the rule with meaning and with a relevant context. I propose the term "institutional organisation" to refer to what Neale indicates as an "institution". A distinction between organisation and institution also occurs in Bromley's writings. For Bromley the term "organisation" refers to a

> physical manifestation of a set of "working rules for going concerns" (Bromley 1985, 786).

---

[2] Though I must admit that one always can discuss whether a rule really is one rule or a set of rules and, hence, whether an institution really is one institution or a set of institutions.

Bromley explicitly stresses the difference between organisations and institutions (Bromley 1989, 23). Organisations obtain their meaning from institutions. Their existence and operation depend upon a set of institutions that defines what they will do, how they will do it, how they will relate to the outside world, and how they will remunerate their employees.

1.2 Institutions as Historical Entities

Both Bromley's and Neale's interpretation of institutions show that institutions are social entities. Habits of private individuals, for instance one's habit of going to the cinema every Saturday night, do not count as institutions, however regular and meaningful the habitual action may be (Goodin 1996, 21). Both Neale and Goodin note, moreover, that institutions are historical entities. They are artifactual residuals of past actions and choices (Goodin 1996, 20).

According to Neale, this implies that institutions can change, but that we cannot indicate something like their origin. The concept "origin" assumes that

> a historical happening has had full scientific determination and that we can demonstrate this determination on the basis of well-documented data. In ethnology or history, only too often, the hunt for the "true cause" lies in completely non-determined, because non-charted, realms of hypothesis, where speculation can roam freely, unhampered by fact (Malinowski, cited in Neale 1987, 1194).

Because of this impossibility of indicating origins of institutions, Neale strongly rejects the assumptions of "new institutionalists" that institutional changes are "rational" answers in service of economic efficiency.

Neale's interpretation of institutions as historical entities parallels Goodin's. According to Goodin, any actual instance of institutional change is almost certain to involve a combination of accident, evolution and intentional intervention (Goodin 1996, 24-28). The problems that social groups face, the solution they concoct, and the way that they implement those solutions are all subject to accident and error. But, Goodin adds, the accidents and errors are rarely purely stochastic; and even when they are, they nonetheless typically arise in the backwash of intentionality, through the oversights and miscalculations of purposive agents.

> Institutions are often the product of intentional activities gone wrong – unintended by-products, the products of various intentional actions cutting across one another, misdirected intentions, or just plain mistakes [...]. To explain how those outcomes came about, we must refer essentially to intentions and the interactions among intentions. The explanation is still intentional in form, even if the outcome is not intended. An institution can thus be the product of intentional action, without its having been literally the intentional product of anyone's action (Goodin 1996, 28).

To recapitulate, institutions as historical entities are what I called, in the previous chapter, "interaction things". The way both Neale and Goodin interpret the historicity of institutions seconds Arendt's interpretation of institutions (i.e. political events) as unpredictable, without author, and as reflections of human intentions.

1.3 Institutions as Simultaneously Restricting and Enabling Entities

Institutions constrain and liberate at the same time (Neale 1994, 402-406). Bromley's analysis of institutions shows that this is even true in a double sense. In the first sense, one party's restriction constitutes another party's freedom. In the second sense, institutions offer opportunities through their meaningful restrictions. I will, mainly with the help of Bromley, clarify both dualities in the following paragraphs.

According to Bromley, institutions as entitlements are 'working rules' (Bromley 1989, 43)[3]. Working rules indicate what

> individuals *must* or *must not* do (compulsion or duty), what they *may* do without interference from other individuals (permission or liberty), what they *can* do with the aid of collective power (capacity or right), and what they *cannot* expect the collective power to do in their behalf (incapacity or exposure) (Commons 1968, 6; cited in Bromley 1989, 43).

In other words, institutions as legal relations define the rights, exposures to the rights of others, privileges and responsibilities of people.

Since institutions as entitlements are collective rules that define socially acceptable individual and group behaviour, they are sets of *dual* or *mutual* expectations[4]. The right, for instance, of one family to the raspberries from their own garden correlates to a duty for all non-family members not to take raspberries from this garden. Bromley, following the legal scholar W.N. Hohfeld, postulates four fundamental legal relations (Bromley 1989, 44-46). 1) The *right* of one party (a person or a group) Alpha correlates to a *duty* for the other party (all other persons belonging to the same community, but not being or belonging to Alpha) Beta. 2) The *privilege* of Alpha correlates to *no right* for Beta. Alpha is free to behave in a certain way with respect to Beta. Alpha is, for instance, free to sell raspberries to X, Y, or Z without the consent of Beta. 3) The *power* of Alpha to create voluntarily a new legal relation affecting Beta correlates to Beta's *liability*. Beta is enforced to comply to the new legal relation. 4) The *immunity* of Alpha correlates to the absence of power to Beta. *No power* means that Beta may not voluntarily create a new legal relation affecting Alpha. Immunity means that Alpha is not subject to Beta's attempt voluntarily to create a new legal relation affecting him. Beta has, for instance, no power to sell Alpha's raspberries or Alpha is immune against Beta's try to sell Alpha's raspberries. Hohfeld's four types of legal relations are each illustrations that one party's restriction is another party's opportunity and *vice versa*. This clarifies the first sense in which institutions limit and enable simultaneously.

---

[3] John R. Commons initiated the term (Bromley 1989, 43).

[4] On other occasions, Bromley points to institutions as entitlements as triadic, rather than dyadic, relationships (Bromley 1989, 71). Institutions as entitlements define relationships between two parties Alpha and Beta, guaranteed by a third entity, namely an external authority. The two parties together with the external authority form the three necessary elements of an institution understood as an entitlement or a legal relation. In other passages, Bromley defines the three elements of this triadic relationship as 'the object or circumstances of interest, the individual or group related to that interest, and all others who have a duty to respect the right' (Bromley 1997, 50).

Bromley continues to explain that the four types of legal relations can be grouped in two ways. To start with, legal relations can be static or dynamic. The first two types of legal relations are static. They define the choice sets of the different parties within a specific set of legal relations. The latter two correlates are dynamic. They concern changes in a specific set of legal relations. They concern, what Bromley calls, "institutional transactions" or "implicit rights transfers". The four fundamental rules can also be subdivided into active and passive ones. The first and third types are active. They represent imperative relations subject to an external authority (for instance, the state). The second and fourth kinds are passive. They are not themselves subject to direct legal enforcement. They set the limits of the activities of the external authority in that they define the types of behaviour that are beyond the interest of the state. They describe the choices that a party can make independent of existing laws. They are, according to Bromley, in a sense statements of 'no law' (Bromley 1989, 46).

This latter way of grouping legal relations shows that they are not only dual relations in the sense that they connect Alpha's right, privilege, power and immunity to Beta's duty, no right, liability and no power respectively. Precisely by setting limits to the freedom of a person or group, they define (and protect) degrees of freedom. This means that the right of Alpha does, for instance, not only correlate to the duty of Beta. Alpha's right at the same time correlates to Alpha's privileges or degrees of freedom or choice sets. And Alpha's power to change some legal relations correlates to his immunity against Beta's trials to prevent these changes. All actions of Alpha that are compatible with his rights and duties, with his powers and liabilities are "free" (or "autonomous") actions, i.e. actions for which no law exists[5].

Neale puts the second sense in which institutions restrain and enable at the same time more explicit than Bromley does. Because institutions provide order and meaning to human action, they offer opportunities for creativity, for individual and ever new variations in choice, style, goal and realisation (Neale 1994). Or, in Goodin's words, the same factors that constrain individual and group actions also shape the desires, preferences, and motives of those individual and group agents (Goodin 1996, 20).

Bromley stresses that institutions always have these enabling and limiting sides and have both sides always in a double sense. When institutions are considered statically, they turn out to reflect collective decisions in restraint and liberation of

[5] Bromley also uses the concepts "actual" and "presumptive" rights to indicate "rights" and "privileges" respectively (Bromley 1991, 50). "Actual rights" correspond to "rights". (Actual) rights are protected by an authority system. Since, however, a law is not always sufficiently clear or is not capable of dealing adequately with new situations, a grey area often exists in which the institutional setting of rights and duties leaves room for interpretation. The law can, for example, be clear about Alpha not trespassing on Beta's land, but quite unclear about Alpha's chemicals drifting to Beta's land and causing harm. In both instances, Alpha "trespassed" on Beta's land, once physically and once by allowing Alpha's actions elsewhere to harm Beta. In the latter kind of situations we find ourselves in the domain of "presumptive rights" on the part of the perpetrator and no rights on the part of the victim. Such situations come down to situations of "privilege" (for Alpha) and no rights (for Beta).

individual action. When they are considered dynamically, institutional changes reflect collective decisions in expansion and reduction of individual action (Bromley 1989, 38; 54). A reduction in the range of choice of one decision unit (often) means an expansion of the range of choice of another one. A legal ban on burning leaves from Alpha's yard in the autumn, for instance, means that the range of choice of Alpha has been diminished, but the range of choice of Alpha's asthmatic neighbour Beta has been enhanced.

I should stress the political relevance of previous analysis of institutions as both restricting and enabling in a double sense. This analysis implies an important correction to prevailing discourse. It shows that solutions to political problems are not a matter of regulating or deregulating existing markets. For this often seems to be the point of contention between social-democrats on the one hand and liberals on the other. The question is not whether we need *more or less* rules (or institutions), often interpreted as more or less coercion (to refer to Buchanan's terminology) and less or more (economic) freedom or autonomy. The question is *which* rules with which accompanying degrees of freedom cause the political problems in question and how these rules and accompanying degrees of freedom should be transformed in order to avoid or reduce them. The question is, in other words, what kind of and whose degrees of freedom are to be politically defined and protected.

1.4 Laws as "Public Facts"

According to Bromley, one element characterising the distinction between institutions as conventions and as entitlements or laws has to do with the underlying preferences of the parties involved (Bromley 1989, 88-103). In case preferences for the regularised aspect of action are in perfect agreement (or can be brought into perfect agreement through a bargaining process between the various parties), there is no need for an authority to introduce and enforce an institution. In that case the institution is called a convention (or "autonomous institution"). In case the underlying preferences are not in (or cannot be brought into) agreement, (some of) the parties involved will make an appeal to an (internal or external) political authority to get their interests legally protected. An entitlement (or a law, or an "imposed institution") is nothing else but a politically recognised and enforced institution. Bromley's analysis of the distinction between conventions and entitlements throws light on what political processes, according to Bromley, really are about. They are about the (legal) protection of some private interests rather than others (Bromley 1989, 237).

There is, however, more to say about entitlements. Institutions as laws or entitlements are a "public fact" in a double sense[6]. They are "public" because they

[6] I borrow the term "public fact" from Taylor (Taylor 1966, 109, cited in Schmid 1987, 28). I prefer this term to the term "public good", because the term "good" has an economic connotation. Public goods are as much economic goods as are private goods. The difference between both depends on the set of property rights attached to both. (We will come back to this topic when dealing with Bromley's explanation of property regimes.)

result from political rather than from "autonomous" or "private" – in the economic sense - processes. The term "public" refers to the political processes through which public preferences for private choice sets are developed out of private preferences. Entitlements are legally protected private interests. As such, they reflect political or public preferences for the protection of particular private interests. (I prefer the verb "reflect" to "express" because the former takes better account of unconscious or non-voluntaristic elements in the "results" of political actions.) At the same time, they condition the private choices that individuals make in order to satisfy their private preferences. (I will come back to the meaning of entitlements as public preferences and to their role in conditioning private choices in section 2.1.2).

We just concluded that entitlements reflect political preferences for the protection of particular private interests. This statement, however, is at a rather abstract level: it does not consider the concrete persons who are in a position to have these particular private interests. Therefore, laws are also public in the sense that they are impartial. They hold for all members of a polity[7]. Legally protected interests or rights can belong to individuals, to all members of a polity, or to a group within a polity. Rights can thus vary from strictly private to fully public or something in between. Anyhow, once a right is assigned to either an individual, a group or all members of the polity, it holds for the whole polity. All members are, indeed, deemed to recognise and to respect the rights assigned to all or particular other members.

1.5 Summary

I propose the following definition of an institution. An institution is a *social rule* (in singular) guiding people's actions and the *folk views* justifying and explaining the rule and its relevance in a particular situation. This definition considers institutions as the symbolic dimension of human actions. This symbolic dimension of human actions is the counterpart of their ecological (or physical or material) dimension. Institutions are historical entities: they are the often unintended result of intentional interaction. As such, they correspond to Arendt's interpretation of political entities as unpredictable, irreversible and not really "made". Institutions restrict and enable in a double way. First, one party's restriction corresponds to another party's liberation. Second, institutions define people's degrees of freedom or their autonomy. Institutions make people free by limiting their freedom. Institutions do not simply coerce, they liberate simultaneously. Institutions, finally, are "public facts" in the double sense that they result from political interaction and that they hold for all members of a political community. (The latter does, however, not exclude that institutional rights can be assigned to either an individual, a group or to all members of a polity. See further in chapter 7.) I introduce the concept "public fact" to distinguish institutions from "public goods". Public facts are political entities, while public goods are economic entities. (We will come back to the topic of public goods in section 2.1.3 of this chapter and in chapter 7.)

---

[7] In one passage, Bromley himself also refers to 'the collective good we know as *the legal foundations of the economy*' (Bromley 1991, 106; the italics are his).

2 INSTITUTIONAL ORGANISATION AND ECOLOGICAL PERFORMANCE OF AN ECONOMY

2.1 Economic Institutions

As I explained in section 1.1 of this chapter, I propose to define economic institutions as institutions referring to economic characteristics of human actions. This definition cannot escape a characterisation of what is deemed typically economic. And this characterisation depends, in its turn, on the perspective from which we look at human action. Given the three first perspectives mentioned in the previous chapter, economic institutions can either be the institutions defining what counts as an economic good or service, or the institutions conditioning the rationality of economic action, or the institutions defining economic decision units. In the following paragraphs I will deal with each of them separately.

2.1.1 Institutions Defining Economic Decision Units

I will lean on Bromley to deal briefly with the kind of economic institutions that are characteristic for the perspective that takes decision units as its constituting element. According to Bromley, one can distinguish two kinds of institutions relevant for economic decision units (Bromley 1989, 43). The first define a decision unit *vis-à-vis* other decision units. The second spell out the internal nature of an economic decision unit. In case of a corporation, the first type of institutions articulate the necessary steps which must be followed to become a corporation and to remain one. The second type of institutions give the corporation its structure. They articulate how officers are appointed, how the financial records shall be kept, how administrative decisions are made, and so on.

2.1.2 Institutions Conditioning Economic Rationality

Mainstream (neo-classical) economics defines economic rationality as the rationality typical of *homo oeconomicus*. This rationality is of an instrumental kind: economic man knows how to organise his means in order to fulfil his goals as good as possible. Rational economic man has one motive, namely maximisation of the satisfaction of his private interests. Neale notes that neo-classical economists regard the rationality of economic action as universal over time and place (Neale 1987, 1180-1181; 1188). An institutional perspective, on the contrary, considers economic actions as specific to time and place. An institutional approach focuses upon the rules and opportunities for action and the limits to action, assuming that each individual is always moved by one or another purpose. An institutional investigation does not build its analysis upon the aims or passions of the actors. It does not even need to consider them. It only assumes that economic actors have the desire to continue to participate in existing institutional arrangements, and to use institutions to achieve their personal aims, whatever they may be. According to Neale, activities are governed by rules, not aims or passions. Aims or passions lead people to engage in particular activities, but they do not determine specific actions. What specific actions are chosen depends upon the institutional context: the particular "rules of the game" in the particular system that each individual tries to manipulate in order to realise his goals.

Neale's statements need some elaboration. In the following paragraphs, I will embroider on two examples offered by Bromley to make plausible a) that *economic* rationality comes down to *economising* rationality in a context of particular economic institutions, b) that maximisation of satisfaction can be linked to egoistic as well as altruistic *private* motives, c) that the same motive can urge economic actors to act differently in different institutional contexts, d) that institutional arrangements are reflections of *public* preferences, and e) that we do not need to know the private preferences of separate individuals to know something about the social (or ecological) performance of economies with particular institutional arrangements.

Bromley explores two basic (isolation) games: the prisoner's dilemma and the prisoner's dream (Bromley 1989, 85-88). Consider the prisoner's dilemma. Two prisoners are apprehended for a minor crime, but actually suspected of a more serious one. The two suspects are isolated and told that if they both confess to the major crime they will be convicted of the major crime and sentenced to ten years in prison. If neither confesses each will be convicted of the minor offence and be sentenced to two years in prison. If only one turns state's evidence by confessing to the major crime then the confessor will go free and the other, who remained silent, will go to prison for twenty years. Under the institutional structure of this game, the interest of both suspects to minimise their own time in jail, leads them to confess (whereas had both not confessed their respective prison sentence would have been only two years each). This institutional structure reflects the preferences of the legislature (or the state), namely to extract confessions. By defining the incentive system in a particular way and by isolating the suspects (who are, moreover, assumed not to be particularly true to each other), prisoners act as if they rat on their companion. Under these conditions, the outcome for the prosecuting attorney is exactly coincident with her preferences, though the outcome for the suspects is not at all.

Consider now the prisoner's dream. Imagine a similar situation in which two suspects are apprehended for a minor crime, but thought to be - 'and in fact are', Bromley adds - guilty of a far more serious one. The prosecuting attorney cannot promise leniency in return for co-operation. The sentence for the minor crime is two years in jail, and for the major crime ten years. The suspects are isolated as before, and interrogated. If each acts in order to reduce his time in jail as much as possible (or, in Bromley's words, 'if each is strictly self-interested') the non-confession option is the best choice. The suspects act as if they do not rat - they 'have no incentive to rat' - and so each is given the more lenient sentence for the crime in which they were in fact engaged when apprehended. The more serious crime, 'which they also committed', remains unsolved.

From both games Bromley concludes the following.

> The preferences of the prisoners are invariant across the two games: they wish to minimize their respective sentences. The preferences of the prosecuting attorney can certainly be assumed to be concerned with solving crimes in both instances. The difference in the outcome of the two games has nothing to do with preferences and everything to do with choices; it is the institutional structure that defines the environment of choice - or what I have already termed *choice sets*. Choices are made from the pertinent choice set, and those choices will vary even with the same underlying preferences (Bromley 1989, 87).

Bromley thus demonstrates that choices made within private choice sets cannot be equalled to private preferences. Choices are not (revealed) preferences. Choices are strategies meant to satisfy private preferences and the strategy chosen depends on the institutional environment, i.e. the ensemble of entitlements (and conventions). There exists a difference between (private or "autonomous") preferences for outcomes and (private or "autonomous") preferences among strategies (or choices).

To conclude, institutional arrangements stimulate or incite particular actions. Institutions are incentives. Different institutional arrangements cause individuals to make different choices – to act differently – to satisfy as good as possible their same private preferences (ad c)). From an ecological perspective, it is the strategies or concrete actions chosen by economic actors to satisfy their private preferences that count, not their private preferences themselves. The ecological performance of an economy depends on the private preferences individuals hold *and* on the context of economic institutions that condition the strategies chosen to satisfy these preferences (*). This is why the rationality of *homo oeconomicus* – the scientific model of the conventional approach – is not particularly clarifying with regard to the social/ecological performance of an economy. "Economic rationality" is too abstract a model: it abstracts from the institutional arrangements offering "rational" behaviour concrete content.

Apart from the interesting point made by Bromley that private choices cannot be equalled to private preferences, the two examples are illuminating in another respect. Note, to start with, that both examples have nothing to do with "economic activities" in the sense of "activities occurring within an economy". Though managing a prison certainly shows economic aspects, serving a prison sentence can hardly be considered an economic activity. Nevertheless, the prisoner is considered to show "economic rationality". On closer look, however, this "economic rationality" is the same as "economising rationality". Given that the prisoner has to serve a prison sentence and that the term of the sentence depends on his statements, the prisoner's rational choice consists of choosing the statement that allows him to serve his sentence with least means, i.e. in the shortest time possible. Economic rationality then is the same as economising rationality, i.e. reaching ones goal (and as much goals as possible) with least effort, least cost (ad a)). This kind of economising rationality is, I suppose, rather trivial and has nothing particularly to do with activities in the economic sphere. Acting economically in this sense is always implied in rational actions directed at organising means to achieve ends, i.e. in every notion of instrumental rationality. According to Karl Polanyi, the interpretation of economics as the logic of economising (and thus of maximising) is but one "formal" or "logical" interpretation. This formal interpretation does not tell us much about what people do to provide themselves with the material means of achieving their ends. To this second meaning of economics, Polanyi attached the rubric "substantive". A substantive – or institutional – economics is the study of econom*ies*, of how people go about provisioning themselves, either as individuals or as members of groups with common purposes, and of the institutions governing that provisioning (Neale 1987, 1180). To conclude, the conventional interpretation of economic rationality comes down to instrumental or economising rationality. This economising rationality is not typical for actions occurring in the economic sphere. It is the context of particular economic institutions that makes *economising* rationality become *economic* rationality.

We can illustrate the difference between public and private preferences by making Bromley's examples of the prisoner's game and dream more complex. Consider, to begin with, that the state or the prosecuting attorney has indeed a strong suspicion, but is nevertheless not completely sure that the suspects committed the major crime. The objective of the state (the public preference) is probably not so much to extract confessions, but to administer justice: to convince who is guilty to confess and who is guiltless to deny. Consider, moreover, that the suspects have two private preferences, the one is to be honest and the other is to be free. The relative weight of these preferences depends on the suspect's personality on the one hand and on the specificity of the situation on the other. In case the institutional arrangements are these of a prisoner's dilemma (case A), suspects being more attached to their freedom than to their honesty will confess, whether they are guilty or not. Suspects being more attached to their honesty than to their freedom will certainly confess in case they are guilty. In case they are not guilty they will only deny on condition that their preference for honesty is so strong relative to their preference for freedom that they are prepared to risk a high price (in terms of years in jail) for it. In case the institutional arrangements are these of a prisoner's dream (case B), suspects being more attached to their freedom than to their honesty will deny, whether they are guilty or not. Suspects being more attached to their honesty than to their freedom will certainly deny in case they are not guilty. In case they are guilty, the probability that they will confess is relative high since the price they risk in terms of years in jail is relative low.

From these modified, more complicated examples we can learn several things. To start with, the kind of private preferences protected in both cases through the institutional arrangements differ (ad d)). In case A the preferences of the "victims" are politically better protected than these of the "suspects", because the suspects will always - independent of their private preferences - confess in case they are guilty. In case B, the opposite is true: the preferences of the "suspects" are better protected than these of the "victims", because the suspects will always - independent of their private preferences - deny in case they are not guilty. In other words, in case A a crime will not be wrongly denied, while in case B a suspect will not be wrongly sentenced. This illustrates that different institutional arrangements reflect different public preferences. Institutional arrangements as laws or entitlements are not only political protections of given private interests, as Bromley argues (see section 1.4). They are at the same time reflections of public preferences. Between private interests demanding for political protection and laws reflecting public preferences really lie political events. These events define whether and to what extent given private interests will be transformed and/or enforced through the final institutional arrangements. As reflections of public preferences, institutional arrangements condition what kind of private preferences the members of a polity can adequately satisfy. In case A, for instance, institutional arrangements make it much harder for an individual having the private preference for honesty to get it satisfied than in case B. In case A, honest people get demoralised. In the long run, institutional arrangements thus influence the kind of private preferences members of a polity will hold.

Second, the examples show that private choices do not only not coincide with private preferences, as Bromley states. They show even that we cannot simply derive the preference from the choice. Nevertheless, we do not need to know the private preferences of separate individuals in order to be able to comment on the social/ecological performance of a given institutional environment. This brings us to our third observation. If administering justice is, for instance, the higher-order public preference, then institutional arrangements must be so that they stimulate private honesty or, at least, do not punish honest people too heavy. Case B succeeds better in this respect than case A. In other words, the social performance of the institutional arrangements in case B is better with regard to the administration of justice than it is in case A (ad e)). This implies a correction to my earlier conclusion (*). Considered over a longer time interval, we do not really need to know the private preferences of separate individuals in order to understand the ecological performance of an economy. This means that an internal relationship exists between the ecological performance and the institutional organisation of an economy. This conclusion supports my research project. It shows that it makes sense to look for institutional reasons for (the present unmanageability of) the ecological performance of our industrial economies.

Finally, "autonomous" choices are deemed to satisfy private preferences, whether egoistic (one's own freedom) or altruistic (honesty cannot be considered an egoistic preference, I suppose). For that reason it is misleading to indicate economic behaviour (i.e. economising behaviour as incited through the institutional arrangements constituting an economy) as simply "self-interested" or "opportunist". A specific economy turns out either to stimulate or to temper egoistic or altruistic, but certainly private preferences (ad b).

2.1.3 Institutions Defining Economic Goods and Services

To argue that economic goods and services cannot exist without (economic) institutions defining them as such, I will refer to Alan Schmid's analysis (Schmid 1987)[8]. In economic literature, one uses to distinguish between private and public

[8] With thanks to Paul Thompson for referring me to Schmid's work.

goods. The former are then characterised as incompatible in their use (Schmid 1987, 39-61). If A eats, for instance, a bushel of corn, it cannot be eaten by B. The latter goods are characterised as indivisible goods for which non-rivalness in consumption exists (Schmid 1987, 75-94). A classical example is national defence. A's enjoyment of national defence does not interfere with B's enjoyment thereof. Use of national defence is compatible, though the utility of use is not necessarily compatible. A can be happy with the level of national defence, while B can judge the level too high or too low. Both A's and B's enjoyment of national defence can, moreover, not be traced back to a particular unit of input (say a specific bomb or soldier).

Schmid rejects the terms used, namely *private* versus *public* goods, to indicate goods with respective characteristics. According to Schmid, these terms fail to distinguish between what he calls "situation" and "structure" (Schmid 1987, 39-43). "Situation" refers to features of goods that are a matter of physics and biology and inherent in the good. "Structure" refers to institutions or rights connected to goods. In contrast to inherent situational variables, the rights structure is a matter of human choice. It is the rights structure that defines whether a good is private or public. A piece of land, for instance, can be private or public depending on whether rights to use and/or exchange it are assigned to individuals or all members of a polity.

In order to respect the distinction between situation and structure, Schmid introduces the terms "incompatible-use goods" *versus* "joint-impact" goods to refer to inherent or situational features of a good. "Incompatible-use goods" and "joint-impact goods" then have the *situational* features previously ascribed to so called "private" and "public" goods respectively. The terms "private" and "public" refer to *structural* features and reflect public or political choice. The same piece of land can, for instance, be an incompatible-use good if A wants to grow corn on it while B wants to build a factory on it. But as an incompatible-use good it can be private as well as public. In the former case whether corn will be grown or a factory built depends on whether either A or B have the private right to use it. Whether either A or B will earn money from the growing of corn or the building of a factory depends on whether either A or B have the private right to exchange the piece of land. In case both A and B have the right to use the same piece of land, they will have to interact with each other – either by debating or by bargaining – to decide which of both uses will come through. To conclude, it is institutional structure that defines who chooses (who has power) and who has to pay for a specific use of a particular good. It is, in other words, institutional structure that provides situational "things" with economic meaning. Or, in other words, it is institutions that make "things" become economic goods.

I suppose, by the way, that the distinction between situation and structure is not as unequivocal as presented by Schmid. Clean air, for instance, can be both a joint-impact good and an incompatible-use good depending on the uses different users have in mind. If user A wants to use clean air in his production of steel, it cannot be used by user B to breathe it because of the pollution emitted in the production process. In this case, clean air is an incompatible-use good. If both user A and B want to use the air to breathe, it is a joint-impact good, since A's use does not interfere with B's use. (I borrow the example from Schmid himself (Schmid 1987, 86)). This example shows that even the situational characterisation of a good in terms of either a joint-impact good or an incompatible-use good depends on the interests of the user. This characterisation is itself value-related (to use Weber's terminology) and thus non-neutral. It is not simply a matter of physics or biology. Given a particular economic good, one can distinguish between ecological and institutional aspects, but one cannot separate them. Contrary to Schmid's explanation, situation does not precede structure. Situation and structure (or ecological and symbolic dimension) are simultaneous dimensions of an economic good.

To conclude, it is institutions that define material things (and even hardly material things such as, for instance, knowledge) as economic goods. These institutions define whether an economic good is commonly understood as private or public. (I will deal with the problematic aspects of this classification in chapter 7.) Economic goods thus are always characterised by an ecological (or physical or biological) and a symbolic dimension. The institutions constituting the symbolic dimension of a (private or public) economic "good" are "public facts".

2.1.4 Summary

In this section, I defined "economic institutions" as the institutions constituting – depending on the perspective used - either economic decision units, economic rationality or economic goods. I followed Bromley in his argument that two kinds of institutions defining economic decision units can be distinguished. The first kind defines an economic decision unit versus another economic decision unit. The second kind defines the internal organisation of an economic decision unit. I followed Schmid in his argument that economic goods consist of both an ecological and an institutional dimension. It is the institutional dimension that defines a thing as either a private or a public economic good. This institutional dimension itself is, what I called previously, a public fact.

I spent the larger part of this section on an analysis of the relationship between institutional organisation and economic rationality. From Bromley's reflections on the two examples of a prisoner's dilemma and a prisoner's dream, we learned two things. First, we learned that the choices economic actors make cannot be equalled to their preferences. Choices are not revealed preferences. They are strategies chosen to satisfy their private preferences as good as they can given the existing institutional organisation of an economy. Different institutional arrangements urge people to choose different strategies in order to satisfy their same private preferences. From this observation, I concluded that the ecological performance of an economy does not only depend on the private preferences individuals hold, but also on the institutional organisation of an economy. Second, we learned that the conventional (neo-classical) interpretation of economic rationality comes down to economising (or simply instrumental) rationality. The conventional interpretation is too abstract to provide us with insights into the ecological performance of an economy. Only within a specific economic context, i.e., within a specific institutional organisation of an economy does abstract *economising* rationality become concrete *economic* rationality.

Embroidering on the two examples offered by Bromley, we still got more insights into the relevance of an institutional analysis of an economy. To start with, we learned to understand institutional arrangements as reflections of *public preferences* for the protection of particular *private choice sets* (and, hence, of particular private preferences). Institutions as public preferences do not simply protect existing private preferences. Between existing private preferences and institutions as reflections of public preferences lie political processes that transform given and/or create possible private preferences. Politics is not simply a matter of bargaining; it is a matter of deliberating and of judging. This interpretation of institutions as reflections of public preferences shows that it makes sense to look for an institutional expression of the public preference for sustainability. We illustrated, further, that institutional arrangements stimulate some private preferences and temper others. This implies that to understand the ecological performance of an economy in the long run, we do not really need to know the private preferences of separate individuals. It suffices to know an economy's institutional organisation. This is another way to say that an internal relationship exists between the ecological performance of an economy and its institutional organisation. This latter conclusion supports my research question: it shows that it makes sense to look for institutional reasons for (the seemingly unmanageability of) the ecological performance of our industrial economies. The observation, finally, that institutional arrangements can either stimulate or temper either egoistic or altruistic private preferences suggests that it is not necessary for public authorities to adopt a moralising attitude in order to convert egoistic economic actors to ecologically benign behaviour. Public authorities should rather – to use O'Neill's words - create the institutional conditions of sustainable economic practices. They should create the institutions that foster in individuals a wide conception of their interest that simultaneously encourages sustainable practices (O'Neill 1994, 214).

2.2 The Institutional Whole of an Economy

In the previous section, I argued that internal relationships exist between the institutional organisation of an economy and its ecological performance. The line of reasoning is the following. Economic action shows both a symbolic and a material dimension. The symbolic dimension consists of a set of economic institutions. Economic institutions are social entities and they are public facts. They define, in the short run, the strategies economic actors choose to satisfy their private preferences. They condition, in the long run, economic actors' private preferences themselves. Hence, it is economic institutions that make rational economic action concrete. In other words, it is economic institutions that condition the material dimension, i.e., the ecological performance of economic actions. Alternative institutional organisations of an economy will induce alternative ecological performances. The ecological performance of an economy is the counterpart of its institutional structure[9].

In the first part of this section, I will illustrate that the opinion that the ecological performance of an economy is the counterpart of its institutional organisation does not go without saying. I will do this by offering an overview of various models that represent economists' understanding of the relationship between an economy and its (ecological) environment and that define the way in which economists look for solutions to ecological problems. This overview will, at the same time, clarify the peculiarity of the approach proposed in this research project.

In the second part, I will enlarge on the analytical meaning of the particular approach proposed. I suggest that, in order to gain insights into these internal relationships between the ecological performance and the institutional organisation of an economy, we need a picture of the "institutional whole" characterising a specific historical economy.

In the final part, I will reflect on how this "institutional whole" can be understood. In economic literature, I discerned two possible endeavours to grasp - on a theoretical level - something like an institutional whole. The first endeavour understands an institutional whole as a hierarchical whole. The second endeavour understands it as a classificatory whole.

2.2.1 Economy's Ecological Performance

The ecological performance of an economy can mean different things, depending on the measures used to evaluate this performance. One possible measure is the aggregate use of energetic and material resources. Another possible measure is, for instance, bio-diversity. The viewpoint that the ecological performance of an economy – whatever measures used to evaluate this performance – is the counterpart of its institutional organisation is not self-evident in economic literature. To illustrate the particularity of this viewpoint, I will contrast it with some other interpretations as they can be found in economic literature.

In orthodox economics the economy is interpreted as an isolated system in which exchange values circulate between firms and households (see Figure 1) (Daly 1996, 46-47). Though circulation processes regard production and consumption, orthodox economics abstracts from their physical or, better, ecological dimension. Circulation refers to abstract exchange values. According to this model, an econpmy is independent of its ecological environment. Consequently, it is not possible to treat ecological problems within this model.

[9] This idea can also be found in Schmid (1987, 39-43).

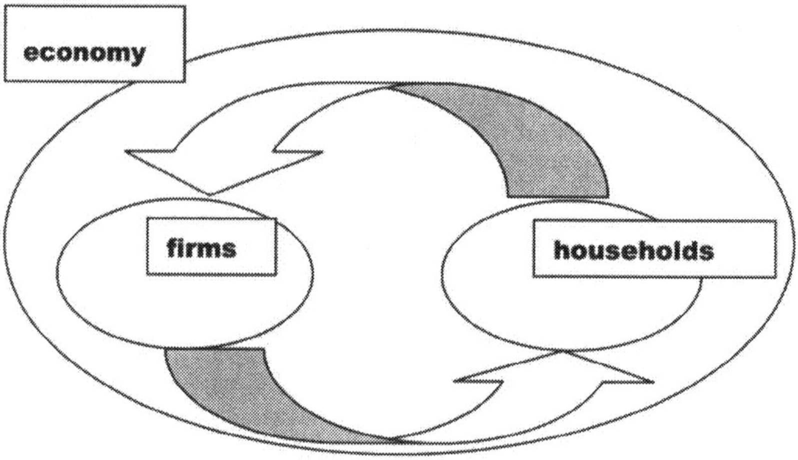

Figure 1: Economy as an isolated system (Daly 1996, 47)

Conventional environmental economics is a correction to this model. It does not consider the economy as isolated, because it depends in its functioning on its natural environment. However, in this corrected model the interfaces between economy and ecology remain external (see Figure 2) (Dietz *et al.* 1994, 19). Nature is understood as a "resource" for economic activities. These parts of nature that function as an "input" of economic production processes are called "resources"; the "output" of production- and consumption processes, namely those things that cannot be used any more, are called "waste". According to this model the interfaces between economy and ecology do not influence the nature (i.e. the institutional organisation) of an economy (and *vice versa)* (O'Connor 1994, 61-62). Problems of pollution or depletion can occur, to be true. These problems, however, do not have consequences for the organisation of the economy.

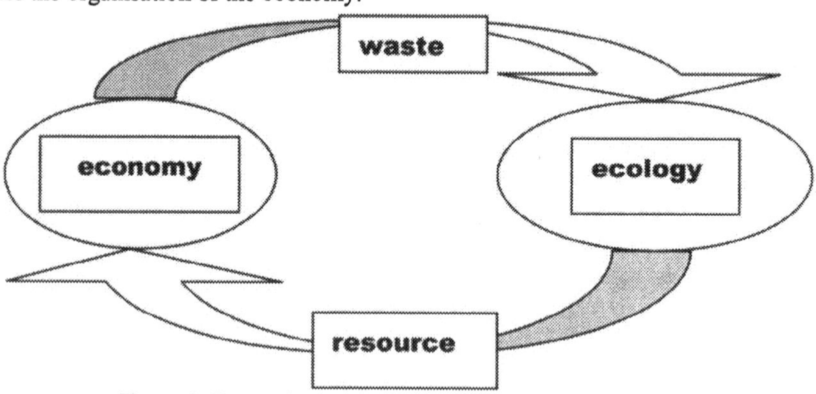

Figure 2: External relationship between economy and ecology (Dietz *et al.* 1994, 19)

Some (ecological) economists (see, for instance, Daly 1996, 49; Dietz *et al.* 1994, 19) understand the economy as embedded in an ecological context (see Figure 3). In this model, the interfaces between economy and ecology are not external any more, but internal. The ecological situation influences the specific organisation of an economy and the economy has, in its turn, an impact on the ecological situation. This model understands economic activities themselves, not merely their "inputs" and "outputs", as ecological entities.

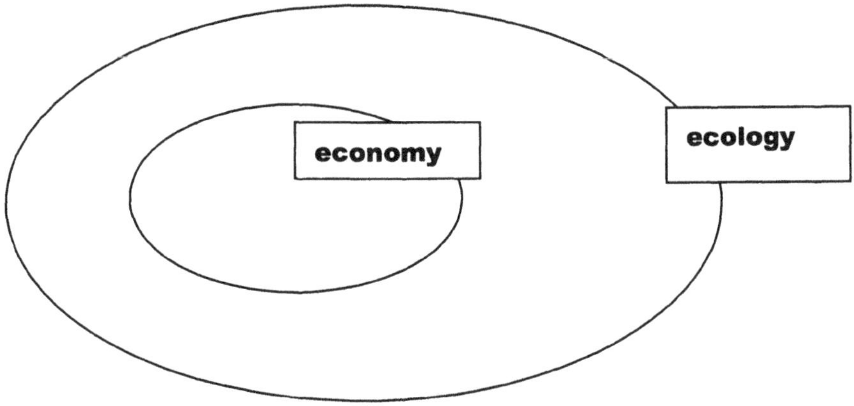

Figure 3: Economy as embedded in ecology

Other (ecological) economists (for instance Munda 1997, 227; O'Hara 1996, 8) understand the embeddedness of economy into ecology less directly. An economy is always embedded into ecology in a historically and culturally specific manner (see Figure 4). This model allows for an analysis of the cultural and historical peculiarities of problems of sustainability.

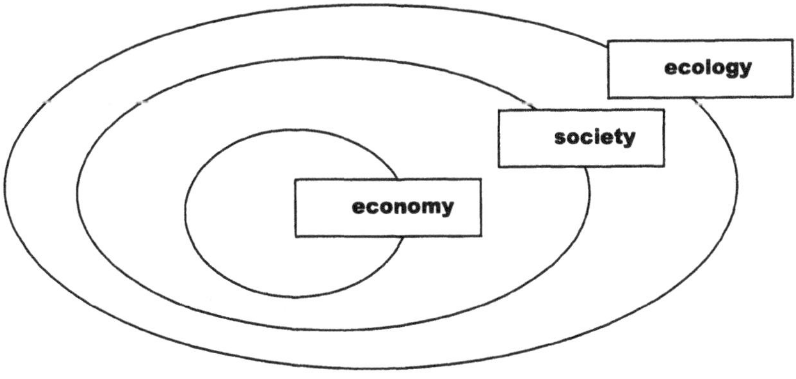

Figure 4: Economy as indirectly embedded into ecology

In this book, I adopt this latter model and I add the polity as the sphere within human reality where legalised economic institutions, and hence the institutional organisation of a culturally and historically specific economy, are debated and decided on (see Figure 5). Since economic power relations influence political power relations, the arrows point from the economic to the political sphere as well as from the political to the economic sphere.

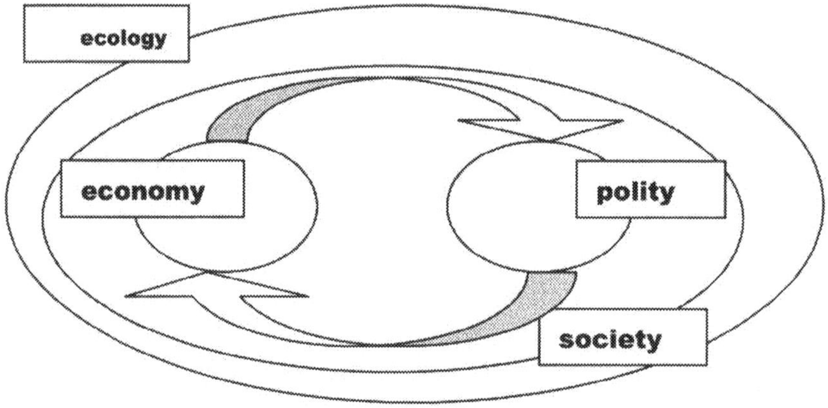

Figure 5: economy and polity as indirectly embedded into ecology

2.2.2 Relevance of the "Institutional Whole"

In this section, I will deal more extensively with the analytical meaning of the statement that the ecological performance of an economy relates to its institutional organisation. This statement means that we need insights into the "institutional whole" constituting a particular economy in order to understand its ecological performance. For, to start with, we need insights into the ensemble of economic institutions, rather than into separate institutions, conditioning the ecological performance of one specific economic action. And, further, it is the accumulating ecological effects of combined economic (inter)actions, rather than the separate effects of isolated economic actions, that matter. I will use some examples in order to illustrate the two previous arguments.

Economic actions have both a symbolic and a material or ecological dimension. This material dimension is responsible for the ubiquitous occurrence of interdependence (Schmid 1987, 10). Interdependence is manifest in the conflicting interests of the parties involved. When person A eats the corn from a particular acre of land, person B cannot meet his interest in eating the same corn. If person A uses his land to build a huge building, it can conflict with B's interest in a scenic view. According to Schmid, it is the inherent situation (or, to use my terminology, the material dimension) that creates interdependence, while it is the public institutional structure (i.e., the symbolic dimension) that gives order to interdependence and determines the opportunity sets of the interdependent parties (Schmid 1987, 189). An opportunity set is defined as the available lines of action open to a party (either an individual or a group), i.e., the lines of action not prohibited by criminal law or violating the private or communal rights of others (Schmid 1987, 6). A party's opportunity set consists of the options for acting without the formal consent of other parties and without other parties getting in the way to the extent defined by the institutional structure. The opportunity set is, to put it in Bromley's terminology (see section 1.3), the ensemble of (individual or group) privileges, i.e. an individual's or group's choice set. The institutional structure determines which effects of A's actions on B must be considered by A and which can be ignored. It determines which effects are costs that are external to the decision maker A (Schmid 1987, 10).

According to Bromley, '[i]t is the *aggregate* of institutional arrangements that determine, at a particular moment, economic conditions. In other words, there is a prevailing structure of norms, conventions, rules, practices, and laws that shape or define the choice sets of individuals and groups in an economy' (Bromley 1993b, 141; the italics are mine). To illustrate the relevance of this *aggregate* of institutional arrangements for a specific economic action, consider the following example. X is a producer of steel. In order to produce steel, X needs several natural resources. He needs ore to refine, water to cool, air to pollute. X's use of water and air are both subjected to specific use rights. X may, for instance, use a maximal amount of water a day out of the nearby river and he may pollute the air up to a maximal level. Ore is something X needs to buy and steel is something X wants to sell. Buying and selling refer to specific exchange rights, to contracting rules, to rules governing information costs, and so on. The production process takes place in X's factory that is equipped with particular technologies and that employs several labourers. Employing labourers implies rules defining labour contracts and circumstances. Using particular technologies assumes, again, rules governing the purchase and use of the machines and instruments representing the technology in question. To recapitulate, in order to produce steel X needs several production factors. The exchange and use of the separate factors are conditioned by various institutions. It is the whole set of relevant institutions – i.e. the whole set of institutions related to each of the production factors – that define the concrete form , and thus the ecological performance, of the economic action called "steel production"[10].

The opportunity set of producer X does, however, not only depend on the set of institutions governing use and exchange of production factors. It also depends on the opportunity sets of other economic actors (Schmid 1987, 7). Suppose a very wealthy activist Z who is dissatisfied with X's legally admitted level of air pollution. Z can offer X to pay in order to reduce the latter's level of air pollution. This offer changes X's opportunity set. X's opportunity set thus depends, besides on the institutions related to production factors, on the actual choices of others acting within their own

[10] It is of course arbitrary to call "steel production" an economic action, because one could call "steel production" a combination of economic actions as well.

opportunity sets. For that reason Schmid states that opportunity sets cannot be described statically or in individual isolation. His statement shows that economic actions and actors are interrelated or interconnected. This implies, at the same time, that the ecological performance of a particular economic action is influenced by (the institutional context of) other economic actions[11].

The general ecological tendencies of ongoing industrialisation, as sketched in chapter 1, moreover suggest that we need insights into the institutional reasons for the ecological performance of a historical economy as a whole rather than of separate economic actions. This hypothesis can be supported by the following examples. First, though the pollution per kilometer car use decreases due to technological innovation, total car pollution rises due to an ever greater mobility (i.e. more cars and more kilometers). Second, home insulation, more energy-saving machinery and appliances, and more energy-efficient production of consumer goods and services did not prevent total energy use in the Netherlands to increase (though the rate of increase declined) (Environmental Balance Sheet 1998, RIVM). Finally, though the ratio between energy use and GDP in the UK between 1700 and 1995 has, apart from an initial rise, been ever declining since 1880, per capita energy consumption has risen by a factor of twenty (Jackson 1998, 10-11).

To recapitulate, in this section I claim that, in order to understand the ecological performance of a particular historical economy, we need insights into the "institutional whole" of this economy, for two reasons. First, because separate economic actions are conditioned by a set of economic institutions defining the use and exchange of various production factors in particular and commodities in general and by other economic actors' actions. Second, because the ecological performance of an economy depends on the accumulated ecological effects of the ensemble of economic (inter)actions rather than on the separate ecological effects of isolated economic actions.

2.2.3 Meaning of the "Institutional Whole"

The hypothesis formulated above, namely that we need insights into the institutional whole of an industrial economy to understand the institutional reasons for its deteriorating ecological performance, may suggest too huge and, hence, an impossible requirement. Therefore, I must explain further what I expect from an analysis of something called an "institutional whole". In order to do that I will tie in with two endeavours (found in economic literature) to describe an overview of the institutions constituting an economy. A first approach understands the institutional whole of an economy as a *hierarchical* whole. A second approach understands this

[11] Ramazzotti agrees that a particular economic action cannot be associated to a single institution, but relates to what he calls an "institutional setup" (a more or less extensive set of interrelated institutions). This is, he writes, a reason why "institutions" are usually defined as "systems of norms" rather than isolated norms. Reference to institutional setups does, however, not solve the problem, since they too are interdependent and can hardly be treated as isolated entities. Therefore, he deems it appropriate to adopt the definition whereby an institution refers to a single rule (Ramazzotti 1999). As I mentioned in section 1.1, I share his argument.

institutional whole as a *classificatory* one: it tries to classify economic institutions into different types. Before enlarging on institutional hierarchies and classifications, however, I should deal with (another) boundary problem established by using the term "economy".

In chapter 2, I already mentioned a boundary problem connected to our value-related interpretation of an economy. I argued, to start with, that the set of phenomena constituting an economy can vary depending on the perspective used. I argued, moreover, that economic and non-economic (for instance, political) phenomena, though they can be distinguished, cannot always be separated. This latter boundary problem relates to our presumed interpretations of the distinction between the economic and, for instance, political sphere. There exists, however, another boundary problem connected to the delineation in time and in space of a culturally and historically specific economy. Nominating an economy as, for instance, feudal or capitalistic, agricultural or industrial, capitalistic or socialistic results from a conceptual reconstruction of history. Retrospectively, historians can discern some characteristics that are deemed typical for certain periods in time and for certain regions. Boundaries between different economic periods in time and between different economic regions are, however, not only fuzzy because of a certain continuity in institutional changes. They are, moreover, arbitrary in the sense that they depend on the concepts used to distinguish between periods and regions.

A hierarchy of economic institutions. The idea of an institutional hierarchy can be found in Bromley's writings. Bromley, following Douglass North, distinguishes an institutional environment from an institutional arrangement (Bromley 1989, 27-28). An institutional environment is the set of

> fundamental political, social, and legal ground rules that govern economic and political activity (rules governing elections, property rights, and the rights of contract are examples of these ground rules) (Davis & North 1970, 133; cited in Bromley 1989, 28).

An institutional arrangement is an arrangement between decision units that governs the ways in which these units can co-operate or compete[12]. According to North,

> [t]he institutional arrangement is probably the closest counterpart to the most widely used definition of the term institution (Davis & North 1970, 133).

The term "ground rules" Bromley uses to define an institutional environment suggests a hierarchy of institutions (rules, conventions, habits, customs, entitlements). This idea of a hierarchy of institutions is confirmed in at least two passages in Bromley's writings.

The first passage relates to his description of institutional change as the *raison d'être* for public policy (Bromley 1989, 32-34). In this passage Bromley proposes to consider the (democratic) policy process in a general way as a process with three levels. First, the policy level is represented by the legislative and judicial branches.

[12] North, as cited by Bromley, defines an institutional arrangement as an arrangement between economic units. I made his definition more general and sharp by omitting the adjective "economic", and specifying that the units meant are decision units.

At this level general statements about the sort of world we want to live in are debated and ultimately formulated. Second, the organisational level is represented by the executive branch. Rules and laws define the organisations of this executive branch, how these organisations will operate, and also what they will do in a programmatic sense. The third level is the operational level, the level of operating units in society such as, among other things, firms and households. The range of choice open to decision units at the organisational level is defined by institutional arrangements at the policy level, while the range of choice open to the decision units at the operational level is defined by institutional arrangements at both the policy and the operational level. The outcomes that result from the patterns of interaction at the operational level (and the organisational and policy level; MD) will be evaluated by the citizens as either good or bad. Bad outcomes will give rise to a collective response through the political process, meant to change the institutional arrangements that define the choice sets of the different decision units.

Bromley's picture of the policy process in general is a first illustration of the idea of a hierarchical ordering of institutions. This illustration of Bromley confirms, to start with, the idea – presented in section 4.4 of chapter 2 - that politics is logically prior to economic actions. Bromley agrees that an economy, and thus markets, are the "result" of politics.

> Public policy is about two central concepts: (1) deciding socially acceptable institutional arrangements (entitlement structures) that both constrain and liberate individual action at the [for instance, economic; MD] operational level; and (2) searching for the boundary between autonomous (market-like) and collective decision making. The first choice will be dominated by concern for what sort of world we want to have, who will participate in that choice, and the weighting of the preferences of the respective constituents. The second choice will be dominated by concern for the operating efficiency of alternative entitlement structures, and by the possible costs of a mistake. States, as manifestations of the hopes and interests of their citizens, retain authority over these two types of choices. There are no divinely inspired guidelines about entitlement structures, or about the boundary between atomistic and collective decisions. These are, of necessity, culturally and situation specific (Bromley 1989, 34).

Stated differently, according to Bromley, a hierarchy between institutions exists in the sense of a priority of (political) preferences for institutional arrangements that define economic choice sets to (economic) preferences for particular choices within institutional arrangements[13],[14].

---

[13] Bromley's stress on this hierarchical order between politics and economy is a counterargument to liberal (in the European meaning of the term) ideology. Liberal ideology believes that the state should set up the conditions for atomistic choice and then step aside and let individuals bargain in order to maximise aggregate satisfaction. When new conditions require any modification of the prevailing institutional structure, the minimal state is supposed to compensate those harmed by the changae. This would prevent the state from willy-nilly shifting economic advantage among the polity. Bromley argues that this liberal ideology sanctifies the status quo. 'In practice it means that all manner of offensive or dangerous activity, just because it is in existence, must be bought off by those who seek relief. [...] The tyranny of the status quo in externality policy, justified by the concept of Pareto irrelevancy, is a serious matter. Such a view of the world subjugates the political process to the market - a breathtaking convolution of reality' (Bromley 1991, 80). (This "breathtaking convolution of reality" is what I called in section 4.4 of chapter 2 a reverse hierarchical relation between polity and economy.)

The second passage that refers to the idea of a hierarchy of institutions deals with the fact that individuals belong to more than one (sub-)group in a society (Bromley 1989, 46). Each (sub-)group has its own conventions and entitlements that both liberate and constrain behaviour. Hence, individuals are subject to several sets of overlapping institutional arrangements. What matters is that, according to Bromley, 'the legal standards of the larger group supersede those of the sub-group' (Bromley 1989, 46). This means that institutional relations that regularise the behaviour between members of a larger group dominate institutional relations that are more typical for the same kind of behaviour between members of a sub-group. The institutional arrangements constituting a local economy within a specific state, for instance, are (or have to become, in order to solve existing tensions) in practice subordinate to the institutional arrangements constituting the national economy.

This passage does not exclude the possibility that one individual belongs to several groups, for instance a group of badminton players and a brass band, that each have their particular institutional arrangements, but between which no hierarchical relationships exists. When playing badminton, the individual behaves in response to the institutional arrangements within his sports club; when playing music, he or she conforms to the institutional arrangements regularising behaviour in the brass band. In other words, actions have their own set of *relevant* institutions. (As Neale explains, it are folk views that inform us about the relevant context for a specific rule. And it is the combination of rule and folk views that constitute an institution – see section 1.1.) However, when a local brass band wants to compete with other local brass bands and, therefore, becomes part of a larger, for instance: national, organisation of brass bands, the institutional arrangements of the local brass band must be made compatible with existing national institutional arrangements. Nor does this passage exclude the possibility that fundamental institutional arrangements regularising behaviour in a particular group, for instance the American economy, induce institutional transformations in other national economies, so that these former institutional fundaments become the fundaments of an internationally operating economy. In other words, institutional arrangements regularising behaviour in some sub-group can become dominant in a larger group in the course of time. However, at any time, every national economy operating internationally must sooner or later either subordinate its national economic institutions to - i. e. make them compatible with - the conventions and entitlements regularising international economic

[14] In a recent article, Bromley explicitly and strongly objects to the idea that political preferences for institutional arrangements derive spontaneously from private economic preferences. 'Smith managed to finesse the essential problem of order by arguing that it was the logical outcome of the age-old problem of provisioning. Political conservatives, libertarians and not a few anarchists, have taken great comfort from this idea. And a fine idea it is. How wonderful to avoid the difficult business of having to agree upon mechanisms for achieving and the rules for evaluating, that order. Much better to let it emerge spontaneously from the material acquisitiveness of all. This is what Hayek called spontaneous order' (Bromley 1998, 325).

behaviour or act politically in order to change international economic conventions and entitlements[15].

The two passages just mentioned – and the reflections based on them – illustrate that the institutional environment of a particular, for instance: local, economy can mean different things. It can mean its local *political* institutional environment or it can mean its wider, i.e. national or international, *economic* institutional environment. Bromley remains silent concerning the nature of these hierarchical relations. Ramazzotti's distinction between a genetic and an order hierarchy is clarifying in this respect (Ramazotti 1999, 5).

According to Ramazzotti, a genetic hierarchy is a formal one. Its concern is not with the content of institutions, i.e. with the direct effects that they exert on their fields of action[16]. It is with the procedures to be followed and with the level of the hierarchy that must deal with specific fields of actions. A constitution, for instance, may assign regional public authorities the task of regulating the health service, independently of how the regulation is going to be in practice. Or, to refer to Bromley's example, between the institutions conditioning political action and economic institutions resulting from these actions consists a genetic hierarchy. An order hierarchy, on the contrary, focuses on the effects of the rules. In an order hierarchy, the extension of an institution's effect defines its rank. Some rules are mere specifications of more general rules. In many countries, for example, basic constitutional principles (e.g. the equality of human beings independently of gender, race, religion, etc.) are stated that bound all other laws. No matter how the latter laws are specified, they cannot contrast those principles. They rather have to actualise them. The effects of the general principles encompass the effects of specific laws. Or to refer, again, to one of the previous examples, the institutions of the local brass band cannot contradict the institutions of the national organisation of brass bands. Local brass bands can, however, have some supplementary institutions. These latter ones only have a local "field of action". Between national and local institutions exists an order hierarchy.

Ramazotti notes that an order hierarchy is conceptually distinct but may coexist with a genetic hierarchy (Ramazzotti 1999, 5-7). In terms of a genetic hierarchy, a constitution is, for instance, on a higher tier because it is the law that defines the procedure for the creation of ordinary laws. In terms of the order hierarchy, the constitution defines the overall effects to be achieved while ordinary laws may only work on the details. In this respect the constitution also has a higher rank. Between order and genetic hierarchies may occur different types of relations. The former case is, for instance, an example of "nested hierarchical relations": the ranking of the order hierarchy is directly correlated to the ranking of the genetic hierarchy. According to Ramazzotti, two other types of hierarchical relations can exist.

---

[15] Bromley calls the problem of 'overlapping but not coincident opportunity sets' or of 'incongruent institutional structures' a problem of 'institutional dissonance' (Bromley 1985, 790). Institutional dissonance is, in his view, a reason for non-compliance.

[16] I interpret Ramazotti's term "field of action" in the same way as I interpret Neale's concept " relevant context".

"Switched hierarchical relations" exist when an institution on a higher tier of the genetic hierarchy has a lower rank in the order hierarchy. Multinational firms and national economies, for instance, can belong to switched hierarchical arrangements. "Independent hierarchical relations" exist when the fields of action overlap but the institutions belong to genetically independent hierarchies. Consider the case where state laws coexist with religious rules and where both have common fields of action. "Killing" is, for instance, contrasted by the religious rule "thou shall not kill" and by criminal law (as far as situations of peace are concerned). Both religious and state law have a common field of action, but no ranking of them is possible in terms of a genetic hierarchy.

Ramazzotti's concept of an order hierarchy allows him to define "dominant" institutions (Ramazzotti 1999, 3). Dominant institutions characterise different economic periods in history. Different historical economies are defined not just in terms of existing institutions, but in terms of dominant institutions. Dominant institutions are those that are most pervasive (in space) and persistent (in time). The "pervasiveness" of an institution relates to its field of action. A forty-hour working week, for instance, is quite widespread in the manufacturing industry. The institution not to split up a farm when sold or inherited is, on the contrary, a local peculiarity of Southern Tyrol. The former institution is more pervasive, while the latter is very specific. It is therefore reasonable to believe that changes in the former would affect Italy's industrial economy more than changes in the latter. The "persistence" of an institution refers to its existence in time. Institutions are changeable. They arise, transform and disappear. Sharecropping, for instance, is an institution that disappeared altogether as time passed. Money – i.e. the rule whereby a non-commodity means of payment is accepted in economic transactions – tends to persist.

Ramazzotti introduces the concept "dominant institution" in order to explain the scope of institutional change (Ramazzotti 1999, 9-10). If inconsistencies arise between institutions that are not pervasive, its effects will in general not be very extensive, whatever solution arises. And, because the solution will affect only a small section of an order hierarchy, it will be rather easy for it to be enacted. Conversely, if change were to regard a more pervasive institution, the range of dependent overlaps might be very extensive. In such a case, the viability as well as the final outcome of the overall process would depend on possible reactions along all the tiers of the hierarchy.

To conclude, Ramazzotti's distinction between genetic and order hierarchies looks helpful in at least one respect. His definition of "dominant institutions" – a concept that derives its meaning from the concept "order hierarchy" – suggests a particular starting point for investigating the kind of problems I characterised in the introductory chapter as problems of sustainability. Since I accept the hypothesis that problems of sustainability relate to industrial economies, it seems useful to start with an analysis of the ecological performance of these institutions that dominate industrial economies. Looking for "dominant institutions of an industrial economy" thus is a prerequisite.

A classification of economic institutions. Economic institutions can also be classified into different types. Samuels, for instance, distinguishes between property rights, contract laws and institutions defining economic decision units (Samuels 1994a, 10). According to Schmid, the term "property rights" can indicate a lot of things: both tort and contract law, common and statutory (public) law, civil and criminal law, vested and nonvested rights, judicial procedure, and civil rights (Schmid 1987, 5-6). It can also refer to use or exchange rights, to decision rights, to rules defining market competition, to contingent and noncontingent rights, to rules affecting contractual costs, to rules affecting information and uncertainty costs, and so on (Schmid 1987, 189-194). In short, the term "property right" is a very ambiguous concept. Schmid himself proposes to replace it simply by the concept "right" (or institution, or rule) (Schmid 1987, 6). I accept Schmid's proposal, though it does not contribute much to the problem of classifying economic institutions according to their ecological performance. My hypothesis is that such a classification might be helpful to understand the ecological performance of a historical economy. Economic literature suggests, however, that existing conceptual and theoretical work is, in this respect, still in its infancy.

2.2.4 Conclusion

An overview of various models in the history of economic theory representing the relationship between economy and ecology illustrates the peculiarity of the approach proposed in this book. This approach understands an economy as embedded in an ecological environment. This embeddedness is not direct, but mediated through institutions. Institutions are social entities: they emerge in and define a particular historical society. Institutions as entitlements are political entities: it is within the political sphere that economic institutions typical for a particular historical society get enforced or transformed.

Interpreting the relationship between an economy and its ecological performance as internal implies that - in order to gain insights into this internal relationship - we should look for the institutional whole characterising a particular economy rather than for separate economic institutions. For, to begin with, economic action is always conditioned by an ensemble of institutions defining the use and exchange of economic goods in general and of production factors in particular and by (institutionally conditioned) economic actions of other economic actors. Moreover, the ecological performance of an economy does not depend so much on the separate ecological effects of isolated economic actions, but on the combined ecological effects of the ensemble of economic actions.

My proposition to look for the institutional whole characterising a specific economy cannot mean that we should know every separate economic institution, for this is too huge a task. My hypothesis that typical present-day ecological problems – the kind of ecological problems that prompted for "sustainability" as a world-wide political objective – relate to our 200 years old history of industrial economies suggests that a model of the institutional whole compiling, first, typical institutions of industrial economies and, second, economic institutions relevant for the problem of sustainability suffices. Ramazotti's definition of an order hierarchy – in distinction of a genetic hierarchy – allows him to introduce the concept "dominant institution". It suffices to look for economic institutions that dominate industrial economies to gain insights into institutional reasons for present-day sustainability problems. A classification of economic institutions according to their particular contribution to the ecological performance of an economy can help us to get a deeper insight into the kind of (dominant) institutions we have to look for to explain the (seemingly unmanageable) ecological performance of industrial economies.

3 CONCLUSION

In this chapter, I suggest that economists should adopt an institutional perspective on the economic sphere in order to gain insights into institutional reasons for the unmanageability of the ecological performance of our industrial economies. In section 1, I propose an interpretation of the concept "institution" that allows to understand the ecological performance of an economy as the counterpart of its institutional organisation. Institutions are rules guiding human action combined with the folk views that provide the rule in question with meaning and with a relevant context. Institutions constitute the symbolic dimension of action.. This symbolic dimension is social, not individual. Institutions enable and restrict autonomous action at the same time and in a double sense: one party's restriction is another party's liberation and one party's autonomy is always relative to the institutions defining its rights, duties and privileges. Institutions as entitlements are, moreover, public facts, in a double meaning. First, they are the often unintended results of intentional political action. Second, they hold for all members of a political community in the sense that these members have to respect the rights these institutions assign either to one, to more or to all members of this same community.

In section 2, I elaborate on the meaning of economic institutions. Economic institutions are the institutions that define economic decision units, economic rationality and economic goods. In other words, it is economic institutions that make economic action – action conditioned by scarce means and meant to fulfil the actor's private ends – concrete. It is economic institutions that condition the ecological performance of economic actions. Embroidering on the two examples offered by Bromley – the prisoner's dilemma and the prisoner's dream - we learned to understand institutional arrangements as reflections of *public preferences* for the protection of particular (existing or not yet existing) *private choice sets*. This interpretation of institutions as reflections of public preferences shows that it makes sense to look for an institutional expression of the public preference for sustainability. The further insight that institutional arrangements stimulate some private preferences and temper others implies that to understand the ecological performance of an economy in the long run, we do not really need to know the private preferences of separate individuals. It suffices to know an economy's institutional organisation. This is another way to say that an internal relationship exists between the ecological performance of an economy and its institutional organisation. This latter conclusion supports my research question: it shows that it makes sense to look for institutional reasons for (the seemingly unmanageability of) the ecological performance of our industrial economies.

In the history of economic theory, the opinion that an internal relationship exists between the institutional organisation and the ecological performance of an economy is not evident. An overview of deviating views shows the peculiarity of this particular opinion. In order to gain insights into the internal relationships between the ecological performance of our industrial economies and their institutional organisation, we need insights into the "institutional whole" constituting such economies. This image of an "institutional whole" should not be interpreted as if we need to know every economic institution constituting a particular industrial economy separately. My hypothesis that typical present day ecological problems – problems that have a globalising spatial dimension and a long run time dimension – relate to our historical type of industrial economies invites us to concentrate on "dominant institutions". Further, an (ecologically relevant) classification of types of economic institutions can inform us concerning their respective contribution to an economy's ecological performance. Combining an analysis of an economy's dominant institutions with an analysis of the ecological performance of types of economic institutions can help us to explain general ecological tendencies. My reconstruction of both Pearce's and Bromley's writings (in chapter 5 and 7 respectively) is meant to explore to what extent their work contributes to such analyses.

CHAPTER 4

FOUR NORMS FOR A POLITICALLY SUCCESSFUL ECONOMICS

In section 3.1 of the introductory chapter, I mention two criteria with which to evaluate contributions of economic theory to ecological policy. The first criterion is the impact of economic knowledge on final policy results. The second criterion is the capacity of economic knowledge to offer insights into possible ways to reduce the tension between the idea of sustainability and the general evolution of ecological problems. The latter criterion concentrates on the *content* of economic theory. It indicates the substantive kind of economic knowledge we need. This topic is dealt with in the previous chapter. In this chapter, we will investigate which *characteristics* economic science can and should have in order to ameliorate its political impact. This investigation is based on insights borrowed from both philosophy of science (mainly the methodological writings of Weber and Neurath) and political philosophy (Arendt's elaboration on the nature of a deliberative democracy).

Scientific objectivity is commonly understood as implying neutrality. I will argue, in the first section, that, though economic science should be *objective*, it cannot be but *non-neutral*. Objectivity and neutrality are two different things. I will, further, reflect on what a non-neutral scientific objectivity signifies.

In section 2, I will defend, to start with, that economic science should *describe* the economic sphere as part of human reality, but that it should not *prescribe* it. I will defend, moreover, that economic science should *explain* the relationship between the ecological performance of an economy and its institutional organisation, but that it should not *predict* it. These two characteristics taken together express my belief in the relevance of an economic science that provides public policy with *insights*, rather than *instruments*. Scientific knowledge interpreted as a toolbox for public policy hampers typically deliberative processes, for two reasons. First, scientific instruments implicitly define the objectives political actors should have. Second, they are based on particular conditions that are scientifically presumed, but not necessarily socially accepted or politically realised.

In section 3, I will argue that economic science should be rather *impartial* than *partial*. This means that it should supply citizens and official politicians with insights into the relationships between their private interests on the one hand and the publicly defined institutional context on the other, and the (economic) sources of unequal (political) power relationships. Such insights can help political actors to act as (more) free and (more) equal individuals. In other words, it can help them to better realise the ideal of a deliberative democracy.

1 OBJECTIVE

In section 1 of chapter 2, I show that both Weber and Neurath interpret economic (and other social) sciences as conceptual constructs. According to Weber, economic theories are conceptual constructs because theoretical concepts and laws are ideal-typical, i.e. value-laden. According to Neurath, it is the many decisions involved in scientific practice that urge us to see scientific theories as conceptual constructs. This interpretation of social-scientific theories as conceptual constructs demonstrates that economic theories *are not* and *cannot be neutral*. Both Weber and Neurath, however, hold on to the idea that social sciences *can* and *should be objective*. In this section, I will argue, contrary to Weber, that scientific objectivity does not imply a kind of neutrality that is left once the value-relatedness of scientific concepts and laws are recognised. Scientific objectivity does not simply imply empirical validity. I will, further, reflect on what scientific objectivity can mean and argue that such objectivity is, indeed, something scientists should strive for. In other words, I agree with Weber (and Neurath) that economic science should be objective. Scientific objectivity is a first norm for a politically relevant economics.

Weber postulates a logical distinction between the value-relevance of the data which are investigated and the objectivity or "value-freedom" of the investigation itself (see e.g. MSS 21-22, 58, 77-78, 111). According to Weber, the fact that certain values underlying the practical interest for analytical activity are always decisive for the focus of attention of the social science in question, does not prohibit an analytical ordering of empirical reality in a manner that lays claim to validity as empirical truth (MSS 58). In Weber's view, "objectivity" thus means "validity as empirical truth".

What is Weber's criterion for this "validity as empirical truth"? The criterion proves to be "supra-cultural validity". The purpose of all social sciences is, Weber writes, to achieve supra-cultural validity.

> [...] the successful *logical* analysis of the content of an ideal and its ultimate axioms and the discovery of the consequences which arise from pursuing it, logically and practically, must also be valid for the Chinese. At the same time, our Chinese can lack a "sense" for our ethical imperative and he can and certainly often will deny the ideal itself and the concrete value-judgments derived from it. Neither of these two latter attitudes can affect the scientific value of the analysis in any way (MSS 58-59).

Weber thus interprets "objectivity" as empirical validity. Weber's ultimate criterion for social-scientific "objectivity" is its "supra-cultural validity" or, to reformulate it in more modern (and modest) terms, the extent to which social-scientific propositions gain "intersubjective consent". Mathematics and logic seem, according to Weber, to be outstanding means to achieve such supra-cultural validity or intersubjective consent. For it is the kind of laws as found in "pure economics" – laws expressed in mathematical formulas and ordered in a logically consistent axiomatic system – that Weber indicates as objective (GAW 392; MSS 43). Mathematics and logic are, however, but means to gain such consent. Since these means lack for deciding which data to select – this selection often proves to give rise to conflict – intersubjective consent remains a value-laden matter. This makes me conclude that scientific objectivity ultimately comes down to intersubjective consent, not to neutrality. Intersubjective consent functions as an implicit criterion for distinguishing between "objective" facts – statements that succeeded in gaining intersubjective consent - and "subjective" values – statements that did not succeed in gaining intersubjective consent. It functions at the same time as an implicit criterion to distinguish between empirical and mere theoretical truth. Both kinds of truth are characterised by logical consistency. Only the former kind of truth can simultaneously carry off intersubjective consent.

Weber acknowledges that the objectivity of the social sciences is a normative ideal, not a matter of fact. In his view, striving for objectivity remains, nevertheless, scientists' duty. This duty is twofold. The first imperative of an objective scientist is to make constantly clear to the audience and above all to himself exactly at which point his job as an objective scientist stops and when he starts to speak as an evaluating and acting person. The second imperative is to keep his audience and scientific colleagues

> sharply aware at every moment of the standard by which [he judges] reality and from which the value-judgment is derived (MSS 59).

However, a lot of difficulties arise for the scientist who assents to this ideal of scientific objectivity. The temptation always lies around the corner firstly to present "ethical neutrality" - which more often than not is a case of obstinate and deliberate partisanship of powerful interest groups - as objective validity (MSS 6). Secondly, many scientists are inclined to believe that one can derive scientifically valid value-judgements from factual assertions about "trends" (MSS 22). Finally, the scientist's unconsciousness with regard to his own evaluative motives transforms his duty as a scientist into a nearly unattainable ideal. The motives of scientific labour

> often cannot be clarified and analyzed in a tangible and intelligible form in any other way than through the *confrontation* of the standards of value underlying the ideas criticized with others (MSS 59-60; the italics are mine).

In my view such *confrontation* is the only remaining means to distinguish between "objective" and "subjective" statements. Such confrontation will tell us which statements – provisionally - boast consensus and which do not. The former will then be called "objective" and the latter "subjective". Weber himself, however, is not capable of guaranteeing that the former are indeed value-free facts. Since conscious or unconscious consent concerning value-laden statements – consequently called "facts" - cannot be excluded. For that reason, I propose to drop the belief that we are able to separate facts and values completely. Consequently, we should also drop the interpretation of objectivity as value-free or neutral and, hence, as straightforwardly empirically valid.

To conclude, I propose to hold on to the interpretation *and* to the ideal of scientific objectivity as intersubjective consent[1]. Scientific statements can at most gain (provisional) consent within a particular community of scientists. Statements should gain such consent in order to be worth of the label "scientific". For it is this striving for consent that urges scientists to look for the better, i.e., most convincing (value-related) arguments: for the better selection of data and for the better ideal-typical construction of concepts and laws. Mathematics and logic can help in creating such a consent, but they are neither necessary, nor sufficient. The ideal of intersubjective consent or scientific objectivity does, however, not imply an ideal of neutrality. Objective science is and cannot be neutral, because we lack a criterion to separate completely facts from values.

2 DESCRIPTIVE AND EXPLANATORY

Weber makes an effort to stress that ideal-typical social-scientific theories are neither "true" nor (ethically) "ideal". They are logical ideals, but not simply "true" or empirically valid. They are not neutral, but, nevertheless, no ethical ideals. They are, to catch the previous in one phrase, perspectivistic (i.e., value-laden, non-neutral) descriptions. Weber's interpretation of (some privileged) social-scientific theories as toolboxes for public policy, however, pushes these theories from a descriptive into a prescriptive and from an explanatory into a predictive position. In this section, I will defend that politically successful social sciences should aim at description, not prescription and explanation, not prediction. These norms respect the capabilities and nature of both scientific and political practice (the latter understood as deliberative democracy). In a first part, I will explain why Weber's interpretation of "pure economics" as a toolbox for public policy fails. In a second part, I will fall back on Neurath to propose an alternative interpretation of the political relevance of economic theories. While Weber understands economics as providing public policy with prescriptive and predictive "instruments", I propose an interpretation of economics as supplying citizens and official politicians not so much with "utopias", as Neurath does, but with descriptive and explanatory "insights".

2.1 Weber: Pure Economics as a Political Toolbox

According to Weber, the political relevance of the social sciences consists of providing public policy with adequate means for given ends and of informing it about the consequences of using certain means. Weber thus considers social-scientific theories as political toolboxes. However, this political role is not granted to whatever social-scientific theories. It is granted to the "exact", not the historically

[1] Bernstein's book *Beyond Objectivism and Relativism. Science, Hermeneutics and Praxis* more extensively offers philosophical arguments for an interpretation of scientific objectivity as intersubjective consent and for objectivity as an ideal of scientific practice (Bernstein, 1989).

oriented social-scientific theories. It is granted, more precisely, to the pure economics of the theory of marginal utility, not to economic theories investigating economically conditioned or relevant phenomena. In this section, I will explain, to start with, which characteristics of pure economics make it, in Weber's opinion, a suitable theory for providing public policy with instruments. Second, I will present the contradiction in Weber's writings between his conviction that social-scientific theories are ideal-typical and, hence, at most theoretically valid on the one hand and his belief that pure economics is instrumentally relevant for public policy because of its empirical and/or practical validity on the other. Third, I will explain my reservations with regard to this latter belief of Weber and with the more general belief that whatever social-scientific theory can fulfil an instrumental political function. Finally, I will argue that there is some arbitrariness in Weber's presentation of the theory of marginal utility as the one and only politically relevant economics.

2.1.1 Pure Economics: Technically Applicable

According to Weber, the contribution of the social sciences consists of providing public policy with adequate means for given ends and of informing it about the consequences of using certain means. Giving information on adequate means and indispensable consequences is a purely technical problem.

> It would be superfluous to repeat that it is obviously possible and scientifically useful and necessary to establish propositions of the following type: in order to attain the end x (in economic policy), y is the only means, or under conditions b_1, b_2, and b_3, y_1, y_2, and y_3 are the only or the most effective means. [...] Hence it is simply a question of inverting causal propositions; [...]. It is indeed on this account that science is not compelled to formulate these technical teleological propositions in any form other than that of simple causal propositions, e.g., x is produced by y, or x, under conditions b_1, b_2, and b_3 is produced by y_1, y_2, and y_3. For these say exactly the same thing, and the "man of action" can derive his "prescriptions" from them quite easily (MSS 44-45).

This technical conception of the political relevance of social-scientific theories implies that the main point lies on *causal sequences*. Causal sequences are considered a kind of "predictions". They "predict" that x is produced by y, or that x, under conditions b_1, b_2, and b_3 is produced by y_1, y_2, and y_3.. Causal sequences are, hence, the entities that, through inversion, are transformed into scientifically justified means for political ends. In Weber's writings we can discern, however, two types of "causal sequences".

As sketched in section 2 of chapter 2, Weber distinguishes three kinds of social-economic sciences: pure economics, the science of economically conditioned phenomena, and the science of economically relevant phenomena. In Weber's view, the two latter kinds of economics are a kind of historical sciences. As such they are meant to understand the relationships and the cultural significance of individual events in their contemporary manifestations on the one hand and the causes of their being historically so and not otherwise on the other (MSS 72).

In order to gain such historical understanding, one first has to determine "laws" and "factors" (MSS 75). These "laws" are not, however, laws in the sense of exact natural science. They include regular recurrent relationships, regularities which are

> universally valid by means of comprehensive historical induction

or which are

> immediately and tangibly plausible according to our subjective experience (MSS 72-73).

Such causal relationships do not have to be quantifiable in order to be called a "law". They can especially include the *rules* governing motivated conduct (MSS 74).

"Laws" only fulfil a preliminary task in the historically oriented social sciences.

> The knowledge of causal *laws* is not the *end* of the investigation but only a *means* (MSS 79).

These laws make the analysis of an historically individual event possible. This analysis consists of defining the historically given individual *configuration* of those "laws" and "factors" which effect the unique event on the one hand, and of an explanation of the *significance* of the concrete interactions between those "factors" on the other hand (MSS 75-76).

Because of the complexity of cultural reality an individual configuration of causal factors can never be *deduced* form a system of laws, however complete and perfect this system may be. The argument goes the other way round: our intuition of the significance of an individual event makes us select the relevant causal factors and as a consequence a particular configuration of laws lightens up out of the complex multiplicity of causal reality (MSS 76).

> [...] an *exhaustive* causal investigation of any concrete phenomenon in its full reality is not only practically impossible - it is simply nonsense. We select only those causes to which are to be imputed in the individual case, the "essential" features of an event. Where the *individuality* of a phenomenon is concerned, the question of causality is not a question of *laws* but of concrete causal *relationships*; it is not a question of the subsumption of the event under some general rubric as a representative case but of its imputation as a consequence of some constellation. It is in brief a *question of imputation* (MSS 78-79).

Performing this imputation is the second task to be achieved for a social scientist. "Nomological" knowledge only is a precondition for it.

Every individual constellation is causally explicable only as the consequence of another equally individual constellation which has preceded it. The tracing as far into the past as possible of these constellations and, consequently, the exposition of the individual features of those historically developed configurations which are contemporaneously significant is the third task of a social researcher (MSS 75-76). Again, the sequence of historical constellations cannot be deduced from laws, because the reality to which the laws apply always remains an equally *individual* phenomenon whose meaning - and thus whose constellation of relevant factors -

depends on cultural valuations. The concrete historical significance of an individual event does not depend on its generic features, because generic features are features which each event has in common with all other events, past and present, of the same type. The significance depends on the uniqueness of its causal configuration (i.e., of its genetic features) and of its relationships with other events (MSS 76-77).

To conclude, in Weber's view, the historically oriented social-economic sciences are not politically relevant since they do not allow for predictions. Economically conditioned and economically relevant phenomena are unique events that cannot be "predicted", i.e. deduced from a system of laws. They can at most be causally explained in retrospect. Moreover, historical laws are mere – and often not quantifiable - "regularities".

Contrary to the two historically oriented social-economic sciences, "pure" economics is politically valid in an instrumental way. This is due to the special nature of the kind of knowledge it offers. "Pure economics" exclusively consists of "laws", expressed in mathematical formulas and ordered in a logically consistent axiomatic system (GAW 392; MSS 43). In order to allow for such a logically consistent system of "laws", pure economics is based on certain assumptions. Economic theory assumes the existence of

> pure economic interests and precludes the operation of political or other non-economic considerations (MSS 44).

Pure economic interests depend, in their turn, on only one psychic motive: maximisation of the satisfaction of one's own competing desires (GAW 391). Pure economics is about *rational* economic behaviour, i.e., human action which is "caused" by the only economic motive *and* which succeeds in satisfying this motive. Pure economics, i.e., the theory of marginal utility presupposes, among other things, that people are able to act more or less instrumentally, i.e., that they can choose the correct means for a given end by making use of their experience and their capacity to calculate in advance (GAW 390). Economic theory tries to catch this kind of successful, i.e., rational behaviour in a logically consistent axiomatic system.

Pure economics derives its theoretical validity from the logical consistency of its abstract axiomatic system. This theoretical validity is, however, completely independent of its practical relevance. Time and again Weber stresses that pure economic concepts and laws, as all concepts and laws in cultural science, do not have "metaphysical validity", but are ideal-typical. In a certain sense they are "pure fictions", heuristic instruments which enable us to describe and explain empirical reality.

> Pure economic theory, in its analysis of past and present society, utilizes ideal-type concepts exclusively. Economic theory makes certain assumptions which scarcely ever correspond completely with reality but which approximate it in various degrees and asks: how would men act under these assumed conditions, if their actions were entirely rational? (MSS 43-44).

Whether the theory of marginal utility is practically relevant or not depends on two aspects.

First, it depends on the presence of other possible causes – besides the one psychic motive of maximisation of satisfaction of one's own competing desires - which are deemed relevant for the individual event in question.

> The degree of significance which we are to attribute to economic factors is decided by the class of causes to which we are to impute those specific elements of the phenomenon in question to which we attach significance in given cases and in which we are interested (MSS 71).

Second, the extent to which people, urged by their self-interest, behave "objectively rationally" is decisive for the practical validity of pure theory. According to Weber, human conduct often is irrational:

> errors in thinking or calculation can constitute causal factors of the course of action (MSS 42).

Despite this questionable practical relevance of pure economics, it is the logical consistency of its axiomatic system and the mathematical form of its "laws" that, in Weber's view, provide pure economics with its instrumental political relevance. This is because both features together allow for logical inversions, i.e., for "predictions". Logical inversions are a purely technical, i.e., neutral matter. To conclude, for Weber "instrumentality" implies both "neutrality" and "predictive power". It is Weber's instrumental interpretation of a politically relevant social science that urges him to fall back on "pure" or "exact" economics as the only politically relevant social-economic science..

2.1.2 Pure Economics: Theoretically, Empirically or Practically Valid?

How is it possible that Weber is so confident in the political relevance of economic laws? Weber's writings certainly show a contradiction in this respect. His stress on the ideal-typical character of social-scientific concepts, laws and theories cannot be reconciled with his faith in the practical relevance of pure economics for public policy. In the following paragraphs, I will elaborate on this contradiction.

According to Weber, ideal types are arrived at by the accentuation of certain elements of reality which seem important with respect to a specific point of view. Hence, they cannot be understood as a reflection of reality (MSS 90-93). They are not *true* (if "truth" is understood as correspondence between statements on the one hand and phenomena in reality on the other). They are a logical ideal: a well defined analytical construct, a limiting concept that allows us to compare reality with it. Ideal-types have a heuristic and expository function. Comparison between the ideal-type and reality, the estimation of similarities and discrepancies, can make the characteristic features of empirical phenomena clear and understandable. An ideal type is not a description of reality but

> aims to give unambiguous means of expression to such a description. [...] It is no hypothesis but it offers guidance to the construction of hypotheses (MSS 90).

Ideal-types thus are *logical* ideals. Ideal-typical theories are at most theoretically valid. They are not empirically valid.

Ideal-typical theories are not *ethical* ideals. They do not present models of what should be done to make them exist (MSS 93-95). The concept "economic value", for instance, does not point to an objectively valid "value", to an ethical imperative which should influence price formation. Ideal-types do not correspond to ideas, thoughts or ideals, which an historically decisive number of persons have in mind and which are therefore characteristic of their culture either (MSS 94-96). One can indeed construct an ideal-type out of significant ideas which more or less people in a certain epoch have. However, again, this ideal-type does not reveal actually existing ideas, nor their average or their common features, but at most it makes their revelation possible. In other words, ideal-typical social-scientific theories are not necessarily practically valid either.

Weber's stress on the nature of ideal types is meant as a warning against possible misuses of science.

> Nothing, however, is more dangerous than the *confusion* of theory and history stemming from naturalistic prejudices. This confusion expressed itself firstly in the belief that the "true" content and the essence of historical reality is portrayed in such theoretical constructs or secondly, in the use of these constructs as a procrustean bed into which history is to be forced or, thirdly, in the hypostatization of such "ideas" as real "forces" and as a "true" reality which operates behind the passage of events and which works itself out in history (MSS 94).

Belief in the "truth" of ideal types makes people treat them as practical models. Ideal-typical presentations

> regularly seek to be, or are unconsciously, ideal-types not only in the *logical* sense but also in the *practical* sense, i.e., they are *model types* which [...] contain what, from the point of view of the expositor, *should* be and what *to him* is "essential" [...] *because it is enduringly valuable.* [...] Here it is no longer a matter of the purely theoretical procedure of treating empirical reality with respect to values but of *value-judgments* which are integrated into the concept [...]. Because the ideal type claims empirical *validity* here, it penetrates into the realm of the evaluative *interpretation* [...] (MSS 97-98).

Despite his stress on the ideal-typical nature of the social sciences – a matter of theoretical, not empirical nor practical validity -, Weber shows not much reluctance to interpret the political relevance of pure economics instrumentally. This latter interpretation betrays his implicit belief in the empirical and practical validity of (pure) economic "laws". As I explained in section 1 of this chapter, it is the "objectivity" of pure economics, due to its logical consistency and its mathematical form, that, in Weber's view, stops the gap between theoretical and empirical validity. It is historical developments that stop the gap between theoretical and practical validity. Weber observes that as a matter of fact empirical reality more and more resembles theoretical economics.

> The historical peculiarity of the capitalistic epoch, and consequently also the meaning of the theory of marginal utility for the understanding of this epoch, rests on the fact that [...] under the present conditions of life the approximation of reality to the theoretical propositions has been continuously growing, drawing the fate of ever larger strata of humankind into it, and, as far as one can see, it will go on (GAW 395).

Historical economic reality evolves more and more into a direction which leaves economic actors the choice between

> economic expulsion or the observation of very definite maxims of economic acting (GAW 133).

Nevertheless, Weber's belief in the empirical and practical validity of pure economics remains at odds with his rejection of the notion that social-scientific "laws" are laws in the sense of exact natural science. According to Weber, natural sciences try to attain

> a purely "objective" (i.e., independent of all individual contingencies) monistic knowledge of the totality of reality in a *conceptual* system of metaphysical *validity* and mathematical *form* (MSS 85).

Time and again Weber stresses that all concepts and laws in cultural science do not have "metaphysical validity", but are ideal-typical. In a certain sense they are 'pure fictions', heuristic instruments which enable us to describe and explain empirical reality. Weber calls the wrong supposition that concepts and laws in the cultural sciences are similar to those in the exact natural sciences a 'naturalistic prejudice' (MSS 88).

2.1.3 Two Objections

For two reasons Weber's instrumental interpretation of the political relevance of pure economics is problematic. It is problematic because pure economics *is not* simply empirically valid. Consequently, its predictive power is limited. It is problematic because it *is not* straightforwardly practically valid. Pure economics assumes values – the values constituting its perspective - that are not necessarily socially accepted nor politically aimed at. These objections do not only hold for pure economics in particular; they hold for social-scientific theories in general[2]. I will deal more extensively with the first objection in the next subsection 2.2. I will enlarge on the second objection in the following paragraphs.

The non-neutrality of ideal-typical social science prohibits a purely technical political use. Only when the values underlying a political objective (for instance the introduction or transformation of a particular institution) are compatible with the values constituting the theoretical perspective, will it be possible to use ideal-typical economics as an unproblematic "technique". This compatibility can, however, hardly be realised. The complexity of human reality (i.e., the complexity of the whole set of values constituting human action) offers an insurmountable impediment in this respect (MSS 56, 11-12). On the one hand, the value-relatedness of the concepts and laws of pure economics cannot become perfectly clear. The demand for complete transparency of the values defining the perspective of pure economics not only overlooks implicit norms and values which are imposed on students educated in a disciplinary specialisation, but also ignores the possibility of collective

[2] Similar objections hold for an instrumental interpretation of the natural sciences. For an elaboration of this topic see, for instance, Gremmen (1999) and Radder (Korthals 1989).

oblivion of the evaluations underlying a specific scientific interest[3]. In other words, one cannot completely distinguish between scientific facts and scientific values. On the other hand, the evaluations underlying the political goal can never become completely transparent. One cannot completely distinguish between political facts and political values either. As long as the values constituting both the theoretical perspective and the political objective are not exactly the same, scientific instruments do not precisely connect to political questions. This discrepancy between theoretical and political values prohibits a purely technical or instrumental use of science in the political sphere. One can never guarantee, as Weber suggests, that for politicians

> all that remains is to choose between several economic means, when these differ only with respect to their certainty, rapidity, and quantitative productiveness, and are completely identical in every other value-relevant aspect (MSS 37-38)[4].

Only when these conditions could be met, could a given means be evaluated as "technically most correct".

> In every other case, i.e., in every case which is not purely a matter of technique, the [technical, economic] evaluation ceases to be unambiguous and evaluations enter which are not determinable exclusively by economic analysis (MSS 38).

Undoubtedly, those "other cases" are mainly the case, since perfect consciousness of and complete conformity between the evaluations underlying the political goal and economic theory cannot be taken for granted. This means that a logical positivistic *Weltanschauung* does not follow from "objective" economics (in Weber's sense): pure economics cannot be used as a neutral instrument for the realisation of political goals. On many occasions, Weber seems perfectly aware of the problems related to an instrumental use of "objective" economics within public policy. He often stresses that the constructs of pure economics which are useful for analytical purposes cannot be made the sources of practical value-judgements:

> even indisputably "technically correct" economic actions are not validated through this quality *alone* (MSS 37, 38).

Nevertheless, this awareness remains without further practical recommen-dations.

2.1.4 A Historically Contingent Multiplicity of Economic Paradigms

Weber grants a privileged political role to pure economics. This privilege, which is due to the axiomatic, law-like construction of the theory of marginal utility, limits

---

[3] 'All research in the cultural sciences in an age of specialization, once it is oriented towards a given subject matter through particular settings of problems and has established its methodological principles, will consider the analysis of the data as an end in itself. It will discontinue assessing the value of the individual facts in terms of their relationships to ultimate value-ideas. Indeed, it will lose its awareness of its ultimate rootedness in the value-ideas in general' (MSS 112).

[4] On the one hand, such a lack of conformity can make economists' often heard complaints that politicians mistakenly ignore their recommendations understandable (see ,e.g., Dietz & van der Straaten 1992). On the other hand, an instrumental political use of economic theory hides the partiality in the conformity between the scientific interests and the interests of particular, often economically and politically powerful, groups.

the scope of possible political questions that can be successfully posed to the social-economic sciences. The political perception of social-economic problems becomes, moreover, one-sided under influence of the one-sided exact-economic point of view. Politicians can, for instance, more often than is necessary, take over the belief in the invariability of specific factors (e.g., wants and resources, i.e. those factors which the theory of marginal utility considers as given) and in the manageability of specific goals (economic growth or economic efficiency, rather than the reduction or just distribution of scarce resources, goods or labour power). The privileged political position of pure economics thus not only limits the kind of political problems that can be scientifically dealt with. It also reduces the way in which political problems can be defined. A multiplicity of economic theories, on the contrary, could avoid the necessity of such two-fold reduction.

Though Weber recognises the possibility of a multiplicity of scientific paradigms, he does not seem to consider the political importance of the particular kind of scientific multiplicity that is available. It looks as if he lets paradigmatic developments take their course. Weber stresses that one must not misunderstand the proper task of the social sciences as a continual chase for new viewpoints and new analytical constructs (MSS 111). He tries to limit the number of scientific ideal-types. The construction of abstract ideal-types is only a means, not an end, he writes (MSS 92). An unimpeded proliferation of concepts, laws and theories which are related to different values is, anyhow, only a theoretical possibility which never takes place actually. Scientific communities are much more uniform than the abstract possibility of an infinite multiplicity of concepts and laws may suggest. Scientific research reaches out for "guiding" or "cultural" values:

> in the cultural sciences concept-construction depends on the setting of the problem, and the latter varies with the content of culture itself (MSS 105).

Apparently, the choice of a perspective from which to interrogate reality is not totally free, but the result of some historical cultural characteristics which transcend the scientist's individual free will. Whether an ideal-type, be it a concept, a law or a theory, is scientifically fruitful or not can not be decided beforehand. It depends on its

> success in revealing concrete cultural phenomena in their interdependence, their causal conditions and their *significance* (MSS 92).

Whether this criterion of success applies to a specific ideal-type can only become clear *a posteriori*. Selecting adequate ideal-types is a question of experience and of scientific craftsmanship.

In section 2.2, I will contrast Weber's rather passive conception of the political importance of paradigmatic multiplicity with Neurath's arguments in favour of an active search for "gaps" between various paradigmatic approaches.

2.1.5 *Conclusion*

Weber grants a privileged political role to pure economics. This privileged role relates to Weber's particular instrumental interpretation of the political relevance of social-scientific theories. In his view, social-scientific theories can only contribute to public policy on condition that they are empirically and practically valid. The first condition should guarantee the predictive power of the theory in question. The second condition should make sure that the instruments derived from the theory can be considered "neutral". The latter means that a conformity exists between the values underlying the scientific instrument on the one hand and the political objective on the other. In Weber's view, pure economics satisfies both conditions. The empirical validity of pure economics is satisfied through its logical consistency and mathematical form. Its practical validity can historically be recorded.

I object to this instrumental interpretation of the political relevance of social-scientific theories, for two reasons. First, as contradictions in Weber's writings already suggest, logical consistency and mathematical form do not suffice for empirical validity, i.e., for "truth" as correspondence between conceptual construct and empirical reality. Consequently, the predictive power of pure economics is questionable, as it is of all social scientific theories. Second, the impossibility of complete evaluative transparency of both the scientific perspective and the political objective prevents us to assume the practical validity of scientific instruments straightforwardly. Moreover, as Weber himself admits at times, political objectives cannot simply be assumed to conform to historical trends. Politics does not necessarily look for institutional adaptations that allow for an extrapolation of historical trends. It can as well look actively for institutional transformations that restructure historical tendencies. Science should respect politically defined objectives. An instrumental interpretation of the political relevance of economics does not imply respect for , but prescription of political objectives. A politically successful economics, on the contrary, should look for scientific knowledge that helps citizens and professional politicians to clarify, to adjust and, possibly, to realise their own objectives. This implies that scientists should actively look for paradigmatic approaches that are suited to deal with politically defined problems. This active search for suitable paradigms is at odds with Weber's passive interpretation of the coming into existence of economic paradigms.

Previous objections to the interpretation of a politically successful economics as a provider of predictive and prescriptive instruments urge me to look for an alternative conception. Neurath's writings set us up a long way in that direction.

2.2 *Neurath: Economic Theories as Scientific Utopias*

At first sight, Neurath's stress on "prediction" as the central goal of science seems to support Weber's instrumental interpretation of science. On further consideration, however, it turns out that for Neurath "prediction" is a necessary part of *scientific* practice. At the same time, Neurath insists on the limited predictive power of science within *political* practice. Despite this limited power for political prediction,

Neurath's interpretation of scientific "prediction" and his pleading for scientific utopias help us to clarify the way in which science can be politically successful.

2.2.1 *The Scientific Meaning of Prediction*

'"Making predictions" is', according to Neurath, 'what all of science is about' (Neurath 1931b, 53). Before being able to make predictions one first has to formulate "laws". Predictions can be deduced from laws, but laws cannot be deduced from a set of observation statements. "Induction" leads to laws (and this is always a matter of decision; see section 1.2 in chapter 2).

Laws do not express causality, but correlations. Causality, the idea of a gapless and all-embracing sequence of cause and effect, is too much a remnant of metaphysics (Neurath 1930, 45; 1941, 224). Moreover, it suggests an - empirically undemonstrated - asymmetry: a "cause" determines or, at least, influences an "effect", not vice versa (Neurath 1944, 948-950). For that reason Neurath proposes to drop the causality-related terminology and to replace it with statistical expressions, which are more appropriate for expressing the lack of knowledge inherent in induction.

Only content - or synthetic - statements can qualify for laws (Neurath 1929, 308; 1931b, 56; 1934, 104-105). Analytic statements are tautologies: they do not add anything meaningful. According to Neurath, it is a basic error of metaphysics to suppose that thinking or, more precisely, logical deductions lead to knowledge out of its own resources without using any empirical material. Logical investigations cannot arrive at new contents by an inference from given states of affair.

> [A]ll thought and inference consists of nothing but a transition from statements to other statements that contain nothing that was not already in the former [...] (Neurath 1929, 308).

The scientific world-conception knows only laws, i.e. synthetic, empirical statements, and auxiliary tools, i.e. the analytic statements of logic and mathematics[5].

Laws are directives for finding predictions of individual courses of events, which in turn are tested - and subsequently accepted, or not - by protocol statements. This statement of Neurath reveals his view on the relevance of scientific "predictions". Scientific "predictions" are a necessary element in the testing of science.

The success of scientific predictions further depends on two main factors: 1) the combination of disciplines, which are applied to make one single prediction, and 2)

[5] Neurath's conviction that laws can only take the form of synthetic statements, which always are uncertain to a certain degree, does not imply that analytic statements, the statements of logic and mathematics, are completely certain or indubitable. A statement that is understood to be analytic today can be declared synthetic tomorrow. It is always possible that someone feels obliged to correct a mathematical or logical proposition on the basis of specific protocol statements (Neurath 1934, 104). Symbolic logic and mathematics, the auxiliary tools of unified science, are themselves historical events (Neurath 1936c, 146).

the definition of the proper object of the disciplines used. First, one cannot presuppose that any forecast can always be settled by means of one single science (Neurath 1931b, 53; 1931c, 329). In order to make one definite prediction one often needs many laws from many theories. Neurath's pleading for a "unified science" – see further in section 2.2.3 - is precisely connected with this: it makes the linking of laws of all sciences with each other possible. Second, the area of study of a particular discipline cannot be delimited from the start. This area can only be defined at the end when one surveys and analyses the results of the science. The success of prediction determines whether a specific demarcation is scientifically justified (Neurath 1931c, 365, 368). And since the success of predictions also depends on the combination of laws from different theories, it is rather useless to design new boundaries between individual disciplines.

> Longer experience teaches us that we avoid pseudo-problems of all kinds if, in the analysis of sciences, we set out from predictions, their formulation and their control. But it is precisely this starting point that is little suited for the delimitation of special disciplines (Neurath 1936a, 132).

2.2.2 *Pseudo-Rationalism*

According to Neurath, political practice is, as is scientific practice, a matter of action. A characteristic of action is that it is unavoidably based on decisions. When the motive for a decision is a principle of a more general kind, Neurath calls it an "auxiliary motive". He distinguishes different kinds of auxiliary motives: drawing of lots (the auxiliary motive in its purest form), turning to instinct (which effectiveness is often exaggerated, since instinct must fail with respect to the complex rational relationships created by the consciously shaped institutions of the social order and modern technology (Neurath 1913a, 5)), believing in oracles, omens, prophecies and the like (great military leaders, politicians and other men of action 'are often much more superstitious than corresponds to the spirit of their age, and [...] the forms of their superstition sometimes are strangely primitive or archaic' (Neurath 1913a, 6)), turning to some authority, such as a father confessor or some other adviser, but also using the simplicity principle or the majority principle in a democracy, and, last but not least, relying on science.

Neurath calls the use of this latter auxiliary motive a kind of pseudo-rationalism. It leads to self-deception and to hypocrisy, since science, as a kind of action, is itself the result of many decisions.

> Most of our contemporaries rely on their insight and want to leave the decision in all things to it once and for all. [...] Men of this type are mostly of the opinion that if difficulties turn up, sharper thinking will have to lead to the goal; they completely fail to see that even the sharpest thinker can end up with several conclusions of equal value if premises are lacking. [...] Education and character support these errors which Descartes, who is usually considered to be the father of rationalism, managed to keep free of in the field of practical action (Neurath 1913a, 7-8).

Pseudo-rationalists pretend to have adequate knowledge where strict rationalism excludes it on purely logical grounds. 'Rationalism sees its chief triumph in the clear recognition of the limits of actual insight' (Neurath 1913a, 8).

Empirical rationalists must, for several reasons, acknowledge the limitations of scientific predictions[6]. To start with, they have strictly logical reasons. Science is, indeed, itself a kind of action (see section 1.2 in chapter 2). Secondly, science is a form of practice embedded in a social-historical context. Science is a human enterprise dependent on historically contingent ordinary language and on the limitations of human thinking. Scientific theories are, moreover, linked to the various interests of different social groups. Thirdly, social changes can occur by an invention of an individual. Inventions introduce novelty and novelty poses another limit to social-scientific prediction (Neurath 1931c, 405). Social changes can, finally, occur by "chance". This means that small differences in initial conditions can result in hugely different final situations. Social sciences can at most discuss possible outcomes out of a multiplicity of initial conditions. They can never calculate final conditions out of precise initial data (Neurath 1944, 957). Nevertheless, many scientists are inclined to treat everything as calculable, to postulate complete scientific definiteness (Neurath 1930, 45; 1931c, 407; 1936a, 136). Thus they create a new idol and try to replace the former priest or philosopher by the professor. They are pseudo-rationalists.

> The pseudorationalist discredits logical empiricism when he wishes to bring the unambiguity of action into connection with an unambiguity of a deduction from the data of experience [...] (Neurath 1935a, 118).

2.2.3 Unified Science

It is beyond question that, despite the limitations of scientific prediction, Neurath considers science as politically most relevant. Science - in its logical empiricist variant - offers intellectual aid for forming public and private life (Neurath 1929, 305). In Neurath's view, a close connection exists between practical life and science (Neurath 1931c, 364-365; 1936b, 142). The social sciences in particular are a tool for social struggles (Neurath 1931c, 403-405; 1931d, 88; 1946b, 245).

> [S]ince sociological investigations play a certain role as stimuli and as aids for the shaping of life, an advance in sociology is very closely connected with social struggles (Neurath 1931d, 88).

Hence, a struggle between sociologists cannot be avoided, since they reflect 'the much stronger' social conflicts (Neurath 1929, 317; 1931c, 361)[7]. According to Neurath, it is the non-neutrality of science that explains its political relevance.

---

[6] Note that Neurath uses the term "logical empiricism" as an equivalent of the term "empirical rationalism".

[7] Despite Neurath's recognition of the non-neutrality of science, he pleads for a "value-free" science: a science for which the selection of questions does not influence the content of the answers. At the same time, it seems as if Neurath understands this idea rather as an ideal than as a matter of fact: 'It is clear that such a work [i.e., the search for a unified science; MD] is conditioned by emotional elements, as all human behaviour in history is; even the simple choice of questions to be treated is in itself not scientifically justifiable. But that does not change anything in the essential difference that exists between one mode of exposition using emotional elements and another *taking care to avoid them*' (Neurath 1936b, 142; the italics are mine). Neurath's interpretation of "objectivity" as a matter of accepted coherence, allows me to apply the same line of reasoning to Neurath's use of the term "value-freedom" as I did to Weber's use of it. Hence, I cannot consider another interpretation of "value-free" science than a science

> The assumption that scholars enjoy a kind of social extra-territoriality is above all a product of that period which was inclined to accord an exceptional position to scholars, as substitute priests, and was ready to use scientific assessments as a basis for taking political measures; but this was done not because politicians wished to be scientific but because they knew that scholars are ultimately politicians (Neurath 1931c, 406).

It is the empirically recorded political relevance of scientific theories that makes Neurath plead for a unified science.

> The endeavour is to link and harmonise the achievements of individual investigators in their various fields of science (Neurath 1929, 306).

In order to achieve this goal, one needs at least a unified language and the unified syntax offered by modern symbolic logic (the project of logical empiricism; see also section 1.2 in chapter 2). Both together allow for the linking of laws of different disciplines, or, in other words, for a unified science.

Adherents of a unified science take an encyclopedia as their model. They do not believe in the traditional ideal of a system free from internal contradictions and based on secure foundations (Neurath 1936b; 1936c; 1937a; 1937e; 1946a)[8]. Unified science aims at a survey of the different branches of knowledge. This survey cannot be a system, 1) since different disciplines use different languages, 2) because a unification of science shows that there remain gaps between areas in which a certain, local axiomatisation and systematisation exist, and 3) because successful scientific work undertaken in different parts of science does not prohibit the appearance of contradictions between them. The idea of a system as a model of unified science is too absolute. From the fact that a particular discipline succeeds in giving its theory the form of a system of statements, one cannot conclude that this specific system is the beginning of a complete and definite system of unified science, for two reasons. First, the system of a particular discipline is itself not unshakeable or definitely free from contradiction; it is never absolutely true. Second, one cannot decide scientifically between different systems of particular successful disciplines (Neurath 1916; 1934, 104). Consequently, the unified science movement

> does not propose a "superscience" which is to legislate to the special sciences' (Neurath 1937a, 172). The program of unified science does not aim at a systematisation from above. Neurath thus distances himself from what he calls the metaphysical project of logical positivism (Neurath 1937e, 203-204). The logical positivism of, for instance, Auguste Comte and his successor Wilhelm Ostwald aimed at an all-embracing system, a pyramidal edifice of the sciences. The logical empiricism of Neurath, on the contrary, 'accepts that the vast mass of the groups of statements are, as it were, *in one plane (Neurath 1937e, 204)*.

Unified science shows no symmetrically pyramidal edifice, but a "mosaic pattern", a "complicated network".

---

boasting on intersubjective consensus (though that has little to do with value-freedom; see also section 2).

[8] In his earlier writings, Neurath still speaks of a "system" of physicalism (and of the possible existence of different such systems) (e.g., Neurath 1935a, 117). From 1935 onwards, however, he explicitly distances himself from the idea of a system of science (see his 'Pseudorationalism of falsification' (Neurath 1935b), an essay in which he criticizes Popper's *Logik der Forschung*).

Unified science strives intensively after a systematisation from below. It takes as its point of departure the mass of given statements. With the help of "auxiliary processes", such as statistics, mathematics, modern symbolic logic and a unified scientific language, empiricist scientists try to link the laws of different disciplines and to establish unity among the particular sciences step by step (Neurath 1936b, 139; 1936c, 146; 1936c, 153-156). For this unification of the sciences the unity of auxiliary processes is essential. At the same time, precisely this unifying activity directs scientific work towards gaps and contradictions. Whereas previous encyclopedic enterprises

> give a retrospective synthesis, so to speak, this new work will have to show above all in which direction new ways open themselves, where the problems lead, and where, from the point of view of a unified science, unsuspected possibilities can be discovered (Neurath 1936b, 140).

A unitary approach is a necessary condition to classify the systems of hypotheses of the different social-scientific theories. Classifying these systems is a necessary condition to make manifest lacking, possible systems of hypotheses. Neurath compares the classification of social-scientific hypotheses with the classification of natural-scientific ones (Neurath 1944, 972). In his essay 'On the classification of systems of hypotheses (With special reference to optics)', he comments that a comparative study of existing systems of hypotheses leads to a survey of all groupings of individual views that are possible in principle (Neurath 1916). One first has to analyse the elementary notions of each system. On the basis of all elementary notions one can give a complete survey of logically possible combinations of these notions, without giving preference to one or another combination[9]. Planning science then means filling the gaps with lacking combinations[10]. This kind of planning is a 'purely technical question' (Neurath 1928, 262).

2.2.4 *The Political Relevance of Scientific Utopias*

In Neurath's view, the particular development of science into unified science consolidates the close connection of theoretical and practical workers.

> Technology with mechanics is the science of the engineers (machine-technicians); biology is the science of medical men and breeders (body-technicians), *and sociology is now the science of statesmen and organizers (social-technicians)* (Neurath 1931c, 329; the italics are mine).

The social sciences thus occupy a special place within the political arena. Social-scientific theories are needed to "plan" society (Neurath 1931c, 417).

Planning science is a prerequisite to "plan" society (Neurath 1944, 959-972). In order to plan science, one starts with a classification of given systems of hypotheses.

---

[9] Giving preference to some combinations and talking about eclecticism with regard to other combinations results, according to Neurath, from the use of "crude dichotomies". 'Dichotomies, however, are not only crude intellectually, but also mostly the product of scientific pugnacity. One characterises the opponent as pungently as possible for the purpose of beating him down as forcefully as possible. [...] Thus dichotomies are a result of a warlike spirit' (Neurath 1916, 15).

[10] On the relation between classification and planning, see also Reisch (1994), p. 168.

These given systems of hypotheses refer to the past and to the present. Social scientists who do not want to put their professionalism in the service of a scientific transfer of traditions and existing institutions also work for, at least the nearest, future. They act as a social engineers. They develop a "history of the future" by developing scientific utopias. Utopias are 'all orders of life which exist only in thought and image but not in reality', of which one can hardly say beforehand whether they will someday, somewhere become true (Neurath 1919b, 151). Utopias are constructions of social engineers, just like machines are constructions of technical engineers. In the words of Reisch, a social engineer provides us with 'options for actions' (Reisch 1944, 167).

Scientific utopias are (social) plans derived from lacking combinations of systems of social-scientific hypotheses. Like a technical engineer, who can evolve various types of possible aeroplanes, a social engineer can (and should) develop several possible plans or utopias (Neurath 1944, 959). Historians of the future can always tell us various stories about possible futures, just like other historians can tell us several versions of past events (Neurath 1944, 940). For that reason, there does not exist one unequivocal relationship between sociological plans and political decisions. Neurath dismisses social scientists and historians who present only one utopia or one scientific "optimum": their striving bears witness of a metaphysical determinism. The tendency to present one utopia or optimum as the scientifically best solution is a characteristic of the technocratic movement (Neurath 1942, 426-427).

Scientific utopias arise as prophecies that at the same time function as one (out of many) causes of their coming true (Neurath 1919b, 152). Social engineers, who scientifically develop new social orders and institutions, can be better prophets than scientists who want to confine themselves to a description of existing orders or institutions (Neurath 1944, 960). They are, at the same time, better prophets than unscientific utopias which result from a casual psychological mood. Nevertheless, social engineers' ability to predict which plan will be realised is limited, for several reasons. First, social engineers' imagination is historically and socially restricted (Neurath 1944, 960). Second, the phenomenon of human language together with the flexibility and changeability of human societies pose new limitations (Neurath 1944, 967). Third, the social sciences are not very well developed yet (Neurath 1944, 973). Consequently, the classification of systems of social-scientific hypotheses and the construction of lacking combinations can only be very preliminary. Fourth, even in case particular social-scientific correlations are rather well known, one does often not know under what circumstances these correlations will come into appearance (Neurath 1944, 959). The *ceteris paribus* - or *res sic stantibus* - formula is of little practical relevance, when one does not know whether those *res* are the case or not.

Finally, even a complete overview of scientific utopias does not allow for predictions within a political context. This is because of the nature of political events. Political events reflect human judgements – rather than calculations - concerning a desirable societal organisation. Even complete insight would, according to Neurath, not allow for reducing the final (political) decision to a logical conclusion. Each plan shows specific characteristics to different degrees. Each plan has, in Neurath's words, a different "silhouette" (Neurath 1944, 962-963): it reflects a different combination of values. Comparing different silhouettes is not a matter of mathematics.

> The danger arises [...] out of the trial to obtain index numbers through mingling items, which are measured with different units [...]. The big advantage, which offer us statistical correlations and each way of mathematicising, should not tempt us in this respect to sloppiness[11].
>
> [A]rguing in terms of the one best standard can hardly be maintained, and in addition, [...] one cannot compute the various standards elaborated by various experts: technicians stress the importance of technical efficiency as a matter of course, whereas industrial engineers are interested in the assembling of machines and workers, and in the increase of the efficiency of labour; biologists and physicians sometimes propose certain standards of health, architects standards for buildings. But the computation of all these results is not sufficient because the elements in question are interrelated with one another, and also what remains [e.g. personal independence, voluntary co-operation, democracy, etc.] is not covered by this computation at all [...] (Neurath 1942, 422-423).

One can at most compare different silhouettes, but one cannot range them according to a single standard. A social engineer is thus not able to decide scientifically which plan will or should be realised. In the end, political decisions have to be based unavoidably on common-sense arguments. While making plans can be considered a technical matter, choosing among plans is certainly a non-technical question (Neurath 1928, 263). It is political events that determine which out of possible "utopias" should be realised[12].

Despite their politically limited predictive power, Neurath considers scientific utopias as politically indispensable. Although final decisions will be based on common sense arguments,

> the decisions are different when made without comprehensive knowledge, or when made after hearing all the experts. "Brain trusts" of first-class scientists will therefore play an essential, nay fundamental, role by bringing forth whole teams of possible well-

---

[11] 'Die Gefahr rührt [...] vom Versuch her, Indexzahlen mittels Vermischung von Items zu erhalten, Items, die in verschiedenen Einheiten gemessen wurden [...] Der enorme Vorteil, den uns statistische Korrelationen und jede Art der Mathematisierung bringen, sollte uns in dieser Hinsicht nicht zur Schlamperei verleiten' (Neurath 1944, 963).

[12] All the hesitations Neurath mentions concerning a straightforward – instrumental – use of scientific utopias within political practice makes me doubt the adequacy of his term "planning society". My doubts are enforced by a certain ambiguity in Neurath's ideas about "planning the economy". In his scientifically oriented writings, Neurath sketches the task of economics as investigating the effects of different orders of life, i.e. of different combinations of institutions within varying terrains of life, on human happiness (e.g. Neurath 1917; 1931c; 1931d). "Planning" here still means "developing utopias". In his politically oriented writings, "planning the economy" means deciding on the principles that guide production and distribution (Neurath 1919b, 1928). In his political writings, Neurath hardly deals with the political and legal organisation of a "planned economy". Although his scientific writings suggest a close link between the political and legal order on the one hand and the economic order (in the narrow sense of those units where production and distribution are decided on and carried out) on the other, in his politically oriented writings "planning the economy" does not mean any longer "planning the order of life within a given terrain of life".

> analyzed patterns from which, finally, one will be selected by the nation or by regional groups after much discussion and many changes (Neurath 1942, 426).

That is one of the reasons why far reaching information and education is a prerequisite in a society which is inclined at democratic social planning. This information and education is necessary to allow for an input – selection and change of proposed scientific utopias - by laymen.

2.2.5 Conclusion

According to Neurath, "prediction" is a necessary part in the testing of science. Predictive statements derive from synthetic laws. Synthetic laws express empirical regularities rather than cause-effect relationships. The success of scientific prediction depends on the particular combination of laws borrowed from various disciplines and on the particular definition of the subject matter of a specific discipline. It is, in other words, a particular problem– successful prediction of a particular state of affairs in human reality - that defines the subject matter of a discipline and the relevant combination of disciplines. It is not the other way round: neither a pre-defined subject matter of a discipline nor a pre-defined combination of disciplines will automatically lead to successful scientific predictions.

Successful scientific prediction does not imply successful political prediction. Political questions cannot straightforwardly be answered scientifically, for several reasons. First, because of the logical limitations of scientific practice itself. Science is itself a kind of action. Second, because of the social and historical contingency of scientific language, concepts and laws. Third, because of the novelty typical of political action. Finally, because of the unpredictability of political events. (Note that these latter two reasons parallel Arendt's analysis of the rationality of political interaction; see section 4.2 in chapter 2). Denial of this limited predictive power of science within a political context is, according to Neurath, a manifestation of pseudo-rationalism.

This limited political predictive power does, however, not prevent science's political relevance. Neurath even actively aims at ameliorating science's political relevance by launching the idea of a unified science. He considers of unified science as an encyclopedia, i.e., a systematisation from below of existing theories. Such systematisation from below needs some unitary auxiliary tools, such as statistics, mathematics, modern symbolic logic and a unified scientific language. The political relevance of Neurath's project of a unified science is two-fold. First, it makes the linking of laws borrowed from different disciplines possible. It allows, in Neurath's words, for an "orchestration of the sciences" (Neurath 1946a). Second, it makes us discover gaps and contradictions between scientific disciplines and disciplinary paradigms.

According to Neurath, social sciences are not merely politically relevant. They are even politically indispensable. The gaps between disciplines and disciplinary paradigms that emerge during the project of unified science allow scientists to formulate scientific utopias. Scientific utopias describe options for actions, a variety of stories about possible futures. Each utopia represents a particular silhouette: it reflects a particular combination of values. Designing utopias is a means to write a "history of the future". Scientific utopias – in the plural - are thus politically indispensable because they foster political – deliberative – processes. Political knowledge is indeed not – just as little as is scientific knowledge – autonomous. Scientific utopias can, however, not be used instrumentally. They cannot replace political judgements, for two main reasons. First, because their empirical validity can never be guaranteed. One can never precisely know which *res* (of the *res sic stantibus* formula) are the case and which are not. Second, because practical validity of utopian silhouettes depends on political action. It is up to citizens and professional politicians to judge the kind of utopia they prefer to realise. Political actors should select, discuss and adapt scientific utopias. In Neurath's view, scientific utopias thus leave plenty room for the typically political judgement that Arendt is in favour of (see section 4.3 in chapter 2).

2.3 Economic Theories as Political Muses

Previous confrontation between Weber's and Neurath's interpretation of the political relevance of (social-) scientific theories allows us to develop the metaphor of economic theory as a political muse. This metaphor is meant to replace the metaphor of economic theory as a political toolbox. While the latter is supposed to provide public policy with prescriptive and predictive instruments, the former is supposed to offer descriptive and explanatory insights.

In chapter 3, I defended a particular subject matter of economic science. The idea of "sustainability" urges us, my line of reasoning went, to conceive of economics as the study of the ecological performance of the institutional whole constituting our present-day industrial economies. My interpretation of economic institutions as the symbolic dimension of economic actions leaded me, further, to interpret this ecological performance as the counterpart of an economy's institutional organisation. This suggests that the relationship between ecological performance and institutional organisation should not be understood as a cause-effect relationship (Weber), but as a "regularity" (Neurath).

I consider such "regularities", moreover, as understandable. This means that I assume some "rationality" in the empirical regularities relating a particular institutional organisation with a particular ecological performance. Such "regularities" are synthetic statements, not mere analytic ones. They result from a combination of empirical observations and logical deductions[13].

---

[13] This interpretation of synthetic statements as not merely the opposite of analytic statements is in agreement with Neurath's interpretation. Consider, in this respect, his arguments in favour of the term "empirical rationalism". 'Traditionally one looked at "empiricism" as something crude and coarse, not interested in any refinement of arguing, and at "rationalism" as something creating wonderful pyramids of arguments, deducing any detail on the basis of a nicely elaborated set of assumptions or *a priori* declarations. I suggested the expression "Logical Empiricism" for stressing the combination of empiricism and highly evolved deduction. Since in Latin countries there is a fine tradition of

The empirical regularities economics should make understandable are meant to describe – from an inevitably value-laden perspective – relationships between ecological performance and institutional organisation as they can be found in the past and the present. This implies that I conceive of an ecologically relevant economics as a kind of historical rather than "exact" science (Weber). This means that the stress within economics should be on explanation rather than prediction. This, in my view, important distinction can be encountered again in a paper written by Dugger (Dugger 1979, 900-903). This author distinguishes between (institutionalist) "pattern models" and (neo-classical) "predictive models". The former try to explain human behaviour by situating it as accurately as possible in its institutional and cultural context. The latter try to explain human behaviour by deducing it from carefully specified assumptions. In the former case it is the empirical adequacy of the patterns developed that matter, while in the latter case it is the empirical adequacy of the predictions. According to Dugger, pattern models are rather the scientific result of an anthropological method, while predictive models are rather the scientific result of pure mathematics.

Contrary to Neurath, I doubt whether social scientists should, apart from explaining the past and the present, also write a "history of the future" by developing scientific utopias. I suppose that – a multiplicity of - clarifying explanations of past and present suffice to provide a deliberative politics with necessary insights to derive a whole range of utopias on its own.

To recapitulate, a politically successful economics should provide politics with insights rather than instruments. Economic scientists should develop empirically adequate pattern models explaining empirical regularities that relate ecological performance to institutional organisation. Such pattern models provide scientific insights that are not purely analytic. These scientific insights are synthetic ones: they aim at suitable concepts (for instance, types of economic institutions or institutional hierarchies; see section 2.2.3 in chapter 3) that allow us to make empirical regularities comprehensible. Scientific insights are of a historical, rather than mathematical, kind. They offer clarifying views on our past and present. Scientific insights are sources of inspiration that allow a deliberative politics to develop utopias on its own.

Empirical observations support the metaphor of social-scientific theories as political muses. According to Snel, for instance, empirical research shows that social scientists overestimate their capacity to provide public policy with concrete – instrumental – recommendations (Snel 1996, 22). The extent of overestimation becomes clear in the following quotation.

> First, a great deal of sociological research done for application carries no discernible policy implications of any kind; second, in instances where it does, sociology has served as the basis for formulating policy recommendations, less often the basis for enacted policy; and third, most of the recommendations [...] were rejected by policy-making

"rationalism", I suggested the use of the term "Empirical Rationalism" [...] as synonymous with "Logical Empiricism"' (Neurath 1946a, 234; see also Neurath 1938, 836).

> bodies of government as impractical or politically unfeasible (Scott & Shore 1979, quoted in Snel 1996, 22).

According to Nelson, to give another example, economists' important and proper role in public policy is as proponents of a particular framework for thinking (Nelson 1987, 58). It is economists' way of thinking, their view of the world, that feeds policy debate and decision-making with valuable contributions rather than with definitive answers.

3 IMPARTIAL KNOWLEDGE

The term "impartiality" indicates a fourth characteristic of a politically successful economics. This term should, as may be clear from the above section 1, not be mistaken for scientific "neutrality". The non-neutrality of (economic) science refers to the inevitable value-relatedness of whatever theoretical paradigm. The impartiality of science, on the contrary, refers to its ability to disclose (political) power relationships. Building on both Neurath and Arendt, I will inquire into the precise meaning of an impartial science.

Following Arendt, political power can be interpreted as the capacity to realise and preserve a desirable human society. This capacity depends on citizens' abilities to act as free and equal individuals (Arendt 1958, 199-203). In order to clarify what "acting politically as free and equal individuals" means, I should reflect on the meaning of a (desirable) human society. Human society consists of institutions. It is the ensemble of societal institutions that define individuals' choice sets, i.e. the set of individuals' private interests. This ensemble of societal institutions defines at the same time the distribution of choice sets among its members. From this we can conclude that in daily life citizens are neither absolutely free (because they always and inevitably have particular, institutionally conditioned private interests) nor equal (because of institutional – and personal - reasons). Acting politically as free individuals then presupposes citizen's capacity to abstract from their *existing* set of private interests in order to reflect on *desirable* sets of private interests and on *desirable* distributions of them. This capacity to abstract is not meant in an ascetic sense. It is not meant to incite people to deny their institutionally conditioned private interests. On the contrary, it is meant in an intellectual sense. It is meant to incite people to recognise the relationship between their private interests and the institutional context in which they emerge. This intellectual capacity to abstract presupposes, moreover, citizen's capacity to imagine a desirable *institutional organisation of society* as a precondition of desirable private interests and desirable distributions of private interests.

The capacity to abstract from existing private interests depends on citizens' "negative freedom". Citizens are negatively free when they are free of the day-to-day worries related to the necessities of life. Negative freedom allows persons to *postpone* their immediate wills and predetermined, short-term interests and to *imagine* possible wills and private interests. Citizens' negative freedom is, in other words, a precondition for their "positive freedom". Positive freedom refers to citizens' ability to imagine in a creative way what counts as a desirable human society. Politics is, as Arendt explains, about creative realisations of what it can mean to be human. The extent of creativity relates to the multiplicity of perspectives. Consequently, a balanced distribution of opportunities to put forward one's particular perspective related to one's particular experiences contributes positively to citizen's political imagination, i.e. to their "positive freedom". To conclude, political equality – this balanced distribution of opportunities to set forward one's view – contributes to positive freedom. Both negative freedom – the ability to abstract from existing private interests - and positive freedom – disposing of a creative imagination - contribute to political power.

Previous analysis understands political power as a positive concept. This positive interpretation differs from a contrasting interpretation of political power as a matter of coercion (rather than freedom) and of relationships of dominance and subordination (rather than equality). According to this latter interpretation, political actors act strategically (rather than communicatively). They negotiate with each other, taking their existing private interests and the existing distribution of interests as a starting point[14]. They do not act, to use Arendt's terminology, *with* each other, but *for* or *against* each other (for those with the same kind of private interests and against those with a different kind of private interests). I suppose that neither of both interpretations is "realistic", i.e., an empirically valid description of political reality. Real politics probably is a mixture of both. However, I conceive of the former interpretation – remember my plea for deliberative democracy - as a desirable one and of the latter as an undesirable one.

These contrasting interpretations can illustrate the meaning of an "impartial" science. Impartial science tries to strengthen the former kind of politics and to weaken the latter one. In order to do that, it offers insights into sources of political inequality and of lacking political freedom. In order to stimulate political freedom, it clarifies the relationships between the institutional organisation on the one hand and the kind and distribution of existing private interests on the other. Such clarifications can help citizens to abstract, for the sake of politics, from their existing private interests and to imagine different institutional organisations determining different kinds and distributions of private interests (and different ecological performances). In order to stimulate political equality, impartial science points to sources preventing a balanced expression of a variety of perspectives. It is, moreover, tolerant towards differing interpretations of sources of political inequality. These intra-paradigmatic conditions, the formal condition of tolerance and the substantive condition of indicating sources of political inequality, are, hence, accompanied by a disciplinary condition, namely the condition that a multiplicity of disciplinary paradigms is

[14] Consider the following quotation of Neurath, expressing his conception of a "democracy between enemies": 'If in the dead of night bandits stop a railway train and are then confronted with well-armed passengers of unknown numbers, it may well happen that the head of the gang will compromise with the leader of the passengers as follows: when the sun rises, let firearms be counted; the side which has the fewer shall surrender to the other, to avoid pointless bloodshed - democracy between enemies!' (Neurath 1928, 259).

allowed and even stimulated. Contrary to impartial science, partial science considers a specific institutional organisation and, hence, existing (distributions of) private interests as given. It offers insights in how to act (politically) in order to realise a given goal as efficiently and as effectively as possible. It provides political actors with "rational" strategies. Partial science thus takes particular private perspectives as its starting point, rather than abstracting from them through scientifically explaining them.

I should add a final comment on the contrasting concepts "impartial" and "partial" science. This contrast should not be conceived of as a black-and-white difference. Scientific insights will probably always be somewhere on the continuum between the partial and the impartial pole. There exist, moreover, no independent arbitrators to judge whether a particular scientific analysis of political power relationships does justice to the differing experiences of various members of a society. Whether a scientific interpretation of political power is objective can only be settled in a political way. Only a multiplicity of perspectives on power will help to evaluate on the objectivity of a particular scientific analysis. Scientific communities can, in other words, not do without a (typically political) pluralism and tolerance.

4 CONCLUSION

In this chapter, I developed four norms for a politically successful economics. I argued that, in order to ameliorate the political impact of economics, economists should provide political actors with suitable knowledge. Suitable knowledge is knowledge that stimulates rather than replaces political debates. I claimed that scientific insights succeed better in this respect than do scientific instruments.

Scientific insights are perspectivistic descriptions of human reality. They can never be neutral, though they aim at objectivity. Close reading of Weber's writings suggests that objectivity comes down to intersubjective consent. Logic and mathematics can contribute to such consent. They are, however, neither necessary nor sufficient. Objectivity as intersubjective consent within a particular community of scientists is a first norm for a politically successful economics.

Contrary to Weber's view, there is no need to transform scientific descriptions into political instruments. In order to be politically successful, economic theories should not be interpreted as political toolboxes. Weber understands political instruments as inversions of scientific laws. The effectiveness of political instruments depends, to begin with, on the predictive power of scientific instruments, i.e., on science's empirical validity. Weber believes in the empirical validity of pure economics – due to the logical consistency and the mathematical form of this axiomatic system. He does not believe in the empirical validity of the historically oriented economic sciences. For that reason, only pure economics, i.e., the theory of marginal utility is, in Weber's view, suited as a political toolbox. The effectiveness of political instruments depends, further, on their "neutrality". Neutrality means here practical validity or conformity between the values constituting both the theoretical perspective and the political objective. Neither the empirical validity of pure economics (or whatever other economic theory) can, however, be guaranteed: ideal-typical economic theories are never simply "true". Nor their practical validity can be assumed: the value-relatedness of both scientific instruments and political objectives can never be made completely transparent. The transformation of scientific descriptions into political instruments is, therefore, politically illegitimate. It drives economists to prescribe political objectives rather than to describe empirical realities. It drives them, moreover, to privilege scientific descriptions that are mathematical in form and logically consistent. These latter kind of descriptions easily give rise to prediction (in the sense of causal inversion). They do, however, not necessarily explain a lot.

From Neurath, we learned that scientific descriptions should be explanatory rather than predictive. Scientific explanation is a matter of making empirical regularities – or synthetic laws – comprehensible. Prediction is a scientific means to test our understanding of empirical regularities. It can, however, not be used to forecast our future, for two reasons. First, scientific descriptions can never be assumed empirically valid, because they result from many decisions. Second, our future depends on creative and unpredictable political interaction. Scientific descriptions (or insights) can, in Neurath's view, thus never be used instrumentally. Scientific descriptions are, nevertheless, politically indispensable because they foster political debates. According to Neurath, it is scientific utopias (in plural), i.e., stories about possible futures that stimulate political discussion. In my view, however, scientific insights themselves suffice to let political actors develop utopias on their own. Keeping to scientific descriptions or insights prevents scientists from playing a prescriptive and predictive political role. To recapitulate, description rather than prescription and explanation rather than prediction are the second and third norm of a politically successful economics.

Suitable economic knowledge should also ameliorate the quality of political interaction. This quality depends on the political freedom and political equality of citizens and professional politicians. In order to ameliorate political freedom, economic knowledge should offer insights into the relationships between definition and distribution of private interests on the one hand and the institutional context on the other. In order to support political equality, it should inform us on economic sources of unequal political power relationships. Suitable economic knowledge should, in one word, be impartial rather than partial.

Objectivity, explanation, description and impartiality are thus four norms for a politically successful economics. These norms are scientific ideals. Economic theories do not simply realise or fail them. They rather show them to a lesser or fuller degree. For that reason, I do not mention non-neutrality as a separate norm, for non-neutrality is an inevitable characteristic, not an aimed at scientific ideal.

Suitable knowledge does, however, not only depend on the extent to which it satisfies previous norms. It also depends, as I argued in the previous chapter, on its content. From Neurath we learn that this content, i.e., the definition of the subject matter of a scientific discipline and the combination of disciplines used is conditioned by the problem in question, not *vice versa*. Neither a pre-defined subject matter of a discipline nor a pre-defined combination of disciplines will automatically lead to successful, i.e., ecologically relevant scientific knowledge.

The community of ecological economists concentrates on the "orchestration of the sciences", i.e., the problem of trans-disciplinarity . Starting from existing disciplinary paradigms, ecological economists ask themselves which combination of social and natural sciences is needed to provide public policy with ecologically relevant scientific insights. This approach is very important, for economists need, indeed, ecological, physical, chemical and other natural-scientific insights in order to know which kind of ecological performance is problematic and, hence, which kind of economic institutions they should analyse. My research project, however, concentrates on the definition of the subject matter of economics itself, i.e., on the definition of a suitable economic paradigm. My analysis of both Pearce's and Bromley's theoretical work is meant as a contribution to the systematisation of economic paradigms. While "world socialism" is the ideal that structures Neurath's project of a unified science (Neurath 1922; 1928, 270-275), "sustainability" – in the sense presented in the introductory chapter – is the ideal guiding my research project.

CHAPTER 5

A RECONSTRUCTION OF PEARCE'S ECONOMICS

In this chapter, I will reconstruct the writings of David Pearce[1]. I will reconstruct Pearce's work from a particular perspective. I am interested, to start with, in his interpretation of "sustainability". I am interested, further, in the substantive kind of economic knowledge Pearce aims at. My reconstruction will illustrate that Pearce's economics shows more similarities with "environmental economics" than with "ecological economics", though it does not fit completely within Munda's classification (see section 2.2 in chapter 1)[2].

Pearce is Professor of Environmental Economics at University College London and Associate Director of the Centre for Social and Economic Research on the Global Environment (CSERGE). Next to his academic work, he has held a number of positions within rather political organisations. He was, for instance, personal advisor to the Secretary of State for the Environment. He was Commissioner of the World Commission on Forests and Sustainable Development. He was a member of the Sustainable Development High Level Advisory Board to the Secretary General of the UN and member of the Advisory Panel to the Vice President for Sustainable Development of the World Bank.

Pearce's environmental economics is a kind of welfare economics. It is a welfare economics that considers the "public interest" from the perspective of "sustainable development". In order to define "sustainable development", Pearce needs a "materials balance model". A materials balance model is a kind of bookkeeping model that expresses natural capital (energetic and material resources and the

---

[1] I asked Pearce – as I asked Bromley - to comment on my reconstruction of his writings. Contrary to Bromley, he took no notice of my request.

[2] This classification irritates Pearce. It was one of the reasons Pearce mentioned for not taking notice of my request to comment on my reconstruction of his writings. This classification is, in Pearce's view, responsible for 'an inane waste of energy'. According to Pearce, this classification only diverts attention from real-world problem solving. Therefore, Pearce deliberately mixes up the use of both terms. While the publisher of one of his books introduces him as an author with 'a long-established international reputation in environmental economics', the title of the same book sounds as *Economics and Environment. Essays on Ecological Economics and Sustainable Development* (Edward Elgar 2000 catalogue on economics). Though I agree that classifying economists leads to unjustified simplifications and generalisations, I join with the gradually common distinction between "environmental" and "ecological" economics (see section 2.2 in chapter 1). In this chapter, I will show that Pearce can rightfully be considered a representative of "environmental economics". This label should, however, be interpreted as an indication, not an explanation, of what Pearce's economics is about.

assimilative capacity of ecosystems) in physical terms. In order to incorporate such materials balance model into a welfare-economic paradigm, Pearce needs to translate these physical entities into monetary ones. This translation allows for, what is called in Pigovian terms, an internalisation of externalities.

Pearce's welfare-economic approach illustrates, to start with, that he considers the relationship between an economy and its ecological performance as an external one. It is, secondly, based on a particular political assumption. It assumes that adapting the institutional organisation of an economy to the objective of "sustainable development" is a matter of adding economic institutions to the existing whole. It assumes, moreover, that the institutions to add should be derived from an aggregation of private preferences expressed in monetary terms. Pearce's environmental economics is, thirdly, based on the scientific assumption that scientific insights into the relationships between the ecological performance of an economy and its institutional organisation are impossible.

1 ENVIRONMENTAL ECONOMICS AS A "MATERIALS BALANCE MODEL"

According to Pearce, a first step within environmental economics consists of presenting the relationships between an economy and its ecological environment in an input-output analysis[3]. Environmental economics is about *understanding* (and predicting) the *external* relationships between an economy and its ecological *environment.* These relationships can be made visible within a materials balance model. This model can be transformed into an ecological bookkeeping model by extending the original (monetary) input-output analysis with ecological in- and outputs (expressed in physical units). *Understanding* these relationships means having an overview of the regularities between ecological inputs and economic processes on the one hand and between these processes and ecological outputs on the other.

1.1 An Ecological Input-Output Analysis

Pearce interprets an economy as a big box or matrix, made up of a series of smaller boxes or matrices (Pearce *et al.* 1990a, 31). Each matrix expresses an input-output relationship between two classes of elements of the economy. The input classes are commodities, industries and primary inputs; the output classes commodities,

[3] Instead of using the concept "environment", I prefer to use the terminology "ecological environment". This terminology allows us to distinguish between different aspects – either social or ecological - of human "environments". I also replace Pearce's concepts "environmental problems" by "ecological problems", because that is what Pearce means when dealing with "sustainable development". This terminology does not exclude that ecological problems can have and almost always have a social dimension.

industries and final demand[4]. For instance, one matrix expresses the input of commodities into industries, another one the input of primary inputs into final demand, etc. (Pearce *et al.* 1990a, 32). (Remark that not every combination of classes constitutes a matrix.)

Pearce defines the different classes more precisely. A commodity is anything that is processed, exchanged and produced in the economy (for instance, a factory, a machine, a TV set or take-away meal) (Pearce *et al.* 1990a, 31). Coal in the ground

> is not a commodity because it has not been processed nor yet subjected to any exchange within the economy.

Industries are

> institutions that undertake economic activity in the form of production or providing a service.

Primary inputs refer to labour and capital, but not to land. Final demand refers to the set of demands in the economy by final consumers, e.g. households.

To recapitulate, Pearce's description of an economy is a kind of bookkeeping model. This bookkeeping model tries to make the empirical linkages and, hence, regularities between "input" and "output" visible. It is meant to make predictions about the effects throughout the economy of changes occurring in any one sector (Pearce *et al.* 1990a, 33; Lipsey & Steiner 1975, 469).

Pearce's theoretical need to take ecological problems into consideration prompts him to expand the above model of an economy to its ecological "environment". This expansion illustrates Pearce's interpretation of the relationship between an economy and its ecological performance. He sees this relationship as an external one, i.e., as a relationship between an economy on the one hand and an economy's ecological environment on the other. The economy and its ecological environment are deemed to be two systems which both have their own kind of internal relationships (Pearce *et al.* 1990a, 30 figure 2.1).

> Just as within the economy matrix the relationships studied are between economic entities, so within the environment matrix the entities studied appear to have no economic dimension (Pearce *et al.* 1990a, 29-30).

Consequently, in order to take the impact of economic changes on the ecological environment (and *vice versa*) into consideration, Pearce adds two more classes, the classes of "environmental" in- and outputs, to his bookkeeping model. The input of ecological entities refers to all *in situ* natural resources, classified as land, air and water; the output of ecological entities refers to the output of waste products for which the same resources act as "receiving media" (Pearce *et al.* 1990a, 29;34)[5].

---

[4] Pearce's representation of an economy is a (Leontief) input-output table (Pearce 1990a, 33). For more information about Leontief input-output analyses, see e.g. Lipsey & Steiner (1975 [1963], p. 469-473).

[5] Contrary to Pearce, I propose to avoid the terms "environmental goods and services" and to replace them by the terms "ecological entities" or "ecological phenomena". I already argued why I prefer the concept "ecological" to "environmental". I prefer the terms "entity" or "phenomenon" to "good or

(Pearce remarks that all economy boxes are in money terms, while the ecological boxes are in physical terms (Pearce *et al.* 1990a, 34).) The basic aim of Pearce's extension of input-output analysis is to make the linkages between an economy and its ecological environment visible. Such extended I-O analysis

> permits us to reflect on just what the environment does for the economy (Pearce *et al.* 1990a, 35).

1.2 A Materials Balance Model

Pearce's ecological bookkeeping model is based on what he calls a materials balance model (see Figure 1) (Pearce *et al.* 1990a, 40). This model represents the economy-(ecological) environment interactions in a (more or less) circular way.

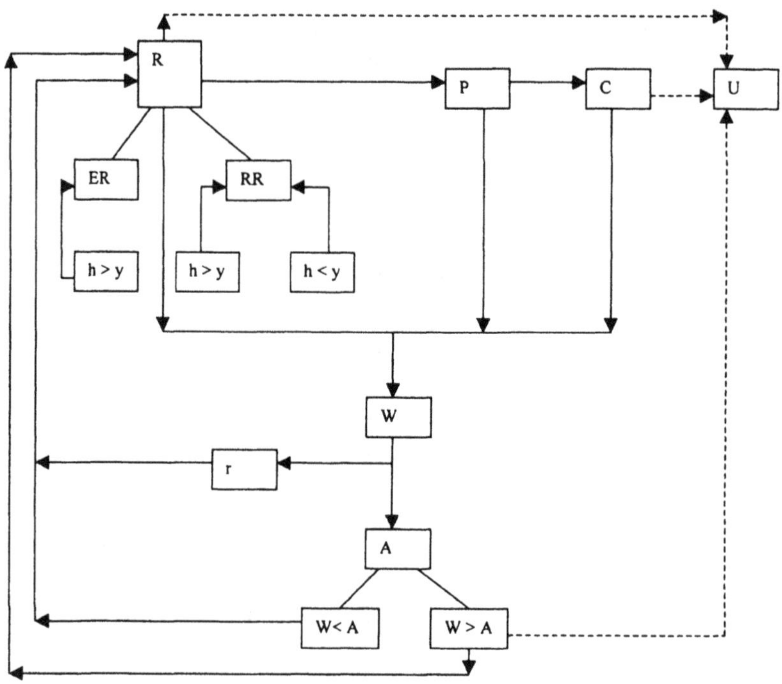

Figure 1: The circular economy (Pearce 1990a, 40)

service", because the latter terms suggest that all ecological entities are *ipso facto* economic entities. Since, as Pearce himself writes, natural resources or waste that are not processed, exchanged or (intended to be) produced are no commodities, one should not label them as "goods or services". As I explained in section 2.1.3 of chapter 3, it is economic institutions that define ecological entities as economic goods or services. This conceptual specification does not exclude the possibility that ecological "phenomena" that are not economic "commodities" nevertheless have an economic (use) value.

Production P is aimed at producing consumer goods C. (In this model, Pearce treats capital goods, K, as a kind of - intermediate - consumer goods. Capital goods are consumer goods that will produce other consumer goods in the future.) The purpose of consumption is to create "utility" U or welfare. R stands for natural resources. W stands for waste. Waste arises at each stage of the production process. The processing of resources creates waste, as does production and consumption. Pearce's materials balance model thus captures at least two functions of our ecological environment, namely the ecological environment as a reservoir of resource inputs to production and as the ultimate repository of waste products.

Pearce describes an economy as circular. He agrees with Boulding that the Earth can be compared with a spaceship (Boulding 1966). The earth has only one external source of energy, solar energy. It moreover has a finite stock of resources. Since, according to the First Law of Thermodynamics, one cannot destroy or create matter and energy, humans have to recycle - or make sure that the environment is able to recycle - the resources used up as much as possible. This recycling makes of the economy a circular system. The box *r* stands for the recycling of waste. As the picture shows, not all waste is recycled in the economy. Part of it ends in the environment. Recycling can never be complete, because of the Second Law of Thermodynamics. This law tells us that materials and energy used in the economy tend to be used entropically, i.e. they get dissipated within the economic system. It is impossible to gather these dissipated materials and energy completely. The reasons Pearce mentions for this impossibility differ. Materials cannot be recycled completely because recycling is too costly or technically unfeasible. Energy cannot be recycled completely because what remains after the use of an energetic resource is not itself an energetic resource.

> Even if we capture the carbon dioxide from burning fossil fuels, it does not create another fuel. We can capture some of the sulphur oxides and recycle the sulphur, but we cannot recycle energy (Pearce *et al.* 1990a, 38).

Pearce's materials balance model analyses the box R a bit further. The resources box R comprises two types of natural resources. Exhaustible resources ER cannot renew themselves. Their regenerative capacity (y) is, from a human point of view, zero. They include such resources as coal, oil, and minerals. Renewable resources RR, on the contrary, have the capacity to renew themselves ($y > 0$). This capacity, however, is only actual on condition that humans do not harvest the renewable resource in question at a rate faster than the rate at which it regenerates. A renewable resource can only be a renewable resource if the rate at which humans harvest it (h) is less than its regenerative capacity (y).

Pearce's model also reflects on the ecological environment as a waste sink. The ecological environment has a capability to take wastes and to convert them back into harmless or ecologically useful products. This capability is called the ecological environment's assimilative capacity. As long as the quantities and qualities of waste disposal are commensurate with this assimilative capacity, the economic system functions - *dixit* Pearce - as a *natural* system (except that it still draws down the stocks of exhaustible resources). The assimilative capacity of the ecological environment is, according to Pearce, itself a renewable resource. This renewable resource can be converted into an exhaustible resource if waste disposal overburdens it.

The utility U in Pearce's model highlights a third function of the ecological environment next to its functions as resource supplier and waste assimilator. The ecological environment supplies utility directly in the form of aesthetic enjoyment and spiritual comfort. This third function can, among other things, be damaged through excessive disposal of waste[6].

1.3 Conclusion

Pearce understands an economy on the one hand and its ecological environment on the other as two separate spheres that, however, show some external linkages. The ecological environment is at the same time a provider of natural resources and a repository of waste. These external linkages show that an economy is dependent on its ecological environment. This dependence can be represented in a materials balance model. In this model an economy is considered to be connected to its ecological environment in a "circular" way. The ecological environment is the sphere where to get natural resources and where to put waste. This dependence can be presented in an Input-Output analysis by adding two classes, the classes of ecological inputs and outputs, to the original Input-Output model. While the latter model is expressed in monetary terms, the former classes are – at least provisionally – expressed in physical terms.

2 ENVIRONMENTAL ECONOMICS AS A KIND OF WELFARE ECONOMICS

Pearce's materials balance model and the accompanying bookkeeping model is but a first step within environmental economics. These models only make the external relationships between an economy and its ecological environment visible. They do not yet offer ways to transform an "unsustainable" economy into a more "sustainable" one, i.e. to make an economy as "circular" as possible (either by recycling as much waste as possible or by harvesting at rates lower than regenerative capacities). And that is what environmental economics is about: it is about "sustainable development". In order to help public authorities to make their economy ecologically more "sustainable" economics should be considered, in Pearce's view, as a kind of welfare economics. Welfare economics is a toolbox for economic policy that is based on neo-classical theory. Environmental economics, as a kind of welfare economics, takes "sustainable development" as its interpretation of

---

[6] Pearce's 1990a materials balance model is misleading in at least one respect. It does not make clear that, in order to recycle waste within the economy, one needs a supplementary amount of resources. In Turner *et al.* (1994, 18), an adjusted materials balance model of a circular economy is presented. In this picture the extra primary material and energy inputs needed for recycling are made explicit.

"the public interest". In the next subsections, I will deal with both Pearce's interpretation of the neo-classical paradigm and with his conception of an ecologically suitable welfare economics.

2.1 *A Neo-Classical Approach*

Pearce is very clear concerning the paradigm he prefers to use for dealing with ecological problems. After a short introduction into different pre- and post-war economic paradigms (Pearce *et al.* 1990a, Chapter 1), he states that

> we have a great deal to learn form our horizon-expanding application of modern [neo-classical; MD] economics, and that the search for "alternatives" is premature (Pearce *et al.* 1990a, 31).

In order to clarify what Pearce means by an expansion of modern neo-classical economics I will compare what Pearce, as an economic scientist, does with Weber's and Robbins' definition of economics (see section 2 in chapter 2). As I mentioned before, Weber distinguishes three kinds of socio-economic phenomena: economic, economically relevant and economically conditioned. In his view, phenomena are (pure) economic insofar as and only as long as our interest is exclusively focused on their constitutive significance in the material struggle for existence (MSS 65). Weber's definition of economic phenomena is an expression of his conviction that social phenomena only have meaning from a specific, value-related perspective. Phenomena are economic on condition that they are human actions taking place under three conditions: 1) competition between different desires which long for satisfaction, 2) limitation of the capacity to desire and of the actual goods and labour forces which are useful for the satisfaction of desires, and 3) a specific kind of coexistence of different people afflicted with the same or similar desires, but equipped with different stocks of goods to their satisfaction, and competing with each other for the means of satisfaction (GAW 389).

Weber's definition of the subject matter of economics partly corresponds to Robbins'. For Weber both the form and the domain define the subject matter of economics. Robbins works with a so-called analytical definition. The analytical definition differs from a classificatory one in that it focuses on the *form* of human action, not on the *domain* in which human actions occur. According to Robbins, every activity, in so far as it involves making choices between alternative means to fulfil competing desires, falls within the scope of economic theory. Robbins' analytical definition allows for an application of economic theory to domains outside the economic sphere. Public-Choice theory is, as I explained in section 3.1 of chapter 2, an example of such application. It is an extension of mainstream economics into the political domain. Weber would not agree with such an expansion of pure economics to domains outside the economic sphere. For him, pure economic phenomena occur in an institutional context that is deliberately created or used for economic ends (MSS 64).

From the brief summary of Weber's and Robbins' definition, I conclude that, in order to define how Pearce understands the subject matter of environmental economics, we should ask for both the domain and the form of human actions Pearce wants to analyse. The latter question can be answered rather quickly. As an adherent of modern neo-classical theory, Pearce focuses, as Weber and Robbins do, on human actions that have the form of making choices under conditions of relative scarcity (Pearce 1993a, 1-4). Neo-classical theory succeeded in describing this kind of economic actions by falling back on the theory of marginal utility. This theory consists of a set of economic laws and is limited to economic actions that answer to certain boundary conditions concerning, for instance, the nature of *homo oeconomicus*. According to Pearce, in its modern version the neo-classical model has *homo oeconomicus* holding the preference structure of indifference and operating on the basis of constrained satisfaction or utility maximisation (Pearce *et al.* 1990a, 10).

It takes a little bit more time to explain Pearce's understanding of the domain of environmental economics. Initially, the concentration of neo-classical theory on scarcity allowed, according to Pearce, for an analysis of both sides of the market, namely supply and demand. Neo-classical economists analyse actions in the real world that result of interactions between productive activity and the preferences of individual buyers constrained by the feasible range of choice and income. Original neo-classical theory is meant to investigate price determination and market structures (Pearce *et al.* 1990a, 10). Or, in other words, the domain of neo-classical theory initially was the economic sphere, of which markets are the central entities. Pearce proposes to expand the original domain of neo-classical theory to deal with ecological problems. The domain of environmental economics covers the economy *and its ecological environment* (Pearce *et al.* 1990a, 29-30). More specifically, environmental economics concentrates on the interactions between economy and ecological environment. This means that environmental economics is not so much concerned with interactions between ecological phenomena that

> appear to have no economic dimension (Pearce *et al.* 1990a, 29-30)

(as, for instance, the interactions between water supply and fisheries, forests and water supply, forests and soil quality, prey and predators, and so on). It rather investigates

> how the demand for steel affects the demand for water, how changing the size of the economy ("economic growth") affects the functions of the environment, and so on (Pearce *et al.* 1990a, 30).

In other words, economists take an interest in ecological phenomena as far as they become more or less scarce. Relative scarcity of ecological phenomena urges economic actors to make choices. To conclude, the relative scarcity of (some) ecological phenomena makes them formally fit for an economic approach. Reformulated in Weber's terminology, Pearce expands the original domain of neo-classical theory, i.e. the market economy, to include ecological phenomena that, because of their relative scarcity, are either economically relevant or economically conditioned.

Expanding the domain of neo-classical theory in order to enclose economically conditioned or economically relevant ecological phenomena is not unproblematic. Within the market sphere individuals have fairly clear information where to base their choices on. Commodities sold and bought on markets tend to be visible, their characteristics are generally well known, and they have a price. Ecological phenomena, on the contrary, 1) often have no price, 2) often have no clear characteristics, and 3) often cannot be understood as market-like commodities. They have no price since markets for them are lacking. They have no clear characteristics since the impacts of ecological phenomena - global warming, for instance - are uncertain and, consequently, there is limited information about the benefits of avoiding damage by undertaking control measures. They often do not act like commodities in a market place, since they have the characteristics of - what Pearce indicates as - "public goods", namely joint consumption and non-exclusion (Pearce 1993a, 3-4). (In section 2.1.3 of chapter 3, I explain why Schmid prefers the term "joint-impact good" rather than "public good". The latter term refers to institutional choices rather than to physical – or ecological – characteristics of the particular ecological phenomenon.) The "relative scarcity" of ecological entities is thus not very clear to economic actors. The discipline of environmental economics considers it as its task to make this relative scarcity more explicit. For that reason, it develops techniques in order to '*impute a value*' to ecological entities (Pearce 1993a; the italics are his)[7]. These techniques are meant to find a willingness to pay measure in circumstances where markets are lacking in order to reveal that information. To conclude, environmental economics searches for techniques that replace market forces in order to supply ecological entities with a monetary, i.e. exchange, value.

These techniques are (or, better, should be, according to Pearce) based on a particular theory of valuation: the theory of Total Economic Value (e.g. Pearce *et al.* 1990a, chapter 9; Pearce *et al.*1993b, 100; Pearce 1993a, 15-22). Total Economic Value consists of use and non-use values. Use values enclose direct (e.g. the output of forest products, energetic and material resources) and indirect (e.g. ecological functions such as watershed protection, storm buffering, waste assimilation) values and option values (values which relate to the desire to keep the possibility for future use open). Existence values are non-use values. They refer to valuations of environmental assets purely for the sake of keeping them into existence, unrelated to either current or optional use. Pearce acknowledges that Total Economic Value does perhaps not enclose yet the complete total economic value. 'Now *total economic value* [...] relates to these individual functions and services (called *secondary*

[7] Note that Allen V. Kneese *c.s.*, who (re-)introduced the materials balance model to 'describe the movements of physical materials through the economy to supplement models describing the movements of dollars' (Ayres 1978, 36-37), disagree completely with Pearce in this respect. They stress that economics becomes ecologically irrelevant as soon as it translates physical ecological scarcities into monetary terms. (With thanks to Jan van der Straaten for this remark. See, for a further elaboration, van der Straaten 1990, 56-60.)

values). But total secondary value does *not* encompass the *primary value* of the system itself, its life-supporting functions and their "glue value" that holds everything together and therefore has economic value. We cannot directly estimate primary value, but it serves to remind us that total economic value is an underestimate of the "true" value of the environment' (Turner *et al.* 1994, 38).

2.2 *Environmental Economics in the Service of "Sustainable Development"*

Following Pearce's explanation, environmental economics is a kind of welfare economics. Welfare economics takes a "public" perspective. It starts from a preliminary belief in the political desirability of economic behaviour (Pearce *et al.* 1990a, 11). It has allocative efficiency as its guiding criterion. This criterion is usually expressed in terms of the so-called Pareto-criterion.

> A Pareto optimum situation is one in which it is impossible to make any individual better off without making someone else worse off, where "better off" means "more preferred" and "worse off" means "less preferred" (Pearce *et al.* 1990a, 11).

This criterion tells us that a Pareto optimum situation is a situation of competitive equilibrium (and *vice versa*), as long as a set of restrictive assumptions, for instance perfect information and absence of externalities, hold true. In case (negative) externalities do occur welfare economics justifies some government intervention. Externalities point to market failures. They are an indication that markets are not maximising collective welfare. Welfare economics considers government to be an ethical agent that is supposed to intervene in the market in the "public interest". Government intervention means regulating markets directly – *via* "Command-and-Control" measures - or introducing economic instruments – property rights, taxes, subsidies - that alter market signals (Pearce 1993a, 5). The task of welfare economists then consists of informing government 1) on the "value", i.e. the costs, of externalities and 2) on the economic instruments available to internalise these externalities, i.e. to transform their "value" into real costs, i.e., into market prices.

Pearce acknowledges the value judgement implicit in the Pareto-criterion. Allocative efficiency says little about the distribution of costs and benefits within a time period or between time periods (Pearce 1993a, 93). Within a time period the use of efficiency as a guide to environmental policy assumes that the prevailing distribution of income is socially acceptable, since it is that distribution which weighs individual preferences. Between time periods, the use of the efficiency concept, manifest in the use of discount rates, biases the outcomes of evaluation in favour of present and against future generations where costs and benefits in the future are both distant and significant. If these latter biases and the former distributions are deemed unacceptable, allocative efficiency should be replaced by another criterion. Both situations count, according to Pearce, as limits to monetary economic valuation.

"Sustainable development" is such an other criterion (Pearce *et al.* 1990a, 24). Sustainable development means, according to Pearce,

> maximising the net benefits of economic development, subject to maintaining the services and quality of natural resources over time (Pearce *et al.* 1990a, 24).

Formulated in other words, economic development is sustainable on condition that the level of well-being increases on the one hand, and that the (natural) capital remains constant on the other hand. Pearce here follows the approach of the World Commission on Environment and Development, which states that sustainable development implies some general rule about not impairing the capability of future generations to achieve the same level of well-being as the current generation (Pearce 1993a, 7-9). This rule is not compatible with cost-benefit approaches which would allow that future generations are made worse off compared to present generations if the gains to the present are deemed to be greater than the costs to the future. With regard to intergenerational problems Pearce chooses for a theory of justice as the guiding ethical principle rather than for utilitarianism. According to this choice what is considered right takes precedence over what is deemed good or, formulated differently, realisation of rights precedes the balancing of goods and bads, of benefits and costs. To recapitulate, Pearce proposes a teleological or consequentialist, more precisely: a utilitarian, approach for matters of intra-generational interest and an approach based on a theory of justice for matters of inter-generational interest.

With respect to his utilitarian approach of intra-generational problems, Pearce initially interprets the concept "well-being" broadly. A rising level of wellbeing encloses a rising level of real income per capita ("economic growth"), but also an ameliorating "quality of life" (concerning the health of the population, educational standards and general social well-being) (Pearce *et al.* 1989,1). From the perspective of neo-classical welfare economics, well being is to be deduced from individual or private preferences (Pearce 1993a, 13). The intensity of private preferences is expressed in terms of willingness to pay and willingness to be compensated. These kinds of willingnesses express the economic value of goods and services. The economic value of goods and services bought and sold on markets equals their market prices. Since for ecological resources markets are often lacking and sometimes impossible (given the physical nature of the resource in question), environmental economics has developed (and is still refining) techniques for defining shadow prices. These techniques are based, as I explain in section 2.1, on a particular theory of valuation: the theory of Total Economic Value (Pearce *et al.*1993b, 100; Pearce 1993a, 15-22). Once ecological values are made explicit, i.e. expressed in monetary terms so that the relative intensity of individual preferences is measurable and the preferences of different individuals can be compared, one can aggregate these values and apply cost-benefit analyses to define the Total Economic Value of a specific (ecological) "good" (Turner *et al.* 1994, 94). Pearce's interpretation of well-being as an aggregate of private preferences expressed in monetary terms – either in market or "shadow" prices - implies that this initially broadly defined concept narrows to an interpretation of it as (ecologically adjusted) economic growth.

With regard to inter-generational ecological problems, Pearce's interpretation of a constant natural capital is rather ambiguous. As mentioned above, Pearce is not always inclined to rely on individual preferences for defining and realising ecological protection. Searching for increasing per capita well-being - of which ecological protection is one aspect - is, in his view, only legitimate on condition that it is compatible with "intergenerational justice". In case a rising level of per capita well-being is not compatible with "intergenerational justice", Pearce presents "keeping the natural capital stock constant" as an acceptable translation of the intergenerational justice objective (Pearce *et al.* 1990a, 238). From this rough translation, Pearce derives some "management rules". The first rule prescribes to make sure that the stock of renewable resources, the assimilative capacity included, does not decline. Therefore, one has to use renewable resources in such a way that the harvest rate is not greater than the natural regenerative rate and to keep waste flows to the environment at or below the assimilative capacity of the environment. The second rule prescribes to ensure that as exhaustible resources are depleted, their reduced stock is compensated for by increases in renewable resources or to allow for the fact that a given standard of living can be secured from a diminishing stock of resources. The second rule allows for substitutability between exhaustible and renewable resources and for substitutability between man-made and (exhaustible) natural capital. Pearce's management rules make this interpretation of a "constant natural capital stock" resemble Munda's idea of "strong sustainability" (see chapter 1). This idea expresses that certain sorts of natural capital are critical and not readily substitutable by man-made capital. Therefore, the stocks of these sorts of natural capital should not change negatively over time. This requirement asks for non-monetary, bio-physical indicators.

However, Pearce leaves the door open for other interpretations of the "intergenerational justice" objective. To start with, Pearce points to three different interpretations of the prescription to maintain the natural capital stock (Pearce *et al.* 1989, 43-44; 1990a 52-53). First, a natural capital stock can be considered constant if its physical quantity does not change. Since there is no way of adding up the different physical quantities, the standard economic approach, however, searches to value each type of resource in money terms and to compute the overall aggregate money value. The constant capital stock requirement then means that the real value of the stock of natural assets is kept constant. Second, a constant natural capital stock can signify that the prices of natural resources are held constant in real terms. On condition that prices reflect absolute scarcity, constant real prices will imply a constant natural capital stock in this sense. Third, maintaining the natural capital stock could be interpreted as a natural capital stock that delivers a constant value of the resource flows. This interpretation allows quantities of natural resources to decline on condition that the prices of these resources rise in such a way that the total value is kept constant. With this latter interpretation, Pearce starts to skate on the thin ice, called "weak sustainability". Because, from an ecological point of view, it does not make much difference whether one holds on to this interpretation of a "constant natural capital" or to an interpretation that allows for substitution between natural and man-made capital. Pearce's latter interpretation quickly comes down to a utilitarian conception of "intergenerational justice". This implies that the distinction between intra- and inter-generational justice becomes obsolete and that "sustainable development" simply comes down to "increasing the (monetary) level of well-being". It comes down to the conventional economist's concept of "optimal allocation". In the words of Beckerman, an interpretation of "sustainable development" as "weak sustainability" makes the independent usefulness of the concept of sustainability redundant (Beckerman 1996, 129)[8];

Pearce admits that the various interpretations of "constant natural capital" imply a relaxation of this requirement How far it is possible to relax this requirement depends, in Pearce's view, on the degree of substitutability between renewable and non renewable resources and between man-made and natural capital, on the power of technological progress to reduce the resource input to a unit gain in the standard of living, and on population growth. At the same time, Pearce warns us to be cautious with relaxing the constant capital requirement, for several reasons (Pearce *et al.* 1989, 37-43; 1990a, 48-52).

First, comparing the efficiency of natural resources with the efficiency of man-made capital is a complex matter. To begin with, substituting man-made capital for natural capital will only be useful if the extra productivity of the man-made capital in question outweighs the extra natural resources needed to produce this capital. Moreover, natural resources fulfil other functions than man-made capital does. Natural capital – for instance, tropical forests, wetlands, the atmosphere and stratosphere, and so on – often fulfils life-support functions – climate regulation, watershed protection, and so on - which are not served by man-made capital. The productivity of man-made and natural capital, therefore, cannot be compared without taking the different "economic" functions of natural resources into consideration. Second, we lack a lot of insights in the functioning of ecological environments on the one hand and in the interactions between an economy and its ecological environment on the other. We face, in other words, considerable scientific uncertainties. Scientific uncertainties imply a danger of making mistakes that cannot be repaired: human interventions can cause irreversibilities. The presence of uncertainties and the awareness of possible irreversibilities together should, according to Pearce, make us circumspect about giving up natural capital. Third, countries which rely rather directly on natural resources - the poorest countries which do not have the money to buy natural resources or vital commodities from other countries or to stimulate the education in and development of technological knowledge - should not be contented with maintaining a natural capital stock which only has a small margin of flexibility to external shocks, such as a few years of

---

[8] With thanks to my colleague Henk van den Belt for this reference. Though I agree with Beckerman's critique on common interpretations of "sustainable development", I do not agree with his conclusion that the only "objective" contribution of economic knowledge consists of helping politicians to realise "optimality", i.e. maximisation of 'the present value of welfare over whatever time period is regarded as relevant given one's views on inter-generational justice' (Beckerman 1996, 139-140).

drought, a war or another dramatic crisis. They would better strive for bigger resource stocks in order to enlarge the margin of flexibility.

Pearce allows for another kind of relaxation of the "constant natural capital" requirement by discussing which stock of natural capital has to be kept constant. Is it the stock existing at the point of time that decisions are being taken or is it a certain desirable stock, more specifically: an economically optimal stock (Pearce *et al.* 1990a, 53-56; 1990b 4-9). An economically optimal stock can be calculated by comparing the costs of natural capital increases - i.e. the forgone benefits of not letting the natural capital stock increase - with their benefits. The natural capital stock is optimal at the level at which the difference between benefits and costs is at its maximum. In reality, two possibilities can occur. Either the existing level of natural capital is lower than the optimal level. In this case the sustainable development prescription of maintaining the existing stock - i. e. of not letting this stock decline - is consistent with the idea of maintaining an optimal stock. In this situation sustainable development means augmenting the stock of natural resources until it reaches the optimum level. Or the existing level is higher than the optimal level. In this case the sustainable development requirement is not compatible with the proposal to maintain the optimal level. This latter possibility shows that the criterion of inter-generational justice can easily be pushed aside for "economic" arguments, i.e. arguments of allocative efficiency. If this is the case the concept "sustainable development" is again redundant and the distinction between inter-generational and intra-generational ecological problems is superfluous.

This distinction between intra- and inter-generational ecological problems is not clear anyway. It is not clear where intra-generational problems stop and inter-generational problems start, because of the simple reason that generations overlap (Pearce 1993a, 11). 'There is', Pearce writes,

> no consensus on how to integrate inter- and intra-generational considerations into economic decision-making about the environment (Pearce 1993a, 11).

This confusion merely contributes to the redundancy of the "sustainable development" idea. Consider, as an illustration, the following example offered by Pearce. Dealing with the problem of chlorofluorocarbons (CFCs) which deplete the ozone layer and thus indirectly cause increases in skin cancer due to higher levels of ultraviolet radiation, Pearce writes :

> Moreover, reducing CFC emissions is unlikely to be a cost-efficient way of preventing cancer even if this is the relationship. More sensible human behavior toward exposure to ultraviolet rays would be cheaper (Pearce *et al.* 1993b, 388).

I do not deny that the present sunbathing behaviour often is exaggerated and not always very wise. However, basing acceptable transformations of the ozone layer on efficiency considerations, thus letting possibly change the originally rather safe human environment so much that humans must adapt their individual behaviour to a more or less great extent, sounds to me as poking fun at the idea of "inter-generational justice".

Pearce gives us some arguments in favour of maintaining the existing stock above the optimal level. First, he points to the problem of identifying the "optimum". The identification depends on which costs and benefits one is willing to take into consideration. It depends, for instance, on whether one is only inclined to recognise direct economic functions or whether one also acknowledges other functions (for instance, the "direct utility" function and life-support functions). Identifying the optimum is defining it and *vice versa*. Moreover, it remains an open question whether life-support functions (such as contributions to geo-chemical cycles) can be expressed in terms of costs and benefits. Second, awareness of uncertainties and irreversibilities pleads in favour of the risk-averse strategy of conserving what there is. Uncertainties are related to our imperfect understanding of the life-support functions of natural environments and to our limited capability to substitute for those functions even if their loss is reversible in theory. Third, optimality tends to be defined in terms of economic efficiency, whereas conservation of the natural capital stock serves other social goals, e.g. distributional goals both within current generations and between current and future generations. Fourth, research on the use of willingness-to-pay and willingness-to-accept measures shows very large discrepancies between willingness-to-pay for a small increase in the size of a specific environmental asset and the willingness-to-accept a small decrease in it. Compensation requirements often are very much larger. This suggests that what exists is seen as a reference point and that attitudes to possible losses of destroying what already exists are quite different to attitudes to possible gains of creating what does not exist yet. Put another way, the discrepancies between willingness-to-pay and willingness-to-accept demonstrate that, according to the perception of many people, the optimal and the existing level coincide.

2.3 Conclusion

Pearce conceives of environmental economics as a kind of neo-classical economics. In agreement with Robbins' formal interpretation of economics, Pearce considers the fact that some people evaluate particular ecological entities or phenomena as scarce as an indication of their fitness for an economic approach. It is, according to both Robbins and Pearce, the formal characteristic of scarcity that defines the domain of economics. This interpretation allows for an expansion of economics from the typically economic domain of market forces to the domain of ecological phenomena. This expansion can, however not occur, without providing scarce ecological phenomena with a price.

"Sustainable development" is the criterion from which to derive prices of scarce ecological phenomena. This criterion means a rising level of well-being – a matter of utilitarianism – with regard to intra-generational ecological problems. It means a constant natural capital stock – a matter of justice - with regard to inter-generational ecological problems. Since Pearce keeps the door open for two kinds of relaxations of the concept "constant natural capital stock", either by defining this stock in monetary terms or by being satisfied with an "optimal" stock, the inter-generational-justice part of "sustainable development" easily vanishes. (The distinction between intra- and inter-generational ecological problems is difficult to make anyhow.) Since Pearce translates, moreover, well-being into the aggregate of private preferences expressed in monetary terms, "sustainable development" comes easily down to "maximisation of welfare", the old-fashioned economist's concept of "optimality". In Beckerman's words, the whole "sustainable development" idea then gets redundant.

3 ENVIRONMENTAL POLITICS

According to Pearce, environmental economics is about providing public authorities with "institutions" – either Command-and-Control measures or "economic instruments" such as property rights, taxes, subsidies – that allow for an internalisation of ecological externalities. In this section, I will argue that an interpretation of ecological problems as a matter of externalities testifies of the ambiguity of the concept "allocative efficiency". This interpretation gives, moreover, rise to a particular interpretation of the *genesis* of economic institutions and, hence, of politics. It gives rise to an interpretation of environmental politics as a matter of economic calculations. This interpretation relates to the assumption that scientific insights into the ecological performance of an economy are impossible. This deemed impossibility leaves two "sustainability" problems unresolved.

3.1 The Ambiguity of the Concept "Allocative Efficiency"

Ecological externalities are (external) relationships between an economy and its ecological environment that are evaluated negatively. In Pigou's words, an external economy (or externality) is

> a service or disservice rendered to persons other than the contracting parties (Pigou 1952, 192; cited in Dietz *et al.* 1994, 44).

External economies can be both positive and negative. Ecological problems are examples of negative externalities. Welfare economics interprets (negative) externalities as "market failures", i.e. as indications that existing markets do not allocate scarce natural resources "optimally". Market failures cause discrepancies between "private" and "social" costs. Consider the following example (Dietz *et al.* 1994, 44-45). When an entrepreneur discharges the heavy metals liberated during the production process in a river, he passes on part of his production costs to society. These production costs are the costs to bring the quality of the water in the river back to the original level. In this case, consumers who buy the products of this entrepreneur do not pay the full price, since the costs of water purification are not included. Because of this discrepancy between "private" and "social" costs, the increasing scarcity of pure water is a blind spot within an economy. Or, in neo-classical terms, the allocation of production factors is not optimal. This neo-classical line of reasoning is ambiguous. To understand externalities as an indication that production factors are not optimally allocated testifies of the ambiguity of the concept "allocative efficiency". I will discuss this statement more extensively.

According to the Pareto-criterion, an allocation of production factors is optimal in case it is impossible to make any individual better off, by allocating production factors differently, without making someone else worse off, where "better off" means "more preferred" and "worse off" means "less preferred" (see 2.2). According to neo-classical theory, private preferences are, however, not known. They can at most be revealed in the choices economic actors make. Consequently, the results of market forces – the commodities produced by producers and bought by consumers – are revelations of this private preferences, though one has to accept that these revealed preferences would perhaps be otherwise in case producers' and consumers' rationality would not have been bounded, transactions costs would have been less, and initial distribution of income would have been more fair. Consequently, either neo-classical theory interprets economic actors' choices as revelations of their preferences (accepting the triple restriction of bounded rationality, existence of transaction costs and a particular initial distribution of income). In that case, whatever results of market forces should be interpreted as Pareto-optimal. Or neo-classical theory interprets the results of market forces as a non-optimal allocation of production factors. This implies that neo-classical theory either "knows" that some choices do not reveal some private preferences (but how can it know?), or that it uses a different criterion to evaluate the results of market forces as non-optimal (e.g., initial distribution of income is deemed unfair, transaction costs are deemed to high, economic actors' rationality is deemed too bounded, or some other – for instance, ecological - reason). If the latter is the case, then the meaning of the concept "optimal allocation" has shifted. Stronger, it has changed its originally independent meaning for a meaning dependent on an external criterion[9].

In order to remove the ambiguity of the concept "allocative efficiency", I propose to reserve this concept for evaluating the separate actions of economic decision units. These actions occur *within* the institutional whole of a specific economy. The allocation of production factors through these actions can only be made more efficient by ameliorating the bounded rationality of individual economic actors. Only individual economic actors can judge whether the choices made satisfy their private preferences in an optimal way. Neo-classical economists can at most help them to make better choices by providing them with more information, i.e. by making their rationality less bounded. Ameliorating this bounded rationality is what neo-classical theory is about. Neo-classical theory and, hence, welfare economics, holds an individualistic perspective. It is meant to help individual economic actors – either households, firms or even public authorities – to manage their scarce resources as economically as possible given their private interests. The concept "allocative efficiency" cannot be used to evaluate the performance *of* an economy as

---

[9] Another interesting analysis of the concept "efficiency" – and comments similar to mine – can be found in Tiles and Oberdiek 1995, chapter 2.

a whole. As soon as one starts to evaluate the institutional organisation *of* an economy, one (implicitly or explicitly) falls back on a different criterion. To recapitulate, allocative efficiency can at most refer to the performance of individual economic actors *within* a given institutional organisation of an economy. Allocative efficiency cannot refer to the performance *of* a given institutional organisation of an economy.

3.2 Economic Institutions as a Matter of Economic Calculations

Since Pearce judges the ecological performance of present-day economies as non-sustainable, he aims at correcting economies. Correcting economies means *adding* institutions – Command and Control measures or "economic instruments" such as taxes, subsidies, property rights – to the existing ones (rather than *transforming* the existing institutional organisation). How does Pearce derive the institutions to add?

In order to understand his line of reasoning , we should first consider an economy that is deemed to show no externalities. In such an economy, prices reveal willingness to pay, say private preferences. These prices result from market forces, say from the given institutional organisation of an economy. Consider now an economy that shows some externalities. These externalities are indications that the existing institutional organisation of an economy should be corrected so that the prices resulting from the corrected market forces reveal private preferences again (or, in welfare-economic language, so that the discrepancy between private and social costs disappears). In order to know which institutions to add, one thus has to know private preferences. Since these private preferences are not revealed in the existing economy, one has to ask for them. Environmental economics has, therefore, developed techniques to let people *state* – rather than *reveal* – their private preferences. These techniques aim at finding a *willingness to pay* measure in circumstances where markets are lacking to reveal that information. Such willingness-to-pay measure asks for a translation of private preferences into monetary terms. According to neo-classical theory, economic values must be expressed in monetary terms in order to make comparisons possible between different kinds of values – the different kinds constituting Total Economic Value -, between the values of different goods and services, and between the values of different individuals. Once private preferences are known in monetary terms, they can be aggregated and cost-benefit analyses can be applied. From this information, economists can deduce institutions to add to the existing institutional organisation so that the calculated environmental protection level can be realised[10].

---

[10] I should remark, that, according to Pearce, definition of the desirable ecological protection level does not necessarily result from economic calculations. His principle of intergenerational justice, translated as a "natural constant capital" allows for a definition in bio-physical terms. This does, however, not alter my argument that, in his view, the derivation of economic institutions allowing for the realisation of this desirable level is a matter of economic calculations. Welfare economics is, after all, about allocative efficiency. The economic institutions economists recommend are those that allow for a cost-effective realisation of desirable ecological protection levels. One could further remark that my argument is at most valid in case economists recommend so-called "economic instruments", rather than Command-

According to Pearce, deciding on economic institutions is a matter of economic calculations. I should deal with this view of Pearce more extensively in order to clarify some of the underlying political assumptions. Pearce's view assumes, to begin with, that people only have private preferences. Private preferences concern wants and desires that can be fulfilled in real or hypothetical market-type situations (Pearce *et al.* 1990a, 237). Each market situation offers a set of goods and services between which individuals can choose given their own income. Private preferences thus regard private choices out of a given choice set. Choice sets themselves depend on the existing (or hypothetical) institutional organisation. Deriving institutions from private preferences thus overlooks the possibility that people can have *political* preferences *for* some *desirable* institutional organisation, rather than *private* preferences *within a given* institutional organisation. Pearce's economic approach closes the possibility off to solve ecological problems by discussing desirable institutional organisations that define different choice sets and different (revealed or stated) private preferences. It denies, in other words, citizens' political autonomy, i.e. their capability to shape their social context through political processes. Though Pearce does not necessarily overlook the logical hierarchy between the political and the economic sphere (the fact that politically decided on – though possibly economically calculated - institutions are logically prior to economic actions), he allows for (what I called in section 4.4 of chapter 2) a reverse hierarchy between both, since he considers of political interests as resulting from predetermined, short-term economic interests. In this respect, his conception of politics comes down to Buchanan's. According to Buchanan, politics is about the kind of legal restrictions we can expect individual actors of the type *homo oeconomicus* to acknowledge and to accept as the political constitution that allows them to strive after their private interests without further restrictions – i.e. without having to care about other people's welfare – and with an optimal realisation of the private interests of all economic actors as a result (see section 3.2 in chapter 2).

Pearce's view assumes, further, a particular interpretation of values. He assumes that values cannot be "rationally" justified, but that people simply happen to have certain values rather than others. For that reason, economic institutions can only be derived from existing private preferences, not from "considered" ones (Pearce *et al.* 1990a, 227; 237). Existing private preferences are preferences conditioned by the existing institutional organisation. They are not reflected on, not debated on within a deliberative democracy. They are not "imagined" as they could be within a desirable

---

and-Control measures. According to Swaney, the distinction between these two forms of economic institutions is overblown (Swaney 1992). He states that the dichotomy between market and command and control is false because both market and regulation are nothing more than sets of man-made rules that govern behaviour. He illustrates his statement with several examples. Consider, for instance, the following one. 'When the FDA proposed regulation to require fast-food restaurants to post nutritional information, was this regulation a market rule to improve market information and efficiency, or was it another example of a command rule, reducing market efficiency? Consumer groups believed the former, and the fast-food industry embraced the latter. Implementation of this rule increased consumer freedom (to make better informed decisions at lower cost), while reducing McDonald's freedom to minimize costs' (Swaney 1992, 626).

institutional organisation. Taking private preferences serious is, according to this value interpretation, what democracy is about.

> We tended not to ask where the preferences came from, or whether they were "good or bad" (subject to the law, that is). This is because cost-benefit approaches try to be "democratic" by using individuals' preferences rather than some expert's view. Otherwise the way is open for the "tyranny of the expert" whereby expert values are imposed on others (Turner *et al.* 1994, 132).

This interpretation of private preferences leads to an interpretation of politics as a *bargaining* process. The most political actors can do is bargaining or negotiating with each other till they reach some equilibrium level. Even stronger, the requirement to express private preferences in monetary terms leads to an interpretation of negotiating as *calculating*. To conclude, Pearce's welfare-economic approach with regard to ecological problems is based on a conception of environmental politics as a matter of economic calculations.

3.3 Adding Economic Institutions: Two Problems of "Sustainability"

Pearce's conception of welfare economics as the theoretical paradigm from which to derive the economic institutions that public authorities should *add* to the existing institutional organisation of an economy leaves two problems of "sustainability" unresolved. First, Pearce's concept of "sustainable development" – a concept that (ultimately) derives ecological conditions from private preferences - can at most by accident contribute to a "sustainable" economy, i.e. an economy of which its ecological performance is manageable or, in other words, an economy in which responsibility towards future generations is not an idle endeavour. Second, Pearce cannot justify why *adding* economic institutions should really *solve* the ecological problems dealt with rather than *keep them down*. I will discuss these two problems into greater detail.

To start with the first problem, my thesis is that the aggregate of people's private preferences – i.e. preferences conditioned by the institutional organisations of existing economies – does not necessarily lead to an ecological performance of an economy that is "sustainable", i.e. "manageable" with respect to both present and future generations. This is because such (aggregates of) private preferences are not necessarily realistic. The ecological conditions needed – given actual technological possibilities - to satisfy such (aggregates of) private preferences may be at odds with existing ecological conditions.

Pearce is aware of this possible shortcoming. In his view, however, this shortcoming is inherently related to present-day common beliefs that ecological problems should be solved in a democratic way. Pearce introduces himself as an adherent of – a non-deliberative version of a - political democracy. He states that "sustainable development" should be the result of a political democracy.

> The social dimension states simply, but powerfully, that a sustained society is also a truly democratic society with rights of expression, dissent, participation, self-reliance

> and equality of opportunity. Political and economic structures have to deliver social as well as environmental sustainability (Pearce 1993c, 185).

At the same time, his confidence in existing democracies is rather simmering.

> Yet, it must be said that the present society is supported by a democracy that is led to believe that its best interests are served by minor adjustments to the status quo.

And Pearce continues expressing his doubts concerning the ecological feasibility of democratic choices:

> However, it is still doubtful whether even the very basic needs of at least one billion of the world's poorest people can really be met without an enormous convulsion in the denial of expectations over future consumption of materials and energy amongst the very wealthy. Moreover, existing experience provides little support for the hope that it is technically possible to bring the existing global population up to the living standards of, say, France, without environmental disruption on an enormous scale (Pearce 1993c, 184).

Second, in case particular ecological problems are internally related with a particular institutional organisation of an economy, the theoretical arguments for justifying *adding* institutions to the existing institutional organisation rather than *transforming* this organisation are lacking. Pearce cannot convince us that economic institutions added will do more than *combating symptoms* rather than *removing reasons*. And empirical data suggest that combating symptoms, rather than removing reasons, is what happens most of the time. Consider again the following statement of the Netherlands' National Institute of Public Health and the Environment: 'The reduction targets for greenhouse gas emissions, acidification and eutrophication will not be met, even after implementation of the measures contained in the national Environmental Policy Plan 3(NEPP3). These measures cannot fully compensate for the increasing environmental burden of the growing economy' (Environmental Balance Sheet 1998).

Pearce acknowledges the "sustainability" problems related to basing ecological policy on (aggregates of) private preferences. His "constant natural capital" proposal is meant as a trial to counter this possible shortcoming. He admits that this proposal formulates ecological conditions - conditions that can be *monitored* via his materials balance approach – that are at most necessary but not sufficient. A sufficient set of conditions would include institutional requirements for implementing sustainable development policy and it may even require systematic changes in social values, Pearce writes (Pearce *et al.* 1990b, 4). To fulfil this *institutional* task, economists lack, according to Pearce, an "existence theorem". An existence theorem would relate

> the scale and configuration of an economy to the set of environment-economy interrelationships underlying that economy (Pearce et al. 1990a, 42).

In my words, it would make the internal relationships between the institutional organisation and the ecological performance of an economy understandable.

Pearce himself does not believe in the feasibility of scientific investigations concerning the relationships between the institutional organisation of an economy and its ecological performance. He states that the scientific elaboration of an existence theorem is an idle endeavour (Pearce *et al.* 1990a, 42). He rejects such institutional investigations as premature undertakings. After a short overview of different economic paradigms - Pearce distinguishes a classical, a marxist, a neo-classical and humanist, an institutional, and an ecological and co-evolutionary paradigm - he concludes

> that we have a great deal to learn from our horizon-expanding application of modern [neo-classical] economics, and that the search for "alternatives" is premature (Pearce *et al* 1990a, 1-28; 31).

Pearce is content with a search for what he deems to be necessary, though not sufficient, sustainability conditions, conditions which he derives from a mixture of economic analyses (cost-benefit, cost-effectiveness, materials balance analyses) and political judgements (concerning the meaning of intra- and intergenerational justice, concerning the scope of relevant valuations, concerning appropriate methods to detect such valuations, concerning prudent behaviour, and so on). He is confident that a neo-classically-inspired trial-and-error approach suffices to deal with ecological problems. Environmental policy

> should be seen as an iterative search process based on a "satisfising" (extended rationality) rather than an optimising principle (Pearce *et al.* 1990a, 20)[11].

3.4 Conclusion

Pearce's welfare economic approach interprets "sustainable development" finally as a matter of "allocative efficiency". It assumes that the institutional organisation of an economy must be corrected in order to allocate scarce ecological resources more effectively. I object to this view. The concept "allocative efficiency" cannot be used to evaluate the ecological performance *of* an economy. In case this performance is evaluated negatively, the criterion used is not "allocative efficiency" but particular ecological standards.

Pearce's welfare economic approach aims, moreover, at ameliorating the ecological performance of an economy by adding institutions to the existing institutional whole. This approach is based on particular political assumptions. It assumes that private preferences - revealed or stated within a given institutional organisation - are politically relevant. It assumes, moreover, that a political democracy consists of respecting and aggregating private preferences. These assumptions lead to an interpretation of the political genesis of economic institutions as a matter of economic calculations.

Finally, Pearce's welfare economic approach cannot scientifically justify that the institutions added will contribute to the ideal of "sustainability" for two reasons. First, because private preferences do not necessarily respect the ecological

[11] I would not deny that environmental policy is an iterative search process, but I state that it makes a difference whether this search process is one-sidedly based on neo-classical insights or that it is also fostered with institutional insights.

conditions needed to satisfy them. Second, because institutions added do not remove reasons for, but at most combat the negatively evaluated ecological performances. These scientific shortcomings relate to the welfare-economic incapability to offer insights into the internal relationships between the institutional organisation and the ecological performance of an economy. According to Pearce, aiming at such insights is an idle and premature endeavour.

4 CONCLUSION

In this chapter, I situated David Pearce's theoretical work in the tradition of environmental economics. Pearce's economics is, indeed, a specialisation of neo-classical economics. It is a kind of welfare economics that considers the "public interest" from the perspective of "sustainable development". "Sustainable development" is a typically neo-classical translation of "sustainability". "Sustainable development" means, according to Pearce, maximising the net benefits of economic development, subject to maintaining the services and quality of natural resources over time. This latter sentence of Pearce suggests that Pearce is in favour of a "strong" rather than "weak" sustainability (which would prevent from classifying his work fully within the tradition of environmental economics). Pearce states that certain sorts of natural capital are critical and not readily substitutable by man-made capital. He defends, therefore, an ecological protection level that shows a non-negative change over time in stocks of specified natural capital. Pearce's argument for a "constant natural capital stock" is, however, open to many interpretations. How to measure whether the natural capital stock is constant? Should the stock of separate natural resources be kept constant or the aggregate stock? Should the (aggregate or separate) stock be measured in physical or in monetary terms? Which stock of natural capital should be kept constant, the existing or the optimal one? These questions illustrate that relaxations of Pearce's original ideal of "strong sustainability" are easily made. "Strong sustainability" easily comes down to "weak sustainability" and "weak sustainability" easily comes down to old-fashioned "economic efficiency".

A particular contrast underlies Pearce's "sustainable development" project. On the one hand, his project is based on the belief that science is capable of monitoring the ecological environment and of managing it at an optimal level. Pearce's ecological Input-Output analyses and his materials balance model are meant to serve these monitoring and managing goals. Pearce's project thus assumes a scientific control of our ecological environment that allows for an optimal (rather than, for instance, sufficient) use of natural resources. It assumes, in other words, a scientific control of our ecological environment that allows for economic growth on the boundary between safe and unsafe natural resource use, though it admits that this boundary is not very well known and that, therefore, irreversibilities cannot be excluded. On the other hand, his project is based on a complete disbelief in the capability of science to provide (comprehensible rather than bookkeeping) insights into the relationships between the institutional organisation and the ecological performance of our economies.

Two political assumptions underlie Pearce's "sustainable development" project. First, Pearce assumes that political democracy is a matter of aggregating the private preferences individuals happen to have. He assumes, more precisely, that ecological policy is a matter of aggregating the private preferences individuals happen to have for the protection of particular natural resources. Second, he assumes that ecological politics is about *adding* economic institutions to the existing whole, rather than transforming this whole. Pearce can, however, not convince us that adding institutions will bring aggregate economic action into a sustainable direction.

Despite previous critical comments, we should recognise that Pearce did pioneering work. To start with, he convinced many of his colleagues that ecological problems are worth of their attention. He integrated ecological problems within the conventional, neo-classical paradigm by interpreting the "public interest" of welfare economics as "sustainable development". He pleaded, further, for a broad interpretation of "the economic value" of ecological entities, by introducing the concept "Total Economic Value". He argued, finally, for institutional adaptations of our industrial economies in order to make them, via trial and error, more sustainable. Many policy documents of various member states within the European Union testify of Pearce's influence. Pearce's interpretation of "sustainable development" undoubtedly prevails within political circles.

CHAPTER 6

THE NATURE OF PEARCE'S ECONOMICS

In this chapter, I will elaborate on the nature of Pearce's environmental economics. In the first section, I will explain that Pearce considers his environmental economics as both non-neutral and objective. Objectivity means, in line with the positive tradition of neo-classical economics, empirical validity. Contrary to the positive tradition, Pearce acknowledges that scientific objectivity does not imply neutrality. Nevertheless, he believes that the specific non-neutrality of his environmental economics is justified, i.e. does not contradict scientific objectivity, because the values underlying his non-neutral perspective are practically valid.

In the second and third section, I will argue that, in line with Weber, Pearce considers his environmental economics as a toolbox for ecological policy. Consequently, he often stops acting as a descriptive scientist and starts acting as a prescriptive scientist. He prescribes the political objectives that should dominate ecological policy. Moreover, Pearce looks in the first place for instruments with which to *manage* people's behaviour into the direction of "sustainable development". His environmental economics cannot provide people with theoretical models that help *explain* the relationships between the existing institutional organisation of an economy and its existing ecological performance.

In section four, I will present Pearce's environmental economics as a partial science. It is a partial science because it does not offer insights into (economic sources of) political power relationships. In line with Buchanan's interpretation of politics, it considers political deliberation as an exercise of balance given existing power relationships.

1 NON-NEUTRAL OBJECTIVITY

In line with the "positive" tradition in neo-classical economics, Pearce believes in the objectivity of his environmental economics. In Pearce's view, economic science is objective on condition that it is empirically valid, i.e. based on empirically observable data, logically consistent and mathematically rigorous. At the same time, he acknowledges the non-neutrality of a welfare economics aiming at "sustainable development" *and* the non-neutrality of the welfare-economical criterion of Pareto-optimality. In Pearce's view, non-neutrality does not contradict objectivity. I agree with this, though I do not agree with the arguments Pearce mentions to justify this combination. According to Pearce, non-neutrality does not contradict objectivity on condition that the non-neutral perspective is practically valid.

1.1 Objectivity as Practically Valid Non-Neutrality

As mentioned in the previous chapter (section 2.2), Pearce acknowledges the value judgement implicit in the Pareto-criterion. Pearce does not have any reservations to call "sustainable development" a value word either. '[I]t embodies', he writes,

> personal ideals and aspirations and concepts of what constitutes the "good" society (Pearce *et al.* 1989, 1).

At the same time, he discerns

> in all writing on sustainable development [...] a common thread, a fairly consistent set of characteristics that appear to define the conditions for sustainable development to be achieved (Pearce *et al.* 1989, 1).

These conditions concern a rising level of well being on the one hand, and keeping the (natural) capital constant on the other hand. This latter observation restores, in Pearce's view, the objectivity of environmental economics. For Pearce considers "sustainable development" as a societal value that can be empirically observed. In other words, Pearce considers "sustainable development" as a practically valid societal value.

Two objections can be made to Pearce's interpretation of objectivity as practically valid non-neutrality. The first objection is one we can directly borrow from Weber. Weber strongly contests the idea that the non-neutrality of science becomes legitimate – i.e., that non-neutral science becomes objective - as soon as the values defining the scientific perspective can be empirically observed (see section 1.1 in chapter 2). Weber argues that a scientist should not be contented with the

> conventional self-evidentness of very widely accepted value-judgments (MSS 13).

On the contrary, he considers the questioning of those things which convention makes self-evident as a specific function of science. Considered from the perspective of a deliberative democracy, Weber is right. Political debates benefit from an input of a variety of (scientific) non-neutral perspectives. One-sided scientific input based on prevailing values limits, rather than stimulates political deliberation.

The second objection regards Pearce's assertion that the values defining his scientific perspective can be empirically observed. I do not agree with this statement, for three reasons. In order to make the concept "sustainable development" operational, Pearce has to make a lot of evaluative choices that are not justified by empirical observations. Such choices concern, to begin with, Pearce's definition of Total Economic Value as the kinds of values economists should take into consideration. They regard, secondly, his interpretation of these values as private preferences[1]. They relate, thirdly, to the use of money as a measuring rod. This requirement is not empirically valid, because it compels people to treat values that are, according to their perception, not commensurate as if they were commensurate or, stated differently, it compels them to treat all phenomena as commodities that can be sold and bought. This requirement denies, for instance, refusals to put a monetary value on buildings or sites of special cultural and historical importance, on specific nature phenomena, or even on human lifes[2]. These refusals can be considered expressions of the conviction that some values are higher-order values than economic valuations and that they, consequently, cannot be treated on an equal footing. Higher-order values refer to values embodied in institutions that logically precede and condition economic valuations. This monetary requirement is, moreover, not empirically valid because of the many empirically unjustified normative choices inherent in the various economic valuation techniques. The simple fact that both (marketed) commodities and (non-marketed) ecological resources can be expressed in monetary terms (due to the invention of certain "techniques" such as hedonic pricing, contingent valuation and the travel-cost method) does not yet justify comparisons between them. Prices depend on specific institutional contexts. For that reason, comparing real prices (related to an existing institutional context) to shadow prices (related to a hypothetical or not even hypothetically existing institutional context) is a kind of deception. The simple fact that both are expressed in monetary terms does not guarantee that their respective monetary units relate to the same standard and, consequently, comparisons are not justified.

To conclude, Pearce acknowledges the non-neutrality of his environmental economics. Since non-neutrality is inevitable, one cannot blame Pearce's environmental economics for that. Contrary to Pearce's conviction, however, his non-neutrality is not practically valid. Even if it were practically valid, Pearce's non-neutrality would not contribute to scientific objectivity. Scientific objectivity is independent of the practical validity of the value-related perspective.

1.2 Objectivity as Non-Neutral Empirical Validity

In the history of economic theory neo-classical theory is commonly considered to be a "positive" science. A positive science is deemed to be both objective *and* neutral. The idea of science underlying neo-classical theory is taken from the natural sciences. According to Robbins, the laws of economics must conform to

[1] Pearce admits that interpreting values as preferences is a non-neutral choice. Consider the following quotation: 'To the economist, economic value arises if someone is made to feel better off in terms of their wants and desires. [...] What economic valuation does is to measure *human preferences* for or against changes in the state of environments. It does not "value the environment"' (Turner *et al* 1994, 38).

[2] 'The same ideas can be found when dealing with the existence of an army, a monarchy, a Rubens painting, a Shakespeare poem, a piece of music by Mozart, the sight of migrating raptors and storks on Gibraltar, an attractive partner, the Amsterdam canals, a Marquez novel, the Matterhorn, Delphi, the Atlantic coast of Portugal, a nation, human rights, or an educational system. There is no price for these goods and that in this view, is the best option' (Briassoulis & van der Straaten 1999, p. 125).

> our conception of science in general: that is to say the formation of hypotheses explaining and (possibly) predicting the outcome of the relationships concerned and the testing of such hypotheses by logic and by observation. [...] I am pretty sure that all the positive propositions of economics conform to this description. In this context, therefore, we may regard them as falling into the same category of knowledge as astronomy, physics, and biology [...] (Robbins 1984, xiv).

In order to attain this natural-science-like goal of objectivity and neutrality, neo-classical theory falls back on the following aids.

It starts from basic assumptions that are firmly grounded in empirical reality. The theory of value, i.e., the theory of marginal utility is founded on the assumption that the different things that the individual wants to do have a different importance to him, and can be arranged therefore in a certain order (Robbins 1984, 75). The theory of production needs a supplementary fundamental proposition, namely that the different factors of production are imperfect substitutes or, in other words, that a multiplicity of production factors exists (Robbins 1984, 76;115). The existence of uncertainty or ignorance concerning future scarcities is the basic proposition of the theory of dynamic change (Robbins 1984, 79;115). According to Robbins these assumptions are all

> assumptions involving in some way simple and indisputable facts of experience relating to the way in which the scarcity of goods which is the subject-matter of our science actually shows itself in the world of reality (Robbins 1984 ,78).

For that reason, pure economics does not need controlled experiments to establish their validity and, for that same reason,

> there is less reason to doubt their real bearing than that of the generalisations of the natural science (Robbins 1984, 105).

The ultimate constituents of the fundamental economic generalisations are known by immediate acquaintance; those of the natural sciences, on the contrary, are only known inferentially. Mind that with "immediate acquaintance" Robbins refers to psychic "evidence"; the basic premises of economics are derived from introspection (Mulberg 1995, 64). To recapitulate, according to Robbins, empirical observation is a first element of an objective and neutral social science.

A second and third aid for attaining an objective and neutral economics are formal logic and mathematics. Once the basic propositions are established, economic laws are logical deductions from these elementary premises (Robbins 1984, 75-83). The truth of these laws depends on the logical consistency of the deductions. Both the evidence of the basic premises and the logical consistency of the deductions guarantee that the truths expressed in neo-classical laws are a-historical: invariable and eternal. Precisely these characteristics lend the truths of pure economics the status of a natural-science-like "law". Formal logic and mathematical rigour are thus, in Robbins' view, two other elements of an objective and neutral science.

A fourth aid regards economic actors' means and ends. Economics considers ends as given data (Robbins 1984, 24-32). It assumes that human beings have ends. This assumption is necessary to define economic conduct and to make this conduct understandable. However, economics is not concerned with these ends as such. This means two things. Firstly, it means that it is not interested in the kind of ends that economic subjects have. It does not assume any specific psychology.

> [E]conomic subjects can be pure egoists, pure altruists, pure ascetics, pure sensualists or - what is much more likely - mixed bundles of all these impulses (Robbins 1984, 95).

Neo-classical economics treats individuals as isolated, autonomous subjects with given ends. For neo-classical theory, the mere existence of ends suffices. Secondly, it means that economists refrain from any judgement concerning varying ends.

> The fact that such data [individual ends; MD] are themselves of the nature of judgments of value does not necessitate that they should be valued as such. They are not judgments of value by the observer [i.e., the scientist; MD]. What is of relevance to economics is, not whether individual judgments of value are *correct* in the ultimate sense of the philosophy of value, but whether they are *made* and whether they are essential links in the chain of causal explanation (Robbins 1984, 90).

Neo-classical economists respect given ends. They do not judge them. The economists' abstinence of judging individual ends is another element that is deemed to ensure the *neutral objectivity* of neo-classical theory.

An analogue story holds for economic means: economic theory considers them as data too (Robbins 1984, 32-35). Economics does not inquire into technical arts of production, nor into the development of these techniques. It does not worry about the nature of scarce material and technical means; it is about conduct as a resultant of conflicting ends within an environment of given material and technical possibilities.

> [T]he problem of technique arises when there is one end and a multiplicity of means, the problem of economy when both the ends and the means are multiple (Robbins 1984, 35).

Finally, neo-classical theory presupposes a particular rationality. It presupposes that economic actors behave economically. Economics does not make ethical judgements concerning the kind of consumers' and producers' ends. It is meant to explain whether the achievement of given objectives happens in an economic way. A producer will produce economically if the type and the quantity of commodities he or she is making to the exclusion of other types and quantities is in conformity with the demands of consumers (Robbins 1984, 50). If production is carried beyond these limits, producers are behaving uneconomically. They produce waste in the sense that productive power is used to produce goods of less value than could be produced otherwise. This uneconomical producer's behaviour results in a definite financial loss for the productive enterprise concerned. In other words, economics states - by definition - that producers are striving for profit maximisation, since that is the way to produce economically. Consumers consume economically on condition that the commodities they buy satisfy their ends most fully, i.e. on condition that they secure their ends with least means (Robbins 1984, 143 ff). Economic(al) consumers are thus aiming at a maximisation of satisfaction.

To conclude, neo-classical theory commonly has an aura of being both neutral and objective because it does not judge, but simply respects the values people happen to have, because economic rationality and other psychic assumptions are "evident", and because of its logical consistency and mathematical rigour. In other words, it is deemed to be both neutral and objective because it is empirically valid: it only "observes" ends, means, economic rationality and other psychic elements, it is logically consistent and mathematically rigorous.

In Pearce's writings one can discern remnants of this conception of neo-classical theory as a "positive" science. This becomes, for instance, manifest in his search for the value of ecological resources. He aims at what he calls "true" values, i.e., values as he finds them - without further judging them - in people's statements.

> The purpose of economic valuation is to reveal the *true* costs of using up scarce environmental resources (Pearce 1993a, 5; the italics are mine).

Gathering and respecting people's values is, in his view, a matter of democracy. That is why he conceives of this endeavour as a neutral enterprise. He, however, overlooks the non-neutrality of the choices he has to make – defining the values that have to be taken into account, defining these values as private preferences, asking people to express their private preferences in monetary terms - before gathering this information. His normative choices follow, indeed, naturally from the non-neutral perspective typical of neo-classical theory. Neo-classical theory starts from given preferences and aims at mathematical rigour. In agreement with this line of reasoning, values have to be asked for and made commensurable by expressing them in one and the same monetary standard.

Contrary to the "positive" interpretation of neo-classical theory, Pearce does not state that the assumption of economic rationality is a matter of neutrality. He, however, defends this non-neutral choice – and his choice for neo-classical welfare economics as a suitable approach to ecological problems – with the following argument. He writes:

> Since any economics needs value judgements, and in the absence of agreed meta-ethical criteria for choosing between value judgements, it cannot be argued that neo-classical economics and its Paretian value judgements are "worse" or "better" than any other economic doctrine (Pearce *et al.* 1990a, 4).

Note that Pearce's defence of the neo-classical choice for the assumption of economic rationality is compatible with his general interpretation of the nature of values (see section 3.2 in chapter 5). Pearce deems this evaluative choice legitimate because he assumes that values cannot be "rationally" justified. Pareto-optimality is a legitimate value because it is a value neo-classical economists simply happen to have.

To conclude, in line with Robbins' interpretation of neo-classical theory, Pearce believes in the objectivity as empirical validity of environmental economics. In order to assure this empirical validity, 1) he *asks* for people's preferences in order to avoid scientists' judgements and 2) he asks to express them in monetary terms in order to allow for mathematical rigour. Contrary to Robbins, he does not interpret scientific objectivity as neutrality. He acknowledges the non-neutrality implicit in the construct of *homo oeconomicus*.

2 PRESCRIPTION RATHER THAN NON-NEUTRAL DESCRIPTION

In section 2.1.3 of chapter 4, I explained why Weber's interpretation of neo-classical economics as a toolbox for public policy is problematic. Instrumental relevance presupposes empirical validity (i.e., correspondence between scientific theories and human reality) and political (or practical) validity (i.e., conformity between the values underlying both the economic and the political perspective). Pearce adopts Weber's interpretation of neo-classical economics as a toolbox for public policy. More precisely, he considers his environmental economics as a toolbox for ecological policy. This implies, to start with, that Pearce does not remain a descriptive scientist, but starts acting as a prescriptive scientist. He acts, in other words, as a political actor in disguise. This implies, further, that he is more concerned with prediction than with explanation. In this section, I will deal with the first implication, while I will discuss the second implication in the following section.

In previous section, I already argued that Pearce's environmental economics is not simply practically (or politically) valid, because it makes a lot of normative choices that do not simply correspond to the choices people happen to make. In order to solve this lack of correspondence, Pearce simply (but implicitly) prescribes the set of values that should constitute political objectives, namely precisely the set of values defining his welfare-economic perspective. Pearce's environmental economics thus is prescriptive, rather than merely descriptive. It has to be prescriptive in order to be able to provide ecological policy with instrumental knowledge.

Pearce's welfare-economic approach prescribes, to start with, that levels of natural resources and private values should be expressed in monetary terms. Neurath would strongly object to this neo-classical convention to reduce everything to one single monetary unit (Neurath 1917, 123-126). In his view, the values of individuals are not commensurable, i.e., not reducible to one common measure. According to Neurath, the book-keeping-method typical of neo-classical economics does not inform us at all of natural processes or human happiness (Neurath 1931c, 342-343). He accuses political economists such as Hume and Smith of mixing time and again notions in kind with money calculations. In his view, these authors gradually introduced a capitalist calculation without adequate discussion of its consequences within the given social order. Finally, everything became reduced to costs and benefits. The application of these terms did not remain restricted to accountancy departments, but their use became generally accepted as adequate means for societal analysis. Economics became chrematistics (Neurath 1917, 123-126).

Pearce's welfare-economic approach prescribes, further, that the political objective of ecological policy is ("sustainable development" that easily comes down to) allocative efficiency. As a consequence, Pearce becomes an active defender of allocative efficiency, as soon as he starts working within a political context. Consider, as an illustration of Pearce playing this role of an active defender of allocative efficiency, the following quotation:

> In practice, standards are rarely set on the basis of cost-benefit considerations. [...] Most countries set standards according to public health criteria and the amount polluters can reasonably be expected to afford [...]. Only by accident, therefore, is the standard-setting procedure likely to produce an optimum [...]. This lack of attention to the efficiency characteristics of setting standards is one of the main criticisms that environmental economists make of real-world environmental policy (Pearce *et al.* 1993b, 204).

Pearce's environmental economics does not only prescribe "allocative efficiency" as the main objective of ecological policy. "Allocative efficiency" functions at the same time as a criterion with which to judge politics. Pearce very often distrusts government interventions because they are considered to yield less *efficient* outcomes than markets do. For that reason he prefers to restrict government interventions to solve environmental problems which cannot be left to market forces (for instance, because they have the character of a joint-impact good). And in those latter cases of unavoidable government interventions, he prefers the economic incentives approach to the regulatory approach (see, for instance, his comments on environmental standard setting in Turner *et al.* (1994, 190-191)). Allocative efficiency thus is the fundamental evaluative criterion with which he judges the outcomes of actual politics. This efficiency criterion can concern the realisation of either intra-generational welfare or inter-generational justice.

In section 3.3.1 of chapter 5, I explained that allocative efficiency, as an independent criterion, only has meaning when referring to actions of economic decision units *within* a particular economy. As soon as one discusses the allocative efficiency *of* a particular economy, the concept loses its independent meaning. Neurath would agree. He objects that economic efficiency does not have meaning without referring to particular units. The (allocative) "efficiency" of a specific economy – a specific "order of life" – does not equal the aggregate of individual values. An economist can at most make "silhouettes" of different orders of life (Neurath 1944, 962-963). A silhouette consists of a description of different features of a specific order of life which are deemed relevant for human happiness, for instance, its illiteracy, health, quality of human relations, freedom, food, shelter, clothing, employment, etc. These silhouettes result from "measurements in kind". A measurement in kind offers an overview of different units (such as the quantity of material and energetic resources present in certain places at certain times, the quantity and kind of labour force, the stage of technological development, etc.) and of their changing presence and application (Neurath 1917, 116-117). Silhouettes are at most comparable with each other, but they are certainly not commensurable.

> There are no units that can be used as the basis of such a decision [to choose one or another order of life; MD], neither units of money nor hours of work. One must directly judge the desirability of the two [or more; MD] possibilities (Neurath 1919b, 146)[3].

In Neurath's view, measurement in kind is unavoidable, since one cannot reduce the efficiency of a silhouette to one unit. Measurement in kind (or "economy in kind") is the opposite of a money economics, which reduces all units to the money standard.

The prescriptive nature of Pearce's environmental economics relates to the ambiguity of the concept "allocative efficiency". This ambiguity parallels the ambiguity of the economic scientist. Either the economist is (in a non-neutral way) descriptive, i.e. he does not evaluate market results according to an (implicit or explicit) criterion that is external to neo-classical theory. In that case, the only thing he can do is, given the existing institutional organisation of an economy, helping economic actors to make better choices by scientifically ameliorating their bounded rationality. Or the economist does evaluate market results – and the political decisions giving rise to them - according to an (implicit or explicit) criterion external to neo-classical theory. In that case, next to being (and being inevitably) non-neutral, he or she is even (though not necessarily) prescriptive. Welfare economists are – even Robbins agrees - in the latter situation. According to Robbins, welfare economics has to abandon the label of a "positive" science. In his view, the *raison d'être* of welfare economics is the desirability to recommend public policy. Economic recommendations, however, can never be 'a matter of scientific demonstration', since it is not simply based on "objective" facts and logical deductions (Robbins 1984, xx), but also on rather arbitrary assumptions (Robbins 1984, 57;63). Welfare economics

> depends upon the technical apparatus of analytical Economics; but it applies this apparatus to the examination of schemes for the realisation of aims whose formulation lies outside Economics (Robbins 194, xxviii).

To conclude, Pearce's environmental economics is prescriptive. It is prescriptive because it is used to evaluate political decisions and prescribe political objectives. Though Pearce concedes at times that citizens can have other political objectives than the objective of allocative efficiency, this latter objective emerges in his political recommendations as the single inclusive objective that is intended to accommodate all other objectives. Pearce's non-neutrality thus becomes problematic as soon as it does not only define the perspective from which to describe, i.e., to do empirical observations, but also defines the criterion with which people should evaluate and citizens and politicians should decide.

---

[3] Consider the following example offered by Neurath and interesting from an ecological point of view: 'More difficult is the case where higher consumption of raw materials goes with less work. The question might arise, should one protect coal mines or put greater strain on men? The answer depends for example on whether one thinks that hydraulic power may be sufficiently developed or that solar heat might come to be better used, etc. If one believes the latter, one may "spend" coal more freely and will hardly waste human effort where coal can be used. If however one is afraid that when one generation uses too much coal thousands will freeze to death in the future, one might well use more human power and save coal' (Neurath 1928, 263).

3 PREDICTION RATHER THAN EXPLANATION

Pearce does not question the empirical validity of his environmental economics. To start with, he considers his materials balance model as a contribution to its empirical validity. This model allows for a constant "monitoring" of ecological phenomena and of economic behaviour in order to be able to constantly re-adjust the relevant economic institutions.

> [...] macroeconomic monitoring is not itself an *instrument* of sustainable development policy, but it is a precondition for rational policy (Pearce *et al.* 1989, 153).

> If an effective management of the natural and environmental and resource base is to be achieved, policy makers need to have access to a consistent, reliable and comparable data set, relating to the availability and use of such resources. Such information is gathered with increasing frequency at the national and international level and it would be difficult to over estimate the importance of these endeavours. One special approach, which is part of this exercise, is an attempt to present the relevant information within an [physical or monetary] accounting framework (Pearce *et al.* 1989, 93)[4].

Moreover, Pearce's belief in the empirical validity of environmental economics implies trust in the predictive power of economic instruments recommended. In his view, economic science is meant to provide public authorities with *rational* advice on

> both their objectives (or more strictly the implications of different objectives) and on the means to achieve these objectives (Pearce *et al.* 1990a, 21).

Environmental economics as an instrumental science is a means to help public authorities to *manage* the environment via a *management* of the actions of producers and consumers.

> While [natural] scientific evidence is essential to identify the extent of the problem, the policy questions are largely ones for social science. The problem can only be addressed through changing human behaviour - altering the demand for environmental services and changing and controlling their supply. Indeed, a major feature of the modern environmental debate is the widespread acceptance of the role which economics must play in analysing causal processes of environmental decay and in formulating policy (Pearce *et al.* 1993d, 2).

Contrary to Pearce, Neurath strongly denies the empirical validity of neo-classical theory. In Neurath's view, neo-classical economics fails as an empirical science, precisely because of its aiming at mathematical rigour and because of its reduction of *economic* rationality to *economical* rationality.

To start with his first reason, Neurath states that neo-classical economics is under the influence of Auguste Comte's idea of a pyramidal structure of unified science. It considers the successful physical sciences as the exemplar of modern science and, impressed by its mathematical form, it introduces money calculations and reduces everything to single index numbers, which allow for a far going mathematisation.

---

[4] Note that Pearce's materials balance model offers at most empirical regularities, but does not provide conceptual knowledge. It does not make – it even does not aim at making – these empirical regularities comprehensible.

> Value systems and whole mountains of value were constructed precisely in order to make mathematical methods applicable. Often this method is worked out very ingeniously, except that it fails just where it should lead to the derivation of complicated relations: namely, for a crisis (Neurath 1931c, 398).

As a consequence of its striving for mathematisation, economics became a theory which worried more about logical consistency than about its practical relevance for societal reality (Neurath 1917, 117).

With regard to the typical neo-classical reduction of the economic subject to *homo economicus,* Neurath states that science must develop from inductive generalisation (empiricism), rather than from abstract deduction (rationalism) (Neurath 1941, 225). The ideal type of *homo economicus* rather resembles a metaphysical synthetic *a priori* that, just like the *a priori* use of mathematical methods, violates empiricist sensibilities (Cartwright *et al.* 1996, 125-127). For on the one hand *homo economicus* is considered an isolated individual, whose values are independent from the values of other individuals. This contradicts Neurath's experience of humans as social beings, who take over the customs of their contemporaries that are influenced by tradition and by their material surroundings. On the other hand, *homo economicus* is deemed an autonomous individual, whose actions are considered to be completely defined by purposive motives. This is in contradiction with social behaviourism that shows human beings partly acting consciously and partly reacting unconsciously to stimuli (Neurath 1917, 109; 1931c, 411). Moreover, the *homo economicus* of neo-classical theory is described as a self-interested individual endowed with economic goods and one overarching motive, the profit motive (Cartwright et al. 1996, 126). This ideal-typical description ignores altruistic motives of concrete living people.

To conclude, Pearce's environmental economics aims – to use Dugger's terminology (see section 2.3 in chapter 4) – for predictive models. It does not try to explain human behaviour by situating it as accurately as possible in its institutional and cultural context. It tries to explain human behaviour by deducing it from carefully specified assumptions. Not the empirical adequacy of the patterns developed matters. For both the basic assumptions – no matter how evident – and the assumption of economic rationality – that comes down to trivial economical rationality (see section 2.1.2 in chapter 3) – are selected from an empirical reality that is much richer. In Weber's view, precisely these selective choices define the perspective of neo-classical theory and are illustrations of its non-neutrality. Neo-classical theory is mainly concerned with the logical consistency and mathematical rigour of its predictions. And Pearce's environmental economics is, in this respect, faithful to its neo-classical roots.

4 PARTIALITY

In section 3 of chapter 4, I worked out the idea of an impartial science as a science that stimulates citizens and politicians to act as free and equal individuals. In order to do that, it offers insights into sources of political inequality and of lacking political freedom. In order to stimulate political freedom, it clarifies the relationships between the institutional organisation on the one hand and the kind and distribution of existing private interests on the other. In order to stimulate political equality, it points to sources preventing a balanced expression of a variety of perspectives. Contrary to impartial science, partial science considers existing (distributions of) private interests as given. It offers insights in how to act strategically, given the existing distribution of political power, in order to realise a given goal as efficiently and as effectively as possible.

Rather than helping citizens to abstract from their existing private interests, Pearce's environmental-economic approach invites them to stick to their given interests. This becomes obvious in his requirement to express values in monetary terms. This requirement asks people to make their valuations fit in their private income.

To start with, this obligation leaves the possibility open that certain people have very little or no money available for something they, however, value very much. So-called "part-whole bias" of the contingent valuation method is illustrative for this possibility (Turner et al. 1994, 126). If people are first asked their willingness to pay for one part of an environmental asset (e.g. one lake in an entire system of lakes) and then asked to value the whole asset (e.g. the whole lake system) the amounts stated may be similar. The reason for this appears to lie in how people allocate their spending. They first divide their income up into several broad budget categories (e.g. housing, food, car, and recreation) and they then subdivide each category between the actual items purchased. Consequently, the more environmental goods and services get endangered and are tried to impute an economic value on, the less money people have available for each good or service given their budget constraints. Put more extremely, the total economic value of environmental goods and services can never exceed the total sum of private incomes (and this is already an unrealistic limit situation, since people often have more urgent needs). The more ecological phenomena are threatened, the less their exchange value will be.

The obligation to express economic values in monetary terms results, moreover, in valuations that privilege the preferences of the wealthier part of the population. Monetary valuation methods take current distributions of income as a starting point. Consequently, it is quite possible that, for instance, the same ecological damage that occurs in or nearby different countries gets completely different economic valuations. Briassoulis and Van der Straaten give the example of the EXXON Valdez oil spill on the Alaskan coast some years ago. As there are many US citizens and as their average income is one of the highest in the world, the (contingent) valuation result was very high. Had the same oil spill taken place on the coast of Denmark (a small country with only 5 million inhabitants and a relatively high income) the outcome would be a relatively low figure. With Gambia and Nicaragua, two small countries with a low level of income, the outcome would have been considerably lower than in the Danish case, and would have been a very small fraction of the Alaskan result (Briassoulis & Van der Straaten 1999, 131)[5].

Pearce's political involvement – Pearce was and is involved with environmental policy within the UK, the EU and of the UN-organisation – provided him with several political experiences that made him sensible for political power relationships. His welfare-economic approach does, however, not supply him with the intellectual aids to analyse (at least the economic sources of) these unequal power relationships. In Pearce's writings one can therefore discern an ambiguous position towards them. Either he provides public authorities with recommendations that he deems correct from his welfare-economic perspective but that are, nevertheless, unacceptable in actual politics (for instance, because of existing power structures or because of existing ideologies, values, world views) and he then blames public authorities for ignoring them. This way to deal with the problem can be heard in the following quotation:

> In practice, standards are rarely set on the basis of cost-benefit considerations. [...] Most countries set standards according to public health criteria and the amount polluters can reasonably be expected to afford [...]. Only by accident, therefore, is the standard-setting procedure likely to produce an optimum [...]. This lack of attention to the efficiency characteristics of setting standards is one of the main criticisms that environmental economists make of real-world environmental policy (Pearce *et al.* 1993b, 204).

Or he adapts his recommendations to (his estimates of) existing power structures in order to augment the chance that public authorities will implement them. This kind of reasoning can be heard in this quotation (dealing with the issue of initial permits):

> The reality of the international political economy is likely to work against any system that allocates permits based on population. Such system would require assurance at the outset that international trade in permits would take place, otherwise the burden of adjustment would fall heavily and rapidly on the countries with high emissions per capita, such as the United States. In those circumstances, such countries are unlikely to agree at the outset. Grandfathering of some kind is likely to be the only initial allocation acceptable to the existing polluters (Pearce *et al.* 1993b, 387).

To conclude, Pearce's environmental economics does not stimulate people to act as free individuals. Rather than helping people to abstract from their private interests – through providing them with insights into the relationships between the institutional organisation of the economy they live in on the one hand and the definition and distribution of private interests on the other -, it stresses and re-enforces the private interests people happen to have. Pearce's environmental economics does not help people to act as equal individuals either. It is not able to offer citizens and official politicians insights into the economic sources of political power relationships. It

---

[5] In Pearce's publications one can find an enumeration of the problems and limitations of the varying monetary valuation methods (e.g. Turner *et al.* 1994, 114-128). In Pearce's view, these limitations are, however, no reason for discrediting these methods. 'However, we remain convinced that such valuation methods have an important role to play and, if carefully applied, provide valid and reliable estimates. Explicit valuation via these methods is preferable to implicit valuations where the link to individuals and their preferences is unclear or non-existent' (Turner *et al.* 1994, 127). Therefore, Pearce pleads for a 'great deal more research' in order to ameliorate the techniques in question (Pearce *et al.* 1990a, 158).

considers political deliberations as an exercise of balance between the various parties in a given power landscape.

5 CONCLUSION

Pearce's scientific approach is non-neutral. According to Pearce, his "sustainable development" ideal and the ideal of Pareto-optimality testify, indeed, of specific ethical choices. Pearce has no problem with acknowledging this non-neutrality. Pearce believes, nevertheless, in the (non-neutral) objectivity of environmental economics. Non-neutral objectivity is, in his view, identical with empirically observable data, logical consistency and mathematical rigour. These three aspects guarantee the non-neutral empirical validity of Pearce's environmental economics. Pearce considers, moreover, that the particular non-neutrality of his environmental economics is justified, for two reasons. First, because he deems the values constituting his particular non-neutral perspective as practically valid. One can, his line of reasoning goes, observe that (most) people aim at "sustainable development". Second, because no convincing arguments exist to prefer another value to the value of Pareto-optimality.

I do not contest that Pearce's environmental economics is, in a certain sense, objective. I do, however, not agree that the non-neutrality of his environmental economics is justified because it is practically valid, for two reasons. First, in order to make the ideal of "sustainable development" operational, Pearce has to make several normative choices that are not necessarily practically (or politically) valid. Second, practical validity of the values constituting a scientific perspective does not yet justify this perspective. I agree with Weber that scientists should not necessarily be contented with prevailing values, but can take a critical stance towards them. A critical perspective is likely to stimulate political debates more than an "evident" perspective.

Pearce considers his environmental economics as a toolbox for public policy. This interpretation causes Pearce on many occasions to stop acting as a descriptive scientist and to start acting as a prescriptive politician in disguise. Pearce does not show much sensibility for political objectives other than (ambiguous) "allocative efficiency". Allocative efficiency is, according to Pearce's environmental economics, an all-embracing objective of ecological policy and a main standard with which to judge actual politics. This interpretation causes Pearce, moreover, to be rather concerned with prediction than with explanation. Pearce is not interested in explaining the internal relationships between the institutional organisation of an economy and its ecological performance. He is rather interested in monitoring the ecological in- and outputs of an economy, in making an inventory of the monetary values people impute to ecological entities, and in prescribing economic instruments that manage people's behaviour as effective and as efficient as possible – given neo-classical assumptions about economic rationality are empirically valid - in the direction of "sustainable development". Pearce's environmental economics is rather of an "exact" than of a "historical" kind

Finally, Pearce's welfare-economic approach is a partial science. It does not offer scientific insights into economic power relationships nor into the relationships between the institutional organisation of an economy and the definition and distribution of private interests. Instead of inviting political actors to abstract from their private interests, it stimulates them to stress the interests they happen to have. Instead of providing political actors with insights that offset existing power relationships, it re-enforces the idea that politics is a bargaining process between various parties with given power and given interests. The interpretation of politics underlying Pearce's environmental economics bears more resemblance to Buchanan's than to Arendt's interpretation.

CHAPTER 7

A RECONSTRUCTION OF BROMLEY'S ECONOMICS

This chapter is a reconstruction of the writings of Daniel Bromley[1]. Bromley is a resource economist. He is professor at the Department of Agricultural and Applied Economics (University of Wisconsin-Madison), where he teaches Institutional Economics and Natural Resource Economics. Next to his teaching and research activities, he works as a consultant within more political contexts such as, for instance, the World Bank and the Ministry for the Environment (New Zealand).

Bromley's economics bears more likeness with ecological than with environmental economics (according to Munda's classification). Bromley's approach to ecological problems is, for instance, an institutional one (see section 1). His institutional analysis concentrates on property rights as one type of economic institutions and on property regimes as a hierarchical set of property rights (see section 2). Bromley recognises the impossibility of a value free science and criticises monetary reductionism (see the next chapter). From his writings one can, however, not unequivocally conclude that Bromley is an adherent of the "strong sustainability" criterion. His abstract interpretation of "sustainability" is not simply compatible with the idea of an "optimal" ecological scale (see section 4.3).

Bromley's institutional perspective makes his approach, from the very beginning, more in agreement with the interpretation (proposed in chapter 3) that the ecological performance of an economy is the counterpart of its institutional organisation than is Pearce's approach. Bromley's analysis of property rights and property regimes gives, for instance, rise to a particular understanding of externalities. This understanding, with which I deal in section 3, is one concrete illustration of this internal connection between ecological performance and institutional organisation. Bromley's analysis of property rights and property regimes is, however, not capable of explaining – what I referred to in chapter 1 as - the growing tension between the idea of sustainability on the one hand and general ecological tendencies on the other. In section 4, I will argue that Bromley's attitude with regard to the distinction between the political and the economic sphere is ambiguous. On the one hand, he

[1] Bromley commented on (an earlier version of) my reconstruction of his writings. I gratefully took his comments into consideration and integrated them as far as possible into the final version presented in this chapter. It goes without saying that I take full responsibility for this final reconstruction.

objects to the conventional idea that institutional changes of an economy are prompted by the only motive of allocative efficiency. He thus denies that the rationality of institutional change is simply economic. On the other hand, he is reluctant in distinguishing between political and economic rationality. In this same section, I will comment briefly on Bromley's own interesting, but abstract interpretation of "sustainability".

1 AN INSTITUTIONAL APPROACH

Bromley's interpretation of an economy is constituted by two elements, namely by the rationality of economic actions and by the ensemble of economic institutions conditioning this rationality. To explain his interpretation of the subject matter of economics, Bromley refers to Oliver Williamson's approach (Bromley 1989, 40). Williamson is interested in economic agents' patterns of behaviour elicited from rules and conventions organising *market* transactions *between* economic decision units and *hierarchical* transactions *within* economic decision units. With regard to economic agents' behaviour, Williamson applies two behavioural assumptions (which Bromley retains): bounded rationality and opportunism.

> The former implies a limited ability of individuals to be perfectly rational in the face of non-trivial information costs, while the latter refers to the seeking of self-interest with guile (Bromley 1989, 40).

These behavioural assumptions make the subject matter of Bromley's economics resemble (a modern version of) what Robbins would call an analytical definition of economics[2]. The study of the rationality of economic agents' behaviour is the first element in Bromley's interpretation of the subject matter of economics.

The second element in Bromley's interpretation of the subject matter of economics regards the institutional organisation of an economy. Bromley defines two kinds of what he considers to be economic activities: commodity and institutional transactions (Bromley 1989, 49). Commodity transactions (or, in Williamson's terminology, market transactions) refer to the selling of goods and services. This kind of transactions comprises all activities that are consistent with the choice sets of independent economic actors, given the conventions and entitlements that define these choice sets. These transactions are in this sense "autonomous". According to Bromley, most of economics is concerned with this domain of commodity transactions. The second domain of economic activity concerns the conventions and entitlements that regularise the market processes through which commodities move. In this domain there are transactions over these conventions and entitlements. Bromley calls them institutional transactions. Institutional transactions are meant to transform the "rules of the game" that offer structure, order, stability and predictability to market processes. These latter transactions are also more ore less "rational" and "opportunist", though the meaning of "rationality" with regard to

---

[2] This interpretation of the subject matter of economics is also called the formal (Dietz *et al.* 1994, 15) approach.

institutional transactions differs from its meaning with regard to commodity transactions. While the latter kind of "rationality" is defined by the institutional structure of an economy, the former kind depends on changing economic conditions (such as technological innovation, population growth and changing tastes and preferences) that urge for institutional adaptations (Bromley 1991, 8).) Bromley pleads for an extension of the subject matter of (conventional) economics to this second domain.

> By recognizing both commodity transactions and institutional transactions, the economist will be able to see markets as manifestations of the legal foundations of the economy, and economics will then be seen not only as the study of the exchange processes that are defined by those foundations, but also as the study of those very foundations (Bromley 1989, 49).

The study of these legal foundations, i.e. of the institutional organisation of an economy, conforms to the ('old') institutional approach.

For both Williamson and Bromley, the analytical and institutional element of the subject matter of economics cannot be separated. The institutional organisation of an economy influences economic agents' behaviour and *vice versa*: the ("rational" and "opportunist") behaviour of economic decision units influences an economy's institutional organisation.

I have two remarks with regard to Bromley's definition of the subject matter of economics. The first remark considers his interpretation of economic rationality as the (analytical) element defining this subject matter. In section 2.1.2 of chapter 3, I explained, with the help of examples offered by Bromley, that economic rationality is the same as economising rationality. I explained, further, that this kind of economising rationality should not be considered as typical for actions occurring in the economic sphere, but is implied in all kinds of instrumental actions. Since the private preferences of economic actors can, in principle, be both egoistic and altruistic, I see no reason to label this economising rationality as opportunistic. The examples offered by Bromley show, moreover, that the choices economic actors make cannot be equalled to their private preferences, that one can even not derive their private preferences from their choices, that one does not need to know their private preferences in order to know what strategies will become dominant in a particular institutional context, and consequently that one does not need to know their private preferences in order to make the social or ecological performance of a particular institutional organisation understandable.

I agree with Bromley that one can discern a typical economic rationality. Typical for an *economic* rationality is that it is an *economising* rationality. This rationality is of an instrumental kind (see section 2.1.2 in chapter 3). Its end is optimal satisfaction of economic decision units' private preferences. This rationality is, however, not necessarily of an opportunistic kind. Economic actors' preferences can be of an egoistic or altruistic kind, but they are certainly private. Economic actors' preferences are, further, institutionally stimulated or tempered. This implies that economising rationality only gains concrete content (and thus manifests a particular social or ecological performance) within a particular institutional context. In other words, *economising* rationality becomes *economic* rationality within a set of economic institutions. This implies, contrary to Bromley's and Williamson's belief, that institutional change is not a simple matter of economic rationality. (I will come back on this topic in section 4.) This economic rationality is, finally, subject to limited information.

My second remark considers Bromley's interpretation of institutional transactions as *economic* activities. I will argue, in section 4, that it is not obvious to label institutional transactions as economic rather than political activities. This second remark does, however, not detract from Bromley's assertion to consider of economics as the study of the legal foundations, i.e. the institutional organisation, conditioning economic activities. Even stronger, since economising rationality only gains concrete content – and becomes really economic – within a particular economy, I believe that this study is the very essence of his approach.

To recapitulate, to present Bromley's approach as an institutional approach does not contradict presenting it as an analytical approach. Bromley's institutional approach allows for making the abstract analytical approach more concrete. It aims at explaining the institutions that give concrete content to economising rationality. In other words, it aims at explaining what makes an abstract economising rationality a concrete economic rationality. Bromley's institutional approach does not imply that economic rationality should be interpreted as an opportunistic rationality. Individuals can try to satisfy egoistic as well as altruistic, but surely private preferences. This does, however, not mean that the institutions conditioning economic rationality directly result from (an aggregation of) private preferences. In section 4, I will explain why we should consider of institutional transactions as showing a political rather than economic rationality. This final remark does not detract at all from Bromley's argument to consider of economics as the study of the institutional context conditioning economic activities.

2 ECONOMIC INSTITUTIONS

Bromley's theoretical work concentrates on property rights and property regimes. He admits that property rights do not represent the whole set of economic institutions. This statement suggests that he has some idea of what makes institutions economic or, in other words, that he has some idea of what distinguishes an economy from other spheres within human reality. I will, therefore, in a first subsection deal with his interpretation of an economy as a particular sphere. In a second subsection, I will elaborate on his conceptual analysis of property rights and property regimes.

2.1 The Economic Sphere

Studying the legal foundations of an economy presupposes some idea of what defines an economy *vis-à-vis* other spheres within human reality. Some passages in

Bromley's writings suggest that the set of ordered relations that constitute market processes are distinctive for an economy (Bromley 1989, 47). A market is a regularised medium for the exchange of entitlements to future benefit streams. Markets themselves are defined by the ways in which those entitlements to future benefit streams are defined, by the way the entitlements to them are transmitted, and by the way these exchanges are enforced. The set of ordered relations that constitutes an economy thus not only comprises the entitlements to future benefit streams. It also contains the legal foundations that define the exchange of entitlements and the ways in which this exchange can be enforced[3].

According to Bromley, the set of ordered relations that constitute market processes covers more than the institutions that define what markets - "market" taken in the broadest sense, to include all voluntary exchange - exist (Bromley 1989, 41). It also covers those institutions that define how economic relations are regulated in areas where markets do not exist. To explain these extra-market economic relations Bromley introduces the concept 'decision unit' (Bromley 1989, 51). Voluntary exchange takes place between decision units that came into existence by convention or by conscious collective action. Individuals can be economic decision units, but also families, firms, schools, hospitals, etc.. Decision units - as well as markets - are social organisations defined by institutions. As mentioned in section 2.1.1 of chapter 3, one can distinguish two kinds of institutions relevant for economic organisations (Bromley 1989, 43). The first define an organisation *vis-à- vis* other organisations. The second spell out the internal nature of an organisation.

Institutional arrangements define the 'choice sets' of decision units, i.e. of consumers and producers (Bromley 1989, 52-54). For consumers, the choice set consists of the set of all feasible bundles x of goods and services in some set X (a set of goods and services). A feasible bundle is a bundle of goods and services out of the set X that a specific consumer finds affordable, given his or her income. If Y represents the consumer's income and $p = (p_1, \ldots, p_n)$ is the price vector for the goods in a bundle, then the consumer's choice set will be the set $B = \{x \text{ in } X; px < Y\}$. For producers, the choice set is the production set, say C. Changes in the aggregate of institutional arrangements change the choice sets of consumers and producers. These changes can follow from the introduction of new techniques that possibly allow for new products. They can also follow from, for instance, a legal ban on a chemical compound that turns out to be carcinogenic.

To recapitulate, in Bromley's view an economy is defined by the ensemble of institutions that define markets - i.e. entitlements to benefit streams, the exchange of entitlements to these benefit streams and the enforcement of this exchange - and

[3] The fact that Bromley defines an economy in terms of market processes, does not imply that he only has market economies in mind (Bromley 1989, 50). Both "centrally planned economies" and "market economies" are about the exchange of entitlements to future benefit streams. The aggregate of institutional arrangements, i.e. the prevailing structure of norms, conventions, rules, practices and laws that shape the choice sets of individuals or groups, differs, however, in both cases. In market economies institutional arrangements rather stress market *processes* than market *outcomes*, while in centrally planned economies rather the reverse is true.

extra-market relations - i.e. the type and internal nature of economic decision units -. Referring to section 2 in chapter 2, Bromley's conception of an economy takes - what I called - the overarching entry of the institutions defining economic goods, economic rationality and economic decision units as the entry constituting his perspective. The economic sphere is the sphere of the production, distribution and consumption of goods and services.

2.2 Property

In his writings, Bromley does not investigate the whole set of institutions constituting an economy. He concentrates on property rights as one important subclass of the institutional arrangements that define an economy (Bromley 1989, chapter 7). In addition to property rights, Bromley mentions 'rules of contract, bankruptcy and credit' (Bromley 1997, 43). The latter rules address transactional insecurity, while the former address possessional insecurity. Bromley calls the ensemble of the latter rules the legal foundations of exchange.

> The legal foundations of exchange concern the fundamental issue of securing contractual behaviour such that individual transactors need not undertake the task of enforcing their own exchange (Bromley 1993b, 148).

To comprehend property rights, one has, Bromley writes, to investigate three sets of variables: 1) the nature and kinds of rights that are exercised, and their correlative duties and obligations; 2) the individuals or groups in whom these rights and duties are vested, and those who play the correlative roles in the collectivity; and 3) the objects of social value over which these property relations pertain (Bromley 1989, 203). Bromley's scientific analysis remains mainly restricted to the first and second element The first element regards a conceptual analysis of "property rights".

The second regards a conceptual analysis of "property regimes". I will deal with both in the following subsections.

2.2.1 Property Rights

Bromley defines property rights as entitlements. Property rights - as all entitlements - only have effect when there is some authority system that agrees to defend a rights holder's interest in a particular outcome. The effective protection the rights holder gains from this authority corresponds to a correlated duty for all others interested in this claim.

> Rights can only exist when there is a social mechanism that gives duties and binds individuals to those duties (Bromley 1991, 15).

Bromley distinguishes between different types of rights. He thereby follows Honoré's analysis of ownership (Bromley 1989, 187). Ownership is, according to Honoré, defined by a list of eleven types of rights (Bromley 1989, 187-190). The right to possess, i.e. the right to exclusive physical control, lies at the centre of the notion of ownership. The right to use is a second characteristic. A third characteristic is the right to manage. The right to manage refers to ancillary rights such as the right to admit others to one's land, the power to permit others to use one's things, and to set limits of such permission. The right to manage is the right to contract with others over the benefit stream which arises from their use of the valuable asset. The fourth and fifth characteristics are the right to the income and to the capital. The latter right comprehends the power to alienate the valuable item, or to consume it, or to destroy it. The sixth characteristic is the right to security: this is immunity from arbitrary appropriation by an external authority. The seventh characteristic, transmissibility to a successor, makes an asset more valuable. One's property diminishes to the extent that transmissibility is restricted. The eighth characteristic is absence of term. Absence of term means that full ownership runs into perpetuity. The interests of an owner are best served by a determinable time horizon, where longer is more valuable than shorter. Perpetuity is the most valuable time horizon. The ninth characteristic concerns the prohibition of harmful use (where the meaning of "harmful use" is a political matter; MD). The tenth characteristic concerns the liability of the owner's interest to be used to settle debts. This characteristic is called "liability to execution". The eleventh and final characteristic is the right to residuary character. This right refers to social rules that govern situations in which ownership rights lapse. These rules decide what to do when, for whatever reason, the pre-existing ownership rights are no longer relevant.

Bromley notes that none of these eleven types of rights is a necessary constituent of ownership as such. Individuals or groups will be recognised to own something in a restricted sense where one or more of these types of rights is not met. Yet the more complete is the list of characteristics, the more thorough is one's ownership of something valuable. And the more thorough one's ownership, the more valuable it is. I guess, however, that ownership cannot exist without the right to possess. The right to possess lies, according to Honoré and to Bromley, at the centre of the concept of ownership. But what does it mean to have a right to possess? Bromley, following Kant, distinguishes between empirical and intelligible possession (Bromley 1991, 5). Empirical possession is about the physical appropriation of something. Physical appropriation, however, is only a necessary , not a sufficient condition for this thing to become my property. Only intelligible possession, i.e. a social convention or contract, constitutes property. The right to possess comes down to the assignment of certain rights with regard to some thing to an individual or a group, the recognition of these rights by the non-owners and the assurance to protect these rights by an authority. To conclude, the right to possess (in a physical sense) turns out to be nothing more than the possession (i.e. assignment, recognition and protection) of certain rights. Ownership thus is a rather abstract concept: it means that certain rights are assigned to a person or a group. The concrete meaning of ownership depends on the kind and content of the (property) rights that are assigned. The fact, for instance, that certain uses of a valuable asset are restricted, reduces the range of choice open to the owner of the asset. It does not diminish the content of ownership (Bromley 1989, 188). Ownership is not the same as absolute control (Bromley 1991, 159-161).

Bromley stresses the distinction between property as a set of entitlements on the one hand and property as related to the notion of ownership on the other. Property as related to ownership refers, according to Bromley's exposition, to the rights, duties, liabilities and privileges of an owner with regard to the thing he or she owns. A person is an owner of some-thing valuable if he or she has specific property rights. This "thing" can be a physical object of value, such as a piece of land or

> an automobile, a house, a Dali original, or a violin (Bromley 1989, 185; 202)

or some thing other than a physical object, such as

> job security, continued access to a stream of revenue from a natural resource, or the future income from one's creative talents (patent and copyright) (Bromley 1989, 185; 202).

Anyhow, ownership refers to the ensemble of property rights with regard to a valuable asset *belonging to a specific owner*, either an individual or a group. Property as a set of entitlements with regard to a valuable asset *tout court* relates to the notion of property regimes. I will deal with this notion in the following subsection.

2.2.2 Property Regimes

Bromley distinguishes between four types of property regimes. What Bromley means by a property regime becomes clear through an analysis of these four types. A property regime turns out to be a hierarchical set of property rights related to one and the same valuable asset and assigned to (a hierarchy of) various decision units. In the next paragraphs, I will first deal with the four types of property regimes Bromley proposes. Secondly, I will explain why a property regime is a hierarchical set of property rights.

Bromley discerns four types of property regimes: state property, private property, common property, and non-property (Bromley 1989, 205)[4]. In the first case an agency has the right to determine use and access rules. Individuals have a duty to observe these rules. In the second case individuals have a right to undertake socially acceptable uses and have a duty to refrain from socially unacceptable uses. Others, i.e. the non-owners, have a duty to refrain from preventing socially acceptable uses, and have a right to expect only socially acceptable uses will occur. In the third case , the group of owners or the management group has a right to exclude non-members of the group, and non-members have a duty to abide by exclusion. Individual members of the group have both rights and duties with respect to the use and maintenance of the thing owned. In case of non-property there is no defined group of owners. Individuals have both privilege and no right with respect to use rates and

[4] Bromley also uses the term "resource management regime" instead of "property regime" in case the valuable asset is an environmental resource. 'A resource management regime is a structure of rights and duties characterizing the relationship of individuals to one another with respect to that particular environmental resource' (Bromley 1991, 22).

maintenance of the asset. Its benefit stream is available to those who use the asset. The asset is an open-access resource[5].

The distinction Bromley makes between state property, private property and common property is more ambiguous than it looks at first sight. The differences are often rather gradual than strict. The habit to call specific property regimes private, common or state property results partly form conventions rather than from analytical dissimilarities. Consider, for instance, the case of common property in the following example offered by Bromley. Bromley writes:

> [...] Consider the extension of exclusive economic zones for fishing access. As certain nations experienced decreased catches with their existing fleets it became of great significance who had access to natural resources that were formerly assumed to be inexhaustible. The extension to 200 miles created a larger zone of common property for each coastal nation as opposed to the former open-access situation. Once the fishing zone was declared to be the common property to a particular coastal state, that nation was then able to define the particular institutional arrangements that would give its citizens access to the resource (Bromley 1989, 218).

This example shows that in case a community happens to be a state, a common property regime is the same as a state property regime. In both the case of a common property regime and of a state property regime, a particular authority has to decide about use and access rules. In case a common (or state) property regime is attached to fishing zones, the public authorities can, for instance, issue or sell quota. These quota define who has access to the fishing zones (namely those who possess quota) and what use of the fishing zone is acceptable (namely a catch rate that does not exceed the quota assigned). Those who possess fishing quota then have the (private) right to use the fishing zone and the (private) right to benefit from the produce of their fishing activities. This latter consideration shows that a common (or state) property regime does not exclude private rights. It only shows that the kind and nature of rights belonging to the state or another community and those belonging to individual members of this community differ. This is already an illustration of the hierarchical nature of property regimes.

Other passages in Bromley's writings support my thesis that the classification of property regimes as private, common or state property is not precise. Bromley writes, for instance, that,

> [f]irst, common property represents *private property for the group of co-owners* (since all others are excluded from use and decision making). Second, *individuals* have rights (and duties) in a common property regime (Ciriacy-Wantrup and Bishop, 1975). In one important sense, then, common property has something very much in common with private property - exclusion of non-owners. In that sense we may think of common property as *corporate group property* (Bromley 1991, 25).

At the same time, Bromley writes:

---

[5] In the history of environmental and ecological economics, Bromley's introduction of the distinction between a common property and a non-property regime implied a fundamental critique of Hardin's arguments – in his article *The Tragedy of the Commons* (1968) - in favour of private property as a means to solve ecological problems (Nelissen *et al.* 1997, 85-86).

> While most think of private property as individual property, note that all corporate property is private property, and yet it is administered by a group. There is also a tendency to consider private property as bestowing full and absolute control on the owner. However, it is well to keep in mind that an owner is faced with a number of strictures and obligations in the use of so-called "private" land and its related natural resources; few owners are entirely free to do as they wish with such assets (Bromley 1991, 24).

Both quotations illustrate that the distinction between a private and a common property regime is not sharp at all. Different rights are assigned to individuals and to groups with regard to one and the same asset.

In section 1.3 of chapter 3, I stress that rights do not only correlate to duties, but also to privileges. A specific right defines the privileges a right-holder has. This latter correlation is helpful to understand property regimes as a hierarchical set of entitlements. Each (property) right is not only assigned to an individual or a group, it is also decided on (or at least acknowledged with) its concrete content. The assignment of a right and the definition (and recognition) of its content is a matter of the collectivity (or an authorised part of the collectivity) to which the right-holder belongs. This means that a hierarchical relationship exists between the right-holder and the collectivity with regard to the right in question. Since each right at the same time correlates to privileges, the right-holder in his, her or its turn can decide on the content and the assignment of the rights that are compatible with the initial right. The right-holder again creates a hierarchical relationship between him-, her- or itself and the person or group to which he assigns the secundary rights. The fact that rights correlate to privileges thus allows for a layering or hierarchy of rights. A property regime refers to the whole hierarchical set of property rights related to a particular valuable asset and assigned to various decision units.

The decision units assigning and defining rights can be political (for instance, a state) or economic (for instance, a firm). Whether they are political or economic depends on the institutional arrangements that define them as either political or economic. Where the polity ends and the economy starts is not a natural, but a (politically) institutionalised fact. I suppose that conventional distinctions between state and private property regimes have something to do with the degrees of freedom left to economic decision units. The smaller the part of the institutional hierarchy that resides in political decision units and the greater the part that resides in economic ones, the more "private" a property regime is. And *vice versa*: the greater the part that resides in political decision units and the smaller the part that resides in economic ones, the more "common" a property regime is. For that reason I deem it adequate to call the distinction between private and state property regimes rather gradual than strict. I do not agree with Bromley's suggestion that a major distinction among (the first three) types of resource management regimes rests with the decision-making process inherent in each property regime (Bromley 1991, 31). Each layer in the hierarchy of institutional arrangements that constitutes a specific property regime allows for (a specific type of) decision-making processes.

2.3 Conclusion

According to Bromley, property rights are entitlements to future benefit streams. These entitlements are related to a valuable asset. An owner is a decision unit – either an individual or a group – that has a right to "possess" a valuable asset. This right to "possess", i.e. to control autonomously, turns out to refer to a set of rights that are assigned, recognised and enforced by an authority.

Bromley's conceptual analysis of property rights shows that it does not suffice to know that a particular decision unit has a right to exchange, use, manage, and so on, a particular valuable asset. One also has to know the precise content of these rights. Under what conditions is the right-holder allowed to exchange? What kind of uses are permitted? What are the boundary conditions for the management of one's possession? The concrete content of (restraining and enabling) rights assigned to a right-holder (either a group or an individual) must be decided on by an authority. This need for defining the concrete content creates a hierarchical relationship between the authority on the one hand and the right-holder on the other. Because this decided on concrete content can never be so concrete that it does not leave open some degrees of freedom – rights imply privileges -, rights-holders can in their turn act as authorities assigning rights and deciding on their content. Consequently, one can imagine a layering of authorities and, hence, an institutional hierarchy. This institutional hierarchy is of a genetic kind (see section 2.2.3.1 in chapter 3). Bromley's analysis concentrates not so much on the concrete content of property rights, but on their formal relationships. The possibility of a genetic hierarchy of property rights follows from the nature of entitlements as both restraining and enabling.

Bromley calls this hierarchy of property rights a property regime. A property regime thus is a hierarchical set of property rights related to a particular valuable asset. The property rights constituting the regime are assigned to various "owners". In short, a property regime refers to a valuable asset, while ownership refers to a particular owner. A property regime relates to a hierarchy of owners. For that reason, ownership as autonomous (or exclusive) control does not imply absolute control.

Bromley's conceptual analysis of property regimes shows, further, that for a specific resource , not so much the type of property regime matters. The designation of a specific type is rather a matter of convention than of analytical distinction. More important than the (analytically vague) type of a property regime is the kind and the concrete content of the different property rights that are assigned to a group, a subgroup or to concrete individuals with regard to one and the same valuable asset. Instead of distinguishing between different types of property regimes, as Bromley does, it is analytically more precise to investigate what (kind and nature of) rights related to one and the same valuable asset belong to a group, to a subgroup or to individuals. In order to solve particular ecological problems, one should, consequently, not spend too much energy discussing whether a common or a private property regime is more effective. One should spend energy discussing the concrete content and the respective owners of the rights that should constitute the property regimes that relate to the ecological problem in question.

From Bromley's explanation, I conclude, moreover, that it is property regimes that define a "thing" as an economic good. Bromley's institutional approach turns out to concentrate on the (hierarchical ensemble of) institutions defining economic goods. In other words, Bromley's institutional perspective is constituted, more precisely, by what I called – in section 2 of chapter 2 – the first entry, namely (the entitlements defining) the "products" of economic action, i.e. commodities or economic goods and services.

It is property regimes that define whether a commodity is, to use conventional economic concepts, a private or a public good. The former commodity is defined by a private property regime; the latter by a common property regime. This conclusion demonstrates that the distinction between private and public goods is analytically as vague as is the distinction between private and public property regimes. This conclusion shows, moreover, that *both the "public" and the "private"* characteristic of economic goods and services is, what I called in section 1.4. of chapter 3, a public fact. In both cases, it is political decisions that transform a "thing" into either a "public" or a "private" good.

Property regimes define the rights and privileges various "owners" of one and the same valuable asset have (and the concomitant duties and non-rights of non-owners). They thus explain the choice sets of economic actors with regard to one asset. Actions of economic actors are, however, linked to more than one asset. Economic actions must, consequently, be compatible with the various choice sets related to the various assets used. An analysis of the property regimes relevant for a particular economic action thus throws light on the *possible* strategies an economic actor can set out in order to fulfil his, her or its private preferences. In other words, it throws light on economic actors' autonomy. Such analysis does, however, not explain plausible *actual* strategies. For the latter kind of explanation, we need further insights into the economic institutions defining economic rationality. I suppose that actual strategies depend on economic actors' income – relative to the income of other economic actors - and on the (kind, magnitude, certainty of) future benefit streams they can expect from their actions. Apart from an analysis of property regimes, we thus need an analysis of institutions defining (future) benefit streams and an analysis of institutional reasons for existing distributions of income. Bromley's approach does not offer us the latter kinds of analyses.

3 THE RELATIONSHIP BETWEEN AN ECONOMY AND ITS ECOLOGICAL ENVIRONMENT

In chapter 3 I argue that an institutional approach towards an economy allows us to comprehend the ecological performance of an economy as the counterpart of its institutional organisation. Two topics in Bromley's writings testify of, and thus support, this hypothesis. The first topic relates to the distinction he makes between "nominal" and "real" boundaries of economic decision units. The second topic regards his treatment of "externalities" (Bromley 1989, 54-57).

3.1 *Nominal* versus *Real Boundaries*

According to Bromley, the nominal boundary of an economic decision unit is the boundary or the frontier that divides market processes from command processes. An economic decision unit is, indeed, defined with reference to the range of choice for command decisions, i.e. extra-market control. This range depends on the constellation of rights that determines the domain over which an economic decision unit has control and in which it is immune for the interference of other parties. The nominal domain of an economic decision unit is that which is presumed by it and which is defended in legislative and judicial proceedings concerning the firm's managerial autonomy from the larger society. The real boundary of an economic decision unit, however, is constituted by the physical (or ecological) and social dimensions of its nominal boundary. When a firm uses in its production process, for instance, a (legally accepted) chemical compound that is found to be carcinogenic then its autonomous choice holds important implications that, according to Bromley, are

> beyond the recognised "boundary" of the firm (Bromley 1989, 55).

This firm uses certain services - and visits disservices on other firms and on consumers - for which contractual agreements and compensation may or may not exist. This domain of all the valuable services used and disservices created by an economic decision unit is its real domain. Legal arrangements define the nominal domain - the domain of autonomous action - of an economic decision unit. Consequently, according to Bromley, collective action to alter the status quo will arise in case there is a divergence between the nominally presumed boundary of decision units and their real boundary as reflected in the scope of costs visited on others in society.

Bromley's definitions of the nominal and real domain of an economic decision unit are confusing. They suggest that the real domain of a decision unit comprises more than its nominal domain (consider the quotation mentioned in the previous paragraph). In fact, however, both domains are the same. The "real" and the "nominal" only refer to different perspectives on the same domain. The latter is the legal perspective: it considers the domain of "autonomous" economic action, i.e. of action that is nominally independent. The former considers the same domain in its physical and social dimension: since nominally autonomous actions interfere on a physical and social level with the actions of other parties, nominally independent decision units are linked physically and socially (Bromley 1991, 78). Bromley's distinction between the nominal and real domain of an economic decision unit does not refer to different domains, but to different perspectives on the same domain. The "real" perspective points to the ecological and social dimension of economic action. The "nominal" perspective points to its institutional dimension. This reformulation illustrates that the ecological and institutional dimensions of economic activities cannot be separated, or, in other words, that the relationship between economy and ecology is an internal one. Collective action does not arise because of a divergence between the nominal and the real boundary of decision units, as Bromley states. It arises because of a divergent appreciation for the physical and social impacts of legal arrangements defining the domain of nominally autonomous actions. An economic decision unit on the one hand and other members of a polity on the other often evaluate the ecological and social impacts of this decision unit's actions differently.

3.2 *Externalities*

This latter view, namely that it is the divergence in appreciation between different parties that matters, reveals itself in Bromley's treatment of externalities. The concept "externalities" originates from the conclusion that (because of the physical and social interdependence of nominally autonomous actions) costs fall beyond the boundary of the decision-making unit that is responsible for those costs (Bromley 1991, 59)[6]. Marshall and Pigou, following Adam Smith, thought of externalities as a divergence between private and social costs. Bromley stresses that to label this divergence in terms of "private" and "social" costs is to miss the essence of externalities (Bromley 1991, 19). What is at issue is the private interest of one party (Alpha) as against the private interest of another (Beta). This conviction of Bromley confirms my interpretation that collective action does not arise from a divergence between the nominal and real domain of an economic decision unit, but from a divergent appreciation for the physical or social impacts of one party's actions between the different parties affected.

Other passages in Bromley's analysis of externalities illustrate that Bromley regards the relationship between an economy and its ecological environment as an internal one. This internal connection becomes manifest in Bromley's arguments 1) that the kind of physical or social interference that occurs, and 2) that whether this interference get solved or not (and to what extent) depends on institutional arrangements. These arguments cannot be found as such in Bromley's writings. For that reason, I will reconstruct them by putting various of Bromley's lines of argument in a different (and sometimes slightly transformed) way together.

To start with, externalities are manifestations of (physical or social) interdependence or interference. Though all "autonomous" actions interfere physically or socially with other "autonomous" actions, not all situations of interference are externalities (Bromley 1991, 63)[7]. Whether physical interference is considered an externality

---

[6] Externalities are not necessarily "negative" or about "costs". They can also be positive, about benefits. However, as Bromley writes, 'while externalities can be either harmful or beneficial, the bulk of the environmental externalities that we deal with are of the harmful kind' (Bromley 1991, 68).

[7] That "autonomous" economic activities always interfere is easier to understand when one takes a specific economic activity as one's starting point of analysis. A specific economic activity always makes use of different resources for which different resource management regimes exist. Since each resource

depends on whether the costs of the physical interference passed on to the other party are deemed legitimate given existing legal arrangements. This can be illustrated with the following (slightly amended) example offered by Bromley (Bromley 1991, 160). Consider a house owner with a (legally protected) privilege to paint his house in whatever colour he likes. In case he is my neighbour and decides to paint his house some outlandish colour that does not match my own aesthetic taste, he burdens me with an externality. In this case two options are - in principle - open to me. Either I can try to buy his house and resell it to someone with an aesthetic taste that conforms to my own taste. Or I can offer my neighbour a sum of money to paint his house a somewhat more conventional colour. Whether these options are feasible - i.e. whether the externality will be solved - depends, among other things, on the relative size of my neighbour's and my own income. A different legal arrangement - for instance, a neighbourhood restriction on house colours - would keep my neighbour from painting his house in an unconventional way. In case he, nevertheless, does paint it this way, the result will not be called an externality, but a violation of the law for which my neighbour will be sanctioned by public authority. This example shows that the term "externality" is reserved for situations of physical (or social) interference that burden second parties with legally legitimate costs. The existing rights structure defines the rights and, hence, - as I argued earlier - the privileges of economic decision units. This means that the rights structure defines the types of behaviour that are beyond the interest of the state, i.e. the types of Alpha's behaviour for which the state declares that it is none of its direct concern if Alpha imposes costs on Beta (Bromley 1991, 18). Precisely these kinds of costs are called "externalities". To conclude, only those situations of interference that are deemed legally legitimate can be considered externalities. Hence, the kind of externalities that will occur depends on existing institutional arrangements.

Whether and to what extent an "externality" will be "solved" within a specific economic situation (this means: without politically defined amendments of the institutional arrangements allowing for the interference concerned) depends on who must pay the (transaction) costs in order to get a solution that is acceptable to all parties, the magnitude of these costs, and whether the injured party is able to pay the costs. Part of the answer to this question depends on the operational rule with which a specific property right is protected (Bromley 1991, 42-51). Remember that having a right means that the collective has agreed to recognise and to protect one's interests in a particular outcome. However, rights (or entitlements) can be given protection in several ways. Entitlements can be protected either by property rules, by liability rules or by inalienability rules. When a right is protected by a property rule,

---

management regime consists of a hierarchy of rights issued to different groups or individuals, a specific economic activity connects, via the resources used, different people. Consider the example of a farmer owning ("privately") a piece of land on which he grows vegetables. In case he uses pesticides, he does not only use this piece of land, but also some water in which residues of these pesticides get left behind. In case this water is used as drinking-water by the people in his region (water in "common property"), it becomes obvious that the growing of vegetables links the farmer to all other people in his region. The urgent question then will be whose rights are legally sufficiently protected: those of the "private" owner of land or those of the "common" owners of drinking-water.

it means that one may not interfere with the protected interests without the prior consent of the interest holder. This means that the costs have to be made - in advance - by the party who wishes to interfere and that these costs are necessary in order to convince the interest holder to accept the interference. When, on the contrary, a right is protected by a liability rule, it means that one may interfere with the protected interest on condition that the interfering party compensates the interest holder. In this case the interfering party again has to pay the costs, but these costs depend on what is considered a fair compensation by an independent assessor, for instance: the public sector, rather than on the whims of the interest holder. When, thirdly, a right is protected by an inalienability rule, this means that the protected interests cannot be interfered with under any circumstances.

In concrete externality situations the interests of one party interfere with the interests of another party. This means that concrete situations are situations of competing interests. Which party will have to pay the costs of the interference depends on whose interests are legally protected by a right. Consider the following example of Bromley (Bromley 1991, 43-45). Assume that Beta lives in a home separated from a lake by a piece of land upon which the owner (Alpha) decides to construct a fence, thereby blocking Beta's view of the sunrise and the boats on the lake. Alpha has an interest in building a fence, while Beta has an interest in an unobstructed view on the lake. If Alpha's interest is legally protected, either by a property or a liability rule, Beta will have to pay in order to protect its own interest. If, on the contrary, Beta's interest is legally protected - for instance, by a zoning ordinance that prevents the construction of fences over two feet high without the prior consent of Beta (in case Beta's interest is protected by a property rule) or else without providing adequate compensation to Beta (in case Beta's interest is protected by a liability rule) - Alpha will have to pay in order to protect its interest. This example illustrates that institutional arrangements (i.e. the rights structure and the rules protecting rights) influence who will pay how many costs to have its own interests protected.

Institutional arrangements define which party has to pay the costs to have its interests protected in a way that is acceptable to all parties, i.e. so that all parties deem their own interests protected in a balanced way. According to Bromley, externalities cannot remain unresolved in case transaction costs are absent and income effects are assumed away (Bromley 1991, 63-64). Since there is an economically appropriate level - i.e. a Pareto-efficient level - of physical interference among atomistic decision units, those directly involved in the interference will bargain out the preferred level (since none of them has to consider transaction costs or restrictions due to his or her own income). We then must conclude, Bromley writes, that the externality has been resolved, even though (some level of) the physical interference is still present. This means that all interdependent decision units have (without costs) bargained away all *relevant* physical interactions and

> by definition there can be no externalities. This does *not* mean that some physical interdependences would not remain; it simply means that our notion of an externality could not exist (Bromley 1991, 64).

Bromley seems to agree with Dahlman that externalities are nothing other than manifestations of nonzero transaction costs (and of the relevance of the wealth position of the different parties) (Bromley 1991, 64). His line of reasoning goes as follows: since in case of absent transaction costs (and of the irrelevance of income effects) all externalities will be bargained away, this means that if externalities are not bargained away, there must be transaction costs (and income effects). Though this line of reasoning is logically correct, it is analytically not sharp. For an independent criterion to decide whether transaction costs exist or not – and hence whether an ecological or social interdependence is an externality or a mere interdependence – is missing. Therefore, I propose to drop the assumptions of absent transaction costs and absent income effects. Even in case of transaction costs and of income effects, a Pareto-efficient level of interference exists and at this level no externalities remain, by definition. This does not mean, however, that transaction costs and income effects are irrelevant. As Bromley explains himself, in case one assumes the absence of transaction costs (and of income effects), the equilibrium level of interference is the same regardless the status quo structure of rights, i.e. regardless whether Alpha's or Beta's interests are legally protected (Bromley 1991, 74-75). In case, on the contrary, transaction costs (and income effects) are relevant, the equilibrium level will be more advantageous (compared with the equilibrium level reached in case of absent transaction costs) to the party whose interests are legally protected and more disadvantageous to the other party, since this latter party has to use part of its income to pay the transaction costs and thus has less to spend to pay for his or her interests (Bromley 76-78).

The idea that externalities are manifestations of transaction costs results from an inaccurate distinction between the term "externality" and the concept "(physical or social) interference". The term "externality" refers to monetary costs, i.e. to prices as revealed on markets (or calculated in cost-benefit analyses). These costs and, consequently, the economically efficient level of interference depend on the institutional organisation of an economy. An economically efficient level of interference does, however, not imply that the non-monetary costs of this interference are well balanced (i.e. are politically or socially acceptable). The following example can illustrate the important difference[8]. Public authorities can decide to levy relatively high taxes on petrol in order to reduce the amount of greenhouse gases produced by national traffic. Because of the non-elasticity of private car use and despite the high taxes levied, drivers use nearly as much petrol and produce nearly as much greenhouse gases as before. The final level of interference consequently will not differ much of the original level. This means that the probably huge, but non-monetary costs that possibly go together with climate changes due to greenhouse gases remain unchanged, though no externality exists: final car use is a Pareto-efficient use[9]. Bromley recognises this important difference

---

[8] I owe this example to Jan van der Straaten, who was patient enough to lead me, an - often impatient and therefore unpleasant - layman in economics, in the way of thinking of professional economists.

[9] Note that this example is characterised by third-party effects, high transaction costs - high information costs have to be spend on uncertainties with regard to the effects of greenhouse gases -, and

between monetary and non-monetary costs of a situation of interference (Bromley 1991, 49). He admits that the prescription to balance interference on efficiency grounds will not always provide a reliable decision aid. Cost-benefit assessments may introduce market/monetary biases which seriously discount non-market/non-monetary aspects of the situation.

> A billboard or an apartment building which blocks a scenic vista has monetary attributes which will be weighted against the "mere" pleasure of a beautiful sunrise; the fetid air which attends the economic activity generated by a kraft-process paper mill is not likely to receive the same weight in the decision process as the jobs that may be jeopardized by a strict air quality policy (Bromley 1991, 49).

A more accurate definition of the concept "externality" - as a situation of legally legitimate physical or social interference that (momentarily) gives rise to monetary costs - will set ecological problems sharper. It will show, first, that viewing an interference as an externality implies a translation into economic terms and, in case of a conventional scientific approach, making solutions dependent on the institutional organisation of an economy. This means that one translates a political problem (a problem concerning the institutional organisation of an economy) into an economic one (a problem asking for a "rational" solution from within existing institutional arrangements). Second, it will show that welfare theory cannot offer (objective) policy prescriptions since externalities get, by definition, solved within an economy (on a Pareto-efficient level). The only thing welfare theory can do is either to offer direction to individual economic agents for judging their bargains (Bromley 1991, 79) or to propose government interventions – i.e. institutional changes - that transform Pareto-irrelevant interferences[10] into Pareto-relevant ones[11], so that the level of interference will shift.

From this line of reasoning of Bromley we can conclude that the concept "externality" refers to a physical or social interference that is deemed legally legitimate, is evaluated as an economic cost, i.e. a cost that can be translated into monetary terms so that an appropriate level of interference can be bargained out. This line of reasoning also shows that the remaining level of interference depends on the existing institutional structure. The prevailing institutional structure defines (real or hypothetical) markets, i.e. monetary costs, and, hence, the outcomes that will be considered efficient (Bromley 1991, 66-67).

> Change the institutional environment and there will be a new [Pareto-]efficient solution

and hence a new level of "appropriate" physical interference (Bromley 1991, 67).

---

possible irreversibilities. According to Bromley, such more complex and more realistic examples are often overlooked in conventional externality analysis (Bromley 1991, 51-54). Traditional examples hold little implication for human health or ecological integrity, one can attach a monetary figure to the damages experienced by the recipient, third-party aspects are generally assumed unimportant, transaction costs are usually not very significant, and, finally, irreversibilities are not considered relevant.

[10] An accurate definition of the concept "externality" prevents me from talking about Pareto-irrelevant externalities, as Bromley - following Buchanan and Stubblebine - does (Bromley 1991, 72). There can at most exist a Pareto-irrelevant interference, not a Pareto-irrelevant externality.

[11] I suppose that this is what economists mean by policy prescriptions in order to "internalise" externalities.

3.3 Conclusion

The distinction Bromley makes between nominal and real boundaries of economic actions shows that economic actions always have, what I called in chapter 3, an institutional and ecological dimension. This implies that nominally autonomous actions inevitably interfere socially or ecologically. Some of these interferences are experienced as externalities. Externalities are legally legitimate interferences that pose unwanted costs on some of the interfering parties and that can be bargained out on existing (or hypothetical) markets. The level of interference that will remain after bargaining depends on which party has to pay the costs, the magnitude of the costs – transaction costs included - , and the relative wealth position of the parties involved. Bromley's analysis shows that both the coming into existence of externalities and whether and to what extent problematic interference get resolved depend on existing institutional arrangements. The latter is an illustration of the internal relationship between an economy and its ecological environment: it demonstrates that the ecological performance of an economy is the counterpart of its institutional organisation.

Since Bromley's analysis of property rights explains *possible*, not *actual* strategies, it explains what kind of ecological interferences *can* occur and whether parties involved have possibilities and what kind of possibilities to prevent or to change the level of these interferences. Bromley's analysis does, however, not explain what kind of ecological interferences are *likely* to occur and to remain. Considered from the global perspective (in time and in place) that I propose to hold in chapter 1, this implies that Bromley's analysis is not able to explain the general ecological tendencies manifest in the history of industrial economies.

4 THE ECONOMIC AND THE POLITICAL SPHERE

Bromley's conceptual analysis of property rights is an illustration of the idea of a genetic, institutional hierarchy. This illustration allows us to comment on Bromley's interpretation of institutional transactions as economic activities. My objection to this general idea is that it does not respect the argument offered in chapter 2 that the economic and political sphere can be distinguished conceptually and that they should be distinguished thus in order to strengthen the ideal of a deliberative democracy. This objection will be the subject of the first subsection. In the second subsection I will investigate whether Bromley's interpretation of institutional change is compatible with the normative ideal of a deliberative democracy. In the final subsection I will explain Bromley's interpretation of "sustainability".

4.1 Institutional Transactions: Economic or Political Activities

Before discussing whether institutional transactions are economic or political activities, let us first investigate what Bromley exactly means by them. Bromley distinguishes between implicit and explicit rights transfers. According to Bromley, a market is a regularised medium for the exchange of entitlements to future benefit streams. Bromley calls such exchanges 'explicit rights transfers' (Bromley 1991, 160). Explicit rights transfers are transfers in which rights to a thing owned are exchanged among willing parties. They are thus the process of shifting the same basic structure of rights and duties among members of a polity. The structure of rights and duties does not change, but the party (Alpha) that enjoys the rights and the party (Beta) that has duties changes. The former owner has moved from a position of having rights to a position of having duty with respect to (the particular benefit stream attendant to) the object, while the new owner now has rights rather than duties. I conclude that for Bromley explicit rights transfers are the same as commodity transactions.

The opposite of explicit rights transfers is implicit rights transfers (Bromley 1991, 161). Implicit rights transfers regard changes in the rights structure. To explain implicit rights transfers Bromley offers the example of the house owner whose neighbour seeks to paint his house in some outlandish colour. Either the house owner can enter into commodity transactions in order to protect his interest in a more conventionally painted neighbour's house. He can buy the house and resell it to someone else or he can offer his neighbour a sum of money to abandon his extra-ordinary taste. Or the house owner can pursue a new institutional arrangement through the city hall. He can try to realise a neighbourhood restriction on house colours. If the house owner succeeds in changing the institutional structure, he has modified the degree of control to be exercised by his neighbour. He changed the institutional structure, i.e. the content of the rights and duties attending to a thing owned, not the parties having rights and duties respectively. I conclude that by implicit rights transfers Bromley means the same as institutional transactions[12].

I agree with Bromley's description of commodity transactions (or explicit rights transfers) as *economic* activities. I do not plainly agree with his description of institutional transactions (or implicit rights transfers) as *economic* activities. In order to explain my reservations I have to come back to my attempts, in chapter 2, to distinguish between the economic and the political sphere. In this chapter, I put forward three partial entries – "products", "rationality", "decision units" - and an overarching one – "institutions" -. Whether institutional transactions are economic or political activities depends on the entry used to define economic or political phenomena respectively. In case "decision units" is the entry chosen, then institutional transactions falling under the control of economic decision units are economic activities and those falling under the control of political decision units are political ones. In case "rationality" is the entry chosen, then institutional transactions – whether occurring in economic or political decision units – are political activities. My argument for this latter statement is that institutional transactions concern the

---

[12] In order to explain the difference Bromley also introduces the concepts 'nominal' and 'real' structure (Bromley 1991, 160). The real structure refers to control, the nominal structure to ownership. Implicit rights transfers (or institutional transactions) are changes in the real structure, while the nominal structure remains unchanged. Explicit rights transfers (or commodity transactions) are changes in the nominal structure – the owner of the rights concerned changes -, while the real structure remains unchanged.

redefinition of the content of rights. Redefining this content is a matter of deliberative - i.e. unpredictable, irreversible, creative – rationality. Though one can, indeed, develop techniques in order to straightjacket the process of redefinition (for instance, by translating preferences into monetary terms, aggregating them and falling back on science to propose institutions as instruments to realise the aggregated outcome) so that the rationality of this process comes to resemble a typically economic – i.e. economising, instrumental - rationality.

To conclude, as soon as economic (as well as political) decision units look for institutional changes, the "rationality" of their actions is rather political. Institutional transactions necessarily result from collective action by members of an authority. This collective dimension is a necessity because this authority must recognise and respect the proposed institutional changes and, if necessary, be prepared to enforce them. Though institutional changes can be initiated by economic (rather than political) decision units and though they can be prompted by existing and dominant economic interests, they have to be accepted, agreed with and ratified by an authority. Economic decision units need to "interact" with other economic decision units in order to define and decide on the content of institutional changes. For that reason, I propose to classify institutional transactions as *political* rather than *economic* activities. Though I admit that this classification stems from the perspective chosen, namely the perspective constituted by the "rationality" entry.

The discussion stirred up by this topic of "institutional transactions" illustrates an argument made in section 2 of chapter 2. It illustrates, to begin with, that the distinction made between the economic and political sphere is a conceptual construct. It illustrates, moreover, that such distinction does not yet allow for a separation between both spheres. Some phenomena prove to belong to a grey zone of neither fully political nor fully economic activities or, formulated differently, to a grey zone of activities that are economic according to one perspective and political according to another. That it is, nevertheless, useful to make this distinction will be demonstrated, in the next subsection, by Bromley's critique on the conventional interpretation of the "rationality" of institutional change.

4.2 *The "Rationality" of Institutional Change*

> [I]nstitutional change is the *raison d'être* for public policy,

Bromley writes (Bromley 1989, 32). According to Bromley, institutional arrangements or, more restrictedly, property regimes are the policy *instruments* meant to realise political *objectives* (Bromley 1989, 144; 1991, 3, 5, 7, 163-168). At first sight, Bromley – contrary to Arendt - understands politics as showing some means/ends rationality. Other passages in Bromley's writings, however, offer us arguments to question this means/ends dichotomy. In this subsection, I will first deal with his interpretation of politics in general. Second, I will deal with his critique on conventional interpretations of institutional change. This critique shows, to start with, that Bromley disagrees with the common interpretation that (allocative) efficiency is the objective of institutional change. His critique shows, further, that an interpretation of the rationality of institutional change as economic rather than political has consequences for the kind of institutional changes that will be taken into consideration.

According to Bromley, in order to look upon politics as showing a means/ends rationality, one needs a criterion to distinguish between means and end. His criterion proves – as will become clear later on – to be borrowed from Lord Robbins. Consider the following quotation:

> We define a *policy objective* as something that appears in the utility function of the decision maker(s) as opposed to a *policy instrument* that will not appear there (Bromley 1989, 144).

Bromley not only admits that

> it is not always easy to maintain a sharp distinction between policy objectives and policy instruments (Bromley 1989, 227).

In another passage he openly criticises (Lord Robbins') means/ends dichotomy because this criterion is far from evident. Let us consider this passage.

According to Robbins' definition of economics, economists are said to study choice among scarce means to accomplish given ends (Bromley 1991, 208-209). The problem is how to differentiate ends from means. To make this differentiation, it is necessary to invoke some external criterion so that the distinction and the linkage between the two is placed in context. Robbins himself states that an "end" is something that enters into an individual's utility function (something individuals care about), while a means is not found there (means are mere instruments – without a value of their own – for accomplishing desired ends). According to Bromley, this is simply a definition, indeed a tautological statement. The problem starts when trying to determine whether or not something is an argument in the utility function of an individual. It cannot be economists' determination for that is to impose the value system of the economist into the analysis. It cannot be asked at all the individuals involved either. I assume that this critique of Bromley does not only apply for the means and ends of economic actors, but also for the means and ends of political actors.

From Bromley's line of reasoning, I conclude that, since we cannot unequivocally distinguish between instrument and objective, we would better drop the whole dichotomy. We would better hold on to the conviction that politics is about institutional arrangements *tout court*, not about instruments on the one hand and objectives on the other. Several passages in Bromley's writings suggest that he would not have that much difficulties with dropping this political means/ends dichotomy. This becomes, especially, clear where he acknowledges the lack of transparency with regard to values underlying both political preferences and institutional arrangements. Bromley plainly states that public policy is about socially acceptable institutional arrangements (Bromley 1989, 34, 244; 1991, 14)[13]. Institutional arrangements reflect, rather than express, public preferences for the protection of particular (egoistic or altruistic) private interests. The verb "reflect" is preferred to the verb "express" because the former takes better account of unconscious or non-voluntaristic elements in the result of political actions[14]. At the same time, institutional arrangements have a certain social/ecological performance that the citizenry will regard as either good or bad. Public evaluation of this performance functions as a feedback mechanism that will possibly lead to further political efforts to change or adapt existing institutional arrangements (Bromley 1989, 33). Note the lack of voluntarism becoming manifest in the obvious need for something like a "feedback mechanism". Bromley is sensitive for this lack of voluntarism which is the other side of the lack of transparency concerning the values underlying institutional arrangements on the one hand and the public preferences for them on the other. Other passages, however, testify that Bromley does not completely abandon the political means/ends dichotomy. I will come back to this topic later in this chapter.

Bromley criticises the conventional economic approach of the public policy problem of institutional change. He criticises the explicit criterion – "objective truth rule" or "decision rule"- conventional economics uses to evaluate the results of political processes. This criterion, economic or allocative efficiency, is, Bromley argues, conventional economists' opinion of the political objective the polity *should* have with regard to the institutional organisation of its economy. The problem with this criterion is not only that it prescribes what objective the polity should have, but also that it is a concept without a clear meaning. According to Bromley, whether a particular economy is allocatively efficient or not does not depend so much on the characteristics of its performance, but of its processes. *On condition that market failures do not occur* – this condition testifies of the ambiguity still present in Bromley's interpretation of allocative efficiency -, the efficient outcome is the outcome resulting from market processes, i.e. from volitional bargains between "autonomous" economic agents. However, "market failures" do occur, sometimes because particular markets even do not or cannot exist (see Bromley 1991, 86-95 for his treatment of 'missing markets'). In that case, citizens and their political representatives look for allocatively efficient institutional changes. Since the meaning of allocative efficiency depends on the process leading to it and since this process cannot simply refer to market processes – markets "fail" -, conventional economic scientists hasten to help the polity and propose cost-benefit analysis. Cost-benefit analysis is deemed a faithful imitation of volitional bargains and, as such, an *analytical* process leading to economically efficient institutional changes (Bromley

[13] In the same passage, Bromley states that public policy is, secondly, about searching for the boundary between autonomous (market-like) and collective decision making. In my view, this so-called second aspect of public policy is simply a reformulation of the first aspect. Institutional arrangements reflect collective decisions concerning the nature of – institutions are preconditions for - autonomous action.

[14] By non-voluntarism I mean that actors cannot simply realise their goals, either because they are not free enough to realise them or because their goals are neither fully known nor completely fixed.

1991, 42). However, cost-benefit analysis can never lead to efficient institutional changes *tout court.* First, cost-benefit analysis cannot be carried out without (implicitly or explicitly) accepting some substantive values defining what is deemed a cost or a benefit. Second, (the magnitude and incidence of) costs and benefits depend on existing institutional arrangements. *Status quo* institutional arrangements on the one hand and dominant values, either within the community of economic scientists or within a particular political community, on the other thus influence the outcomes of cost-benefit analyses.

I will reformulate Bromley's critique on the conventional approach starting from an (unambiguous) interpretation of "allocative efficency" as related to the economic performance *within*, not *of*, a particular economy (see section 3.3.1 in chapter 5). This interpretation is compatible with Bromley's interpretation of allocative efficiency as referring to market *processes*, not *outcomes*. According to this interpretation, market failures (or missing markets) are not indications that an economy fails with regard to its allocative efficiency. As I argued in chapter 5, allocative efficiency *of* an economy has no independent meaning. Market failures only indicate that humans (implicitly) use some substantive criterion to evaluate an economy's performance. This criterion, consisting of a whole set of implicit values, is, however, not transparent to the community of political actors. In other words, the political objective prompting for institutional change is not clear. This illustrates that the political means/ends dichotomy fails. Since the conventional interpretation of economics as a policy science is instrumental, it needs a clear political objective in order to provide politics with adequate means. Since this objective is absent, conventional economics defines it itself, thereby falling back on cost-benefit analysis as the technique deemed appropriate. As Bromley remarks, cost-benefit analysis does not unequivocally allow for allocatively efficient institutional *change*, because allocative efficiency has no meaning independent of the existing institutional organisation of an economy. Moreover, falling back on cost-benefit analyses betrays an interpretation of institutional change as resulting from economic calculations, rather than from political imagination. It betrays an interpretation of institutional change as showing an economic (or, better, economising), rather than political rationality (see also Bromley 1991, 69, 80: on Buchanan and his Pareto-Wicksellian interpretation of efficient institutional changes; Bromley 1991, 218).

That Bromley is sensible for an interpretation of the rationality of institutional change as political rather than economic becomes manifest in his comments on (other) models of institutional change (Bromley 1989, chapter 2). According to Bromley, institutional changes are prompted by changing economic conditions such as new scarcities, new technological opportunities, new distributions of income or wealth, or new tastes and preferences (Bromley 1989, 110).

> Just as [...] institutional arrangements will determine the nature and scope of commodity transactions, the economic conditions at any moment will be important in determining the institutional transactions that will occur, and hence the institutional arrangements that will emerge (Bromley 1989, 110).

In his view, however, no existing model of institutional change is able to capture the "rationality" of these changes. Bromley's critique of the models he discusses comes down to the following arguments. First, the models are circular since the costs and benefits defining whether institutional changes are efficient depend on existing institutional arrangements. (In my words, the models are based on an ambiguous interpretation of economic efficiency.) Second, the models have too restrictive a view on political preferences. Political preferences for institutional change can regard a redistribution of economic opportunity rather than being restricted to either (ambiguous) economic efficiency or redistribution of income. (I will come back to Bromley's explanation of types of political preferences in a later section). Third, political preferences emerge in political processes, they do not simply result from bargains between political agents with uneven (political/economic) power. From Bromley's critique, I conclude that his interpretation of politics resembles Arendt's interpretation of it as a matter of unpredictable events rather than as calculable cause-effect relationships (Bromley 1989, 77-79). In order to strengthen this interpretation, Bromley should consistently drop the political means/ends dichotomy.

According to Bromley, an interpretation of the rationality of institutional change as economic narrows the scope of possible changes. Consider the following quotation.

> It is against the status quo that patterns of interaction will lead to outcomes deemed to be unacceptable. One obvious remedy is for the various parties to attempt to strike a mutual bargain that will improve the situation. However, note that any bargain will always be made from within the existing structure of institutions that defines choice sets. An alternative avenue open to disputants is to attempt to modify directly the institutional arrangements that define those choice sets (Bromley 1989, 54).

This quotation suggests that an economic interpretation of the rationality of institutional change gives rise to minimal adjustments of the existing institutional organisation, adjustments that respect existing power relationships as much as possible[15]. A political interpretation of the rationality of institutional change, on the contrary, allows for more fundamental institutional changes, i.e. institutional changes that redistribute power[16]. This political interpretation presupposes, however, that one has insights into the (social or ecological) performance of existing institutional arrangements prior to looking for institutional change. In his writings Bromley pleads indeed for scientific investigations of (the social or ecological performance of) existing institutional arrangements (rather than of separate institutions since economic behaviour depends on an *ensemble* of institutions).

---

[15] Bromley criticises the Coasian approach concerning institutional change precisely because it falls back on 'direct regulation'. '[In the Coasian approach] a substantive consideration of the institutional arrangements that determine the status quo is dismissed and attention turns to direct regulation of the offending party' (Bromley1991, 100).

[16] The German terms *Ordnungspolitik* and *Prozesspolitik*, to which Bromley refers, indicate, in my view, precisely this distinction between (minimally) adjusting and transforming existing institutional arrangements (Bromley 1989, 225). According to Bromley, quoting Hutchison, the early economists were primarily concerned with *Ordnungspolitik*, while 'it was not until the rise of modern macroeconomic policies in the early 1900s that "extensive and systematic *Prozesspolitik* began to develop" [...]'(Bromley 1989, 225).

4.3 *Sustainability*

Bromley gave no sign that sustainability was a special interest of him until his recent article 'Searching for sustainability: The poverty of spontaneous order' was published (Bromley 1998). In this article he introduces an interpretation of "sustainability" that, though abstract, is interesting for two reasons. First, in a certain sense it respects, better than the conventional "strong" or "weak" interpretation of it, the nature of the relationship between present and future generations. Second, though the political message it provides is abstract, it is fundamental.

To start with the former reason, Bromley defends the idea that we should move beyond the conventional metaphor of sustainability. He objects to the conventional interpretation of sustainability as a problem of allocative efficiency. This conventional interpretation conceives of sustainability, either strong or weak, as about allocating the right quantity and quality of (natural and man-made) capital to the generations living now and in the future. This interpretation requires that the ecological environment is considered a commodity within an economy rather than the counterpart of an economy's institutional organisation. It is a commodity as a capital asset and it provides commodities in the form of ecological goods and services. The ecological environment is deemed to offer autonomous consumers a certain utility that relates to their private preferences rather than it is looked upon as a necessary condition for economic activities. An economy – i.e. the "spontaneous order" constituted by market processes – is considered a kind of machine that converts both natural and constructed capital into goods and services in an allocatively efficient way, on condition that both capital and commodities get "right prices".

Bromley comments:

> While the assumptions of the time machine problem are no more severe than those found in much of economics, when the machine is run with the future in mind, certain rather serious inconveniences arise (Bromley 1998, 234).

Since we do not know what those living in the future might find giving utility nor what they will regard as capital, the idea of "right prices" fails to take us very far. Sustainability as a problem of efficient allocation through the economy-machine is, according to Bromley, a scientific fiction. This scientific fiction only tells us that we must leave something – but what? - for the future. The essential problem of sustainability is that we *do not* and *cannot* know what those in the future would wish for us to do. This is not a mere problem of uncertainty or of risk. It is a problem of lacking information that precludes us from knowing what the economy-machine is expected to do. Bromley therefore proposes to move beyond the conventional metaphor of sustainability because this metaphor is devoid of any positive analytical content for the economist.

Moving beyond this metaphor implies moving beyond the idea of spontaneous order. The order of an economy does not evolve autonomously out of individual economic agents' maximising behaviour meant to solve scarcity problems. The order of an economy is a constructed order. Sustainability must therefore be about a prior constructed order defining a socially acceptable provisioning program for those living now and in the future. This economic order to construct and to reconstruct cannot claim to leave future persons exactly the domain of choice they would select for themselves. This order can at most claim to be a reflection of what *we* deem to be so valuable – settings and circumstances - that they are worth to be left to our descendants. For reasons I will explain hereafter, I consider this interpretation of sustainability as abstract, but fundamental. Bromley himself is at times, however, inclined to detract somewhat from this profundity.

According to Bromley, looking for a constructed order with an acceptable ecological performance is a complex endeavour, for two reasons. First, ecological problems often bind together numerous parties, many of which are not able to enter consensual deliberations to have their wishes expressed or their interests protected (Bromley 1989, 58; 1991, 86-95). While the impotence of contemporary parties could be solved in principle, the impotence of future generations cannot be cancelled out. This is what Bromley calls in his earlier writings the problem of 'asymmetry' (Bromley 1991, 87). For that reason Bromley states that with regard to intertemporal (or intergenerational) problems of ecological interference, one cannot speak of "market failures", but at most of "missing markets".

> If by a market we mean a structured opportunity for two or more agents to exchange ownership of future benefit streams, then there is no market in situations of intertemporal externalities (Bromley 1991, 87).

In order to take this intertemporal dimension into account, Bromley proposes a Rawlsian veil of ignorance to define – politically – suitable institutional arrangements (Bromley 1991, 94)[17]. He concludes that suitable arrangements must be thus that they mean an entitlement of *duty* for the present and *right* – protected by an inalienability rule - for the future, rather than *privilege* for the present and *no right* for the future.

This abstract interpretation of sustainability resembles my interpretation of it, for reasons I will explain. To start with, I interpret sustainability as responsibility towards future generations with respect to the ecological performance of our economies. Such responsibility implies that we keep our present ecological problems manageable, so that we do not load future generations with unknown and perhaps unacceptable risks. This is what I consider to be the meaning of present generations having duty and future generations having inalienable right. The fundamental political message implicit in Bromley's interpretation of sustainability is thus to construct an economic order of which the ecological performance shows at most manageable ecological problems. This interpretation urges us to avoid rather than to tolerate ecological uncertainties with a global dimension (in time and in space). Though one has to concede that is not easy and often not clear beforehand which ecological problems are manageable and which are not, I consider this

[17] For a brief and clear explanation of two possible meanings of Rawls "veil of ignorance" with regard to intergenerational problems, see Beekman (forthcoming)

abstract interpretation of sustainability as politically most valuable. It urges us to reflect on (the ecological performance of) both existing and politically acceptable economies.

However, in the article mentioned Bromley also qualifies his politically fundamental conception of sustainability, arguing that it would be an 'inefficient outcome' (Bromley 1991, 95). For that reason – given, for instance, 'the prevailing technology of pollution abatement' -, institutional arrangements reflecting a right for the future protected by a liability rule suffice in his view. In my opinion, Bromley makes here the same mistake for which he often blames his colleagues. One cannot compare institutional arrangements on efficiency grounds, since the meaning of efficiency differs in both cases. In the first case where future generations have inalienable rights, the criterion for evaluating an economy's efficiency comprises, among other things, keeping a specific natural capital that we deem valuable, e.g. clean air, intact. In the second case, this criterion means, among other things, allowing for a decline of that valuable natural capital, e.g. allowing that the air will in the future be more polluted than it is now, on condition that future generations will be compensated for these costs that we deem ourselves unwanted.. In my view, we cannot circumvent our task of defining politically what kind of economy and, hence, what kind of ecological (and social) performance we deem valuable enough to leave to our descendants. In case we deem clean air a necessary characteristic of it, we should look for institutional transformations, thorough though they can be, that allow this characteristic to be achieved. Efficiency considerations are but secondary. And more important than efficiency considerations are considerations concerning how to organise the transition from one economy into another so that the (monetary and non-monetary) costs and benefits of this transition get fairly distributed. This approach presupposes, however, that we have insights into the institutional reasons for the growing problem of air pollution, rather than into possible (present and future) technologies for abating it.

4.4 Conclusion

In chapter 2, I argued that, in order to strengthen the ideal of a deliberative democracy, we should distinguish between the economic and the political sphere. This distinction applies, hence, also to the "rationality" typical for economic and political actions. In the first subsection, I object to Bromley's classification of institutional transactions (or change) as economic rather than political activities. My objection is based on the argument that the "rationality" of institutional change is political, not economic. It thus only holds in case one is prepared to look upon institutional change from the perspective of "rationality".

Bromley's critique on orthodox economic interpretations of institutional change illustrates that my classification makes sense. Bromley criticises orthodox economists because they prescribe "allocative efficiency" as the only valid political motive for institutional change (or at least the only motive they should recommend on). Bromley's critique comprises two elements. He argues, to start with, that political actors can have other motives for institutional change than the motive of "allocative efficiency". Though he rejects allocative efficiency as the only political objective for institutional change of an economy, he seems to keep to the idea that politics shows a means/ends rationality. Bromley argues, further, that allocative efficiency has no meaning independent of the existing institutional organisation of an economy. He, therefore, blames conventional economists for *constructing* a meaning of allocative efficiency by introducing the technique of cost-benefit analysis. In Bromley's view this construction is biased because cost-benefit analysis implies hidden valuations. And it is biased because it regards politics as an aggregate of volitional bargains. This latter critique testifies that Bromley does not simply comply to the idea that the rationality of institutional change is economic. Nevertheless, despite his argument that allocative efficiency has no meaning independent of the existing institutional organisation of an economy, it looks as if Bromley continues to use the term ambiguously: at times as a criterion for the efficiency *within* an economy and at times as a criterion for the efficiency *of* an economy. This ambiguity becomes manifest, in particular, where he qualifies his original interpretation of sustainability.

I consider Bromley's original interpretation of sustainability as politically fundamental. It admits that sustainability – contrary to weak or strong interpretations of it - cannot be a matter of allocative efficiency, for the simple reason that future generations, since they do not yet exist, cannot bargain on markets. Sustainability is, according to Bromley, about constructing an economic order that we deem valuable enough, given its social and ecological performance, to leave to our descendants. In order to define what "valuable enough" means, Bromley introduces Rawls' veil of ignorance. He concludes that an economic order to leave should reflect duty for present generations and inalienable right for future generations. This implies, translated into my terminology, that present generations have duty to avoid ecological risks that cannot be managed by present generations. This duty can, however, only be realised on condition that we have insights into institutional reasons for empirically observable ecological tendencies (that, until now, we were not able to manage).

5 CONCLUSION

Contrary to Pearce, Bromley can be described as an ecological rather than environmental economist. In one respect, however, his writings are not compatible with this description. Bromley interprets sustainability neither in a weak nor in a strong sense. He rejects the metaphor of sustainability as a matter of allocative efficiency. Instead, he thinks of sustainability as the metaphor voicing our task to construct an economic order that we deem valuable enough to leave it to our descendants. Translated into my terminology, "valuable enough" means, at least, that we take responsibility for the ecological (and social) performance of this economic order. This responsibility implies that we have duty to avoid ecological risks that cannot be managed by present generations. Since, until now, we did not show that we are able to manage present-day general ecological tendencies, this responsibility presupposes that we hurry to gain insights into the relationships between the institutional organisation and the ecological performance of our economies.

Bromley's institutional approach allows for some insights into these relationships between institutional organisation and ecological performance. His treatment of "externalities" demonstrates that the kind and level of ecological interference that can occur and remain is internally related to the institutional organisation of an economy. Through his analysis of property regimes, i.e. that genetic hierarchy of institutions that defines a particular valuable asset as an economic good, Bromley can explain possible, not actual economic actions and, hence, possible, not actual ecological performances. In order to gain insights into actually existing general ecological tendencies, i.e., into the combined rather than atomistic ecological performance of economic actors' actions, I suggest that we need further insights into institutional reasons for existing distributions of income and into the institutional dimension of "(future) benefit streams". I suppose, moreover, that the kind of institutional hierarchy we are looking for is of the kind of an order hierarchy, rather than a genetic hierarchy. For an order hierarchy can learn us something about dominant institutions, and I expect that *dominant* institutions can help us explain *general* tendencies.

Bromley strongly criticises the idea prevailing among environmental economists that ecological policy is about allocative efficiency. He stresses that political actors can have many political objectives other than economic optimality. Bromley is, however, ambiguous in his treatment of economic *versus* political rationality. He has, for instance, no reservations to label institutional transactions as economic rather than political activities. At the same time, he objects to the idea that institutional change is a matter of allocative efficiency. Contrary to Bromley, I argue that a typically economic and a typically political rationality exist (remember chapter 2). I plainly consent that economic rationality is about allocative efficiency. But allocative efficiency only has unambiguous meaning *within* a particular institutional context. Institutional *change* is a matter of political rationality. Political rationality can, indeed, resemble economic rationality depending on the extent that political actors respect existing economic power relationships and aim at optimal satisfaction of private preferences. It does, however, not necessarily resemble it. Political rationality can also question existing power relationships and aim at an institutional realisation of reasoned public preferences. The latter topic will be dealt with again in the next chapter.

CHAPTER 8

THE NATURE OF BROMLEY'S ECONOMICS

In order to explain the nature of Bromley's ecological economics, I have to translate some of the concepts he uses into my terminology. In section 1, I will show that Bromley admits the non-neutrality of ecological economics, though he tries to justify this non-neutrality by defending that the values constituting his normative perspective result from empirical observations. In section 2, I will deal with Bromley's argument that economic science should be objective. His (residual) logical positivist idea that objectivity implies neutrality causes Bromley, however, to wrestle with its meaning. In section 3, I will deal with Bromley's objections to conventional economists' inclination to prescribe the political motive for institutional change. Though I fully agree that it is not the economist's task to prescribe political motives, I deem his endeavour to describe political motives scientifically redundant. In section 4, I will comment on Bromley's stress that science should explain rather than predict. I will argue that Bromley's keeping on to the (political) means/ends dichotomy brings him on the slippery slope of recommending institutional changes, i.e. of predicting rather than explaining. In the final section 5, I will argue that, due to his concentration on property rights and property regimes, the insights Bromley's approach offers us into the relationships between the institutional organisation of an economy and the content and distribution of private interests are restricted. The nature of his ecological economics is, hence, partially impartial.

1 NON-NEUTRAL

1.1 Propagandistic versus Paradigmatic Non-Neutrality

To understand whether Bromley considers of ecological economics as a neutral or non-neutral science, we should refer to his interpretation of the concept "ideology" (Bromley 1991, 205). According to Bromley, ideology can be thought of in two distinct ways. One connotation of the term is that of an emotional or propagandistic position held by someone.

> The *ideologue* is one who engages in a variety of means and tactics in order that the position of others might be altered in specific ways (Bromley 1991, 205).

In Bromley's view, a scientist should try to avoid to be such an ideologue. He or she strives

> to avoid subjectivity and the taint of our personal values having an influence on economic analysis. [...] It is said that we must avoid, at all cost, allowing ideology - by which is meant *value judgments* - to color our analysis (Bromley 1991, 205).

The other interpretation of the concept regards ideology as

> an overall view of, or attitude toward, something (Bromley 1991, 205-206).

The term then refers to a shared system of meaning and comprehension. This system functions as a structure within which information is supplied and processed, directions are given, and justification for certain behaviour is provided. In brief, this second interpretation of "ideology" comes down to what Kuhn defined as a paradigm. To recapitulate, Bromley distinguishes between propagandistic and paradigmatic ideology. In his view, scientists should not be propagandistic ideologues, but they cannot be but paradigmatic ideologues.

Translating Bromley into my own terminology, I conclude that Bromley looks upon economics as a non-neutral science, in the sense that value-laden concepts constitute the perspective from which we look at human reality. A disciplinary paradigm is unavoidably non-neutral or, in Bromley's words, ideological in the second sense. Recognising the non-neutrality of science implies that we cannot maintain – as Bromley does in the previous quotation - that value judgements should not colour scientists' analysis. Value judgements certainly define the way scientists look and, hence, analyse. Recognising this non-neutrality does not imply that scientists engage in a variety of means and tactics in order to alter the position of others in specific ways. The latter problem does not regard so much science's non-neutrality, but scientists' endeavour to augment their political influence by prescribing, rather than describing, political objectives (see further in section 3).

1.2 A Normative Analysis of Institutional Change

In some passages, Bromley explains what the non-neutral perspective constituting his interpretation of economics consists of. He regards (ecological) economics as a kind of policy science. The subject matter of economics as a policy science can be subdivided in the analysis of (existing and possible) institutional arrangements and of institutional transactions (or change) (Bromley 1989, 148-150). Bromley explicitly states that he is concerned with the *normative* content of institutional arrangements and of institutional change (Bromley 1989, 40). His normative analysis of existing and possible institutional arrangements regards, first, their (social or ecological) performance and, second, their framing effect on the meaning of efficiency and optimality and on the problem of collective choice and institutional change.

> By performance I mean more than simply the net national income as reckoned in monetary terms. By performance I mean the full gamut of indicators of well-being that individuals and groups marshal to convey their satisfaction with how things are going. [...] There will be concern with the loss of jobs in the manufacturing sector, there will be concern with regional disparities in economic growth and adjustment, there will be concern with excessive agricultural output, there will be concern with land-use

> tendencies in urban areas, and so on. All of these concerns reflect the outcomes from existing institutional arrangements and patterns of interaction (Bromley 1989 149).

By the framing effect of institutional arrangements on the meaning of efficiency and optimality Bromley means that institutional arrangements – status quo as well as alternative configurations of institutions - define the (monetary as well as non-monetary) costs and benefits in both their magnitude and their incidence. The latter framing effect on the problem of collective choice and, hence, on institutional change is, according to Bromley, a direct consequence of the former framing effect on the meaning of efficiency and optimality since "efficiency" is commonly considered to be the objective of economic policy.

1.3 Four Motives for Institutional Change

In Bromley's view, it is the political objectives as defined by members of a polity that should function as a criterion to evaluate the efficiency, i.e., the social and ecological performance of an economy and of its institutional change. In other words, it is empirically observable political objectives (I will come back to this topic in section 3) that should constitute the normative perspective of ecological economics as a policy science. Bromley strongly objects to the conventional idea that allocative efficiency is the only political objective that economists can recommend on. In order to weaken this conventional idea, he develops four types of political objectives, i.e. four possible motives for institutional change. (Bromley 1989, 128-143).

Conventional wisdom draws, according to Bromley, a distinction between institutional changes that are motivated by allocative efficiency ('pie enlarging' or 'institutional transactions that increase productive efficiency') and those that are redistributive in nature ('merely redividing a fixed pie' or 'institutional transactions that redistribute income'). Recommending on institutional changes motivated by allocative efficiency is considered to be the task of economists. Deciding on redistributive measures is considered to be a political matter. In addition to these two motives, Bromley distinguishes between reallocation of economic opportunity and reallocation of economic advantage. The difference between the two latter motives is related to the social utility function, i.e., Bromley writes, the ensemble of public and private goods deemed desirable in a society. Institutional changes that are meant to ameliorate social efficiency are reallocating economic opportunity. Institutional changes that are meant to protect the interests of economic decision units in a way that is not consistent with the social utility function are redistributing economic advantage. If mine safety is a public or private good belonging to a social utility function, institutional changes meant to realise mine safety are an example of the former case. If miners were able – i.e. spending scarce resources - to achieve an outcome for which there is no argument in the social utility function, the concomitant institutional changes are an example of the latter[1].

Bromley's distinction between the four motives (or types of political objectives) is analytically not sharp. To start with, Bromley uses the term "allocative efficiency" ambiguously. At times, allocative efficiency refers to the efficiency *of* an economy. This is the case where Bromley mentions allocative efficiency as one of the four possible motives for institutional change. I already argued that this kind of efficiency has no independent meaning (see section 3.3.1 in chapter 5). Institutional changes meant for "pie enlarging" or "economic growth" do not contribute to allocative efficiency, since the latter only has independent meaning when referring to economic actions occurring *within* an economy. "Pie enlarging" or "economic growth" are separate criteria. At times, Bromley preserves the term allocative efficiency for economic actions occurring *within* an economy. In these cases, Bromley explains allocative efficiency (Bromley also speaks of 'private economic efficiency' (Bromley 1991, 174)) as a combination of productive and consumption efficiency. It occurs

> when independent producers and consumers take market signals - prices - and adjust their production and consumption decisions such that, at the margin, the gain from one more unit of production (or of consumption) is exactly offset by the added costs of that last unit (Bromley 1991, 174).

Allocative efficiency is about the best attainable combination of goods and services produced and consumed within an economic community, given the availability of particular resource, labour and capital inputs and of particular techniques and given the presence of particular tastes and preferences and of particular institutional arrangements[2].

I keep to my argument that we should preserve the term allocative efficiency for economic actions occurring *within* an economy. Consequently, this kind of

---

[1] 'Imagine that laborers, through threat of a crippling strike, were able to extract work concessions to maintain total daily pay at its current level, but to reduce the work day from 8 hours to 6 hours' (Bromley 1989, 143).

[2] Contrary to what the term "private economic efficiency" suggests, allocative efficiency regards the efficiency within the whole of an economy. The reason why allocative efficiency does not contradict private efficiency is that allocative efficiency derives from the combined (efficient) actions of (nominally) independent, i.e. private, producers and consumers. Under specific conditions, i.e. absence of market failures (and here the ambiguity of the term "allocative efficiency" pops up again), privately efficient - i.e. economising - behaviour is deemed to satisfy the aggregate of individual tastes and preferences in the best possible way. In other words, private economising efficiency is a necessary and sufficient condition for allocative efficiency. Market prices are responsible for this harmonious connection between the private and the common. '[The] argument holds that in conditions of thoroughgoing competition among a number of buyers and sellers the social value of inputs and outputs is correctly reflected in their respective market prices' (Bromley 1991, 174). Allocative efficiency thus is about the best attainable combination of "commodities", i.e. of goods and services sold and bought on the markets that are institutionalised in a particular economy. Pareto-optimality is the criterion for allocative efficiency. The Pareto-principle states that a specific combination of goods and services is Pareto-optimal if no other combination exists that satisfies one economic decision unit's preferences better without satisfying the other economic decision units' preferences worse.

efficiency fails as a criterion to evaluate the performance *of* an economy or *of* institutional change. In order to evaluate the latter, one needs some other, independent criterion.

Bromley proposes to use a social welfare function as an independent criterion to evaluate an economy and its institutional change. A social welfare function is expressed as $W = f(U_1, U_2, \ldots, U_n)$, where U_i represents the utility or happiness of individual *i*. According to Bromley, the social welfare function is an aggregating mechanism for making collective decisions about what ought to be done.

> It is a mechanism for aggregating individual interests to arrive at collective decisions (Bromley 1989, 127).

Which social welfare function is deemed relevant depends, according to Bromley, on the political process (Bromley 1989, 137). The relevant social welfare function results from collective judgements on the strength and relevance of judgements made by the individuals in society. It is an expression of whether or not it is more important to cater to the interests of individual 1 or to those of individual 2. According to Bromley, the social welfare function is a criterion for the social efficiency of an economy. An economy is socially efficient if it contains that combination of private and collective goods that satisfies a particular social welfare function best. Institutional changes that *contribute* to social efficiency reallocate economic *opportunity*, while institutional changes that *detract* from social efficiency reallocate economic *advantage*.

Social efficiency regards, according to Bromley, the best attainable combination of market and non-market goods and services (Bromley 1989, 138). It does not only depend on the (allocative) "efficiency" of economic decision units' behaviour within particular institutional arrangements, but also on the "efficiency" of the institutional arrangements themselves. According to Bromley, citizens consume more than just private goods purchased in commodity transactions (as, for instance, 'coal, food, clothing'); they also consume collective goods that are purchased in institutional transactions (as, for instance, 'literacy, environmental quality, the net wealth position of members in society, the general state of human health, and work conditions of factories, firms, and mines') (Bromley 1989, 136). I object to Bromley's idea that social efficiency is about the best possible combination of private and public *goods*. Social efficiency is about the performance *of* an economy. This performance can be evaluated with regard to an infinite number of standards. These standards are not necessarily met with the help of *goods*, either private or public. The following example, that I owe to Bromley (Bromley 1989, 111-121; 135-139), will help to explain my reservations. I will retell the example in my own words and transform it where necessary in order to adapt it to my own analytical purposes.

Consider a society in which the general level of satisfaction of individuals depends not only on the production of coal, but also on the safety of the work conditions in mines. The social utility function then has the form $U = U(c,s)$ where (c,s) reflects the bundle of coal and safety available in that society. The social efficiency of this society's economy will thus be measured according to two standards, namely provision of coal and safety of miners. Given this (simple) utility function, one has two possibilities with regard to people's interest in "safety in mines". (By the way, one also has two possibilities with regard to people's interest in coal.)

Either the collectivity regards safety of miners as a private interest. In other words, the members of this society have a political preference for considering safety of miners as a private interest. This political preference will be reflected in the institutional organisation of economy A. The institutional organisation of economy A implies no liability on the part of mine owners for accidents that lead to injury or death to miners. Labourers must assume the full risk of work-related accidents and there is no incentive on the part of mine owners to invest in costly safety precautions. The solution left to miners is to bargain with the mine-owners and try to buy a right to their future labour power. Whether these miners will be able to buy this right depends on whether they will be able to raise enough money. What counts as "enough money" depends on the relative income (wealth) of the miners and of the mine owner, on the techniques needed to realise this right – does a hard hat suffice or does one need a complete reorganisation of mining technology -, and on the transaction costs that the miners have to pay in order to bribe the mine owners. Indeed,

> the status quo requires that the laborers initiate the expensive and tedious process of gathering information about the costs and benefits of safety measures, the negotiation of a new safety regime, and the enforcement of that regime (Bromley 1989, 117).

The institutional organisation of economy A thus reflects the political preference for mine safety as a private interest. Whether and to what extent this private interest will be looked after depends on the *allocative* efficiency (i.e. Pareto-optimality) of safety measures and this allocative efficiency depends, in its turn, on the (relative) wealth of the miners and on the magnitude of the transaction costs these miners have to pay. In economy A, the realisation of a safety regime in a mine is an example of an explicit rights transfer, i.e. of a commodity transaction - not of an institutional transaction (as Bromley seems to suggest in some passages[3]). Miners' private interest in safety can be managed with the help of *goods* (a hard hat or an alarm system) or as a counterpart of a different technological (safer machines) or social (shorter working days) organisation. The goods bought to satisfy miners' interest in safety are, moreover, not necessarily private. Depending on the property regime attached to these goods, some rights related to them can be assigned to individuals, others to all miners, still others to miners performing particular work, and so on.

---

[3] For instance in the following passage (Bromley 1989, 146). After distinguishing between four kinds of institutional transactions, Bromley writes: 'These institutional transactions will arise as autonomous responses to new economic conditions and opportunities, or they will arise because of an absence of autonomous change and so they will be imposed from without'. My argument is that a consequent use of the concepts, introduced by Bromley, would denote transactions resulting from 'autonomous responses to new economic conditions [as, for instance, changing preferences concerning mine safety; MD] and opportunities' as *commodity* transactions, not as *institutional* transactions.

Or the collectivity considers mine safety as a common interest. In this case, the members of this society have a political preference for considering the safety of miners as a common interest. This political preference will, again, be reflected in the institutional organisation of economy B in this society. Economy B has an institutional arrangement in which labourers' right in their future labour power is legally protected. This right can either be protected through a legal obligation for mine owners to contribute to an annuity per unit of time worked so as to indemnify workers and their survivors in the event of an accident (Bromley 1989, 112). In this case there is an economic incentive for the mine owners to invest in safety equipment that will reduce the probability of accidents. Or – Bromley does not mention this possibility - this right can be protected through safety precautions that each mine owner is legally bound to take. And the level of the safety precautions can (Bromley 1989, 113) or cannot be derived from cost-benefit analyses. While in economy A the miners must pay for the right in their future labour power (if they can), in economy B the mine owners must (definitely) pay for their labourers' right. In other words, in economy A the mine-owner's right to use his miners' labour power is less restricted than it is in economy B. The activities undertaken to change the initial into the final institutional organisation (for instance, economy A into economy B) are an example of implicit rights transfers or institutional transactions. In economy B, miners' legally protected right in safety can again be realised with the help of *goods* or with the help of a particular technological or social organisation. (The distinction between goods and organisation is, moreover, not strict. Each technological or social organisation shows economic aspects, either in the form of, for instance, costs for machines or information or in the form of costs for more or less expensive labour power.)

To recapitulate, in a particular economy safety can be considered either a private or a public interest. In the former case, individual economic actors should buy and sell rights to safety. Safety is a matter of commodity transactions occurring *within* the institutional organisation of this economy. In the latter case, miners' right in safety is reflected in the institutional organisation *of* this economy. Safety is one aspect of the social performance of this economy. More safety as a common interest is realised through institutional transactions. Miners interest in safety, whether private or public, can be realised either with the help of economic commodities or as a counterpart of a particular social or technological organisation. The property regime attached to the economic commodities meant to realise miners' safety can also vary. Private interests are not necessarily fulfilled with the help of private goods, nor are public interests necessarily fulfilled with the help of public goods. (Anyhow, the concepts private or public good are, as I explained in section 2.2.2 of chapter 7, analytically not precise.)

To conclude, what matters for evaluating the social efficiency of an economy is which interests are politically considered to be private and which are politically considered to be public. The former interests should be satisfied by economic actors *within* the existing institutional organisation of an economy. The latter interests should be satisfied by political actors *through* (changes of) the institutional organisation of an economy. A particular institutional organisation reflects people's political preferences for both private and public interests. Social efficiency does not refer, as Bromley states, to the best combination of private and public goods. It refers to the best institutional organisation of an economy, an organisation that reflects political preferences for a particular combination of private and public interests. These interests can, further, be managed with the help of commodities or (technological or social) organisations.

My reformulation of social efficiency urges me to reject Bromley's classification of political motives for institutional change. I already explained that allocative efficiency cannot be a motive for institutional *change*. Let us, therefore, drop this first motive. A fair distribution of income can be a criterion for evaluating the social efficiency of an economy. This criterion can be politically considered a matter of private or of public interest. If the latter is the case, institutional change contributing to a fair distribution of income should be classified, in Bromley's terminology, as reallocation of economic opportunity. Institutional change detracting from a fair distribution of income should be classified as reallocation of economic advantage. Consequently, Bromley's second motive should not be mentioned separately. It is simply one of possible criteria that can constitute a social welfare function. Finally, one can only distinguish between reallocation of economic opportunity and of economic advantage if one knows the set of criteria that constitute a social welfare function. In section 3, I will argue that this set cannot simply be known. For that reason, I propose to drop also Bromley's third and fourth type of political motives for institutional change. All that remains is people's political preferences consisting of a non-transparent and continuously changing set of values. All an economic scientist can do is to provide political actors with, indeed non-neutral, insights into the social and ecological performance of existing economies. Non-neutral scientists cannot and should not investigate political actors' motives in order to define their own normative perspective. I agree with Weber (see section 1.1 in chapter 2) that one cannot answer scientifically to the question which values must constitute a scientific perspective. I consider, therefore, Bromley's introduction of a social welfare function and a social utility function as superfluous[4].

2 OBJECTIVE

Bromley rejects the logical positivist (and the later logical empiricist) interpretation of objectivity as neutrality, since he denies that (economic) science can be neutral. According to Bromley, this interpretation of objectivity as neutrality still prevails within the community of orthodox economists (Bromley 1991, 207-216). Bromley's rejection of positivism is not a rejection of scientific objectivity. His interpretation of objectivity is, however, problematic.

[4] In his reaction to my analysis of his writings, Bromley argues that the social welfare function and the social utility function are merely economistic metaphors for thinking about whose interests count in a policy, and what goods and services enter into calculation of well being. It is, he writes, an economic way of thinking, but it is not meant to impose economistic criteria.

Bromley distinguishes between the objectivity of the scientist and the objectivity of the science (Bromley 1989, 233; 1991, 223). In his view, the former is a feasible possibility. With regard to the latter, Bromley is ambiguous. The former depends on the extent to which independent investigators can reach similar conclusions about the correspondence of theory and reality (Bromley 1989, 232; 1991, 221). And independent investigators are deemed to reach this similarity on condition that they operate in an 'exemplary, serious, and well-intentioned manner', i.e.

> as *neutral* and as unpremeditated as possible (Bromley 1989, 231-232; the italics are mine).

To conclude, in Bromley's view, an objective *scientist* is a "neutral" scientist. His or her neutrality makes it possible that other neutral scientists will perceive and interpret the world in the same way. Neutrality here refers, according to Bromley, to

> high standards of observation, interpretation and synthesis (Bromley 1991, 226).

This "neutrality" is the opposite of what Bromley calls propagandistic ideology.

Bromley defines the objectivity of the science as a combination of consistency, coherence and correspondence. In Bromley's view, a scientific paradigm (i.e. the shared belief system of scientists) can be consistent - logically valid - and coherent - comprehending all of the phenomena to which it claims relevance - without having something to do with truth.

> An argument can be valid by the rules of logic and still have no connection with the real world;·validity says nothing about truth content (Bromley 1991, 206).

Therefore, in order to guarantee the objectivity of the science, one has to move from internal concerns - consistency and coherence - to external matters, i. e. the problem of concordance.

> Concordance is a matter of how closely a model or theory corresponds to the world it purports to explain (Bromley 1991, 206).

The concrete content of objectivity as, among other things, concordance differs depending on whether one deals with what Bromley calls a 'theory science' or a 'policy science' (Bromley 1989, 231-232; 1991, 221-222). Theory science in economics

> is about discovering what existing theory needs in order that it might more accurately model human interactions,

while policy science in economics

> is about discovering what individuals and groups want (or need) such that they might more easily fulfil their goals and objectives (Bromley 1989, 232).

The objective end product of theory science is the best possible abstract representation of what goes on in daily life, while the objective end product of policy science is policy recommendations that correspond as good as possible with what the individuals affected by the policy problem want to achieve.

Bromley's rejection of logical positivism and logical empiricism allows him to abandon the idea of one true scientific method (Bromley 1989, 231). This enables him to think of, at least, two kinds of economic sciences, the one called theory science, the other policy science. However, the story does not end here. In Bromley's view the policy science is, after all, dependent upon the success of the theory scientist

> for the very essence of policy science is the received orthodoxy that is the domain of theory science (Bromley 1989, 234).

Bromley's reference to "orthodoxy" as the domain of theory science suggests that Bromley has one true method for theory science and one true method for policy science in mind. Although he concedes that different individuals will choose different segments of reality to study, their investigations are meant to contribute to the growth of economic theory science, which serves as the one and only basis for economic policy science (Bromley 1991, 221). In spite of his reference to Feyerabend's philosophy of science (Bromley 1989, 229), it looks as if Bromley holds implicitly to the idea of one true scientific method for theory science on the one hand and for policy science on the other.

Much of the inconsistencies and ambiguities in Bromley's elaboration of "objectivity" would be resolved, if we would distinguish objectivity from neutrality on the one hand and if we would interpret objectivity as intersubjective consent on the other. My latter suggestion is not at odds with Bromley's interpretation of objectivity. In Bromley's view, "neutrality" is a condition for different investigators to reach the same conclusions with regard to their research object. This means that the most important characteristic transforming statements into scientific statements is that they receive independent scientists' common consent. Common consent - or intersubjective consensus - is the criterion; "neutrality" - a neutral scientist is an unpremeditated, non propagandistic scientist - is deemed the means to realise that criterion. According to Bromley himself, however, scientists can never be "neutral" in the sense that the concepts, theories and methods they use are part of a paradigm. Each paradigm implies a lot of - not necessarily consciously - normative, i.e. non-neutral, choices. (Think, for instance, of Bromley's own analysis of the normative choices an economist unavoidably has to make in order to distinguish between means and ends.)

The distinction Bromley implicitly makes between non-neutrality in the first sense of propagandistic ideology and in the second sense of paradigmatic ideology is rather artificial and unclear. For that reason, I propose to drop the distinction and to accept that neutrality is not a feature of scientific objectivity. One can at most distinguish between normative choices that do and others that do not carry off (conscious or unconscious) common consent. The former constitute "objectivity", the latter are a departure from it.

Distinguishing between objectivity and neutrality releases Bromley from distinguishing between the objectivity of the scientist on the one hand and of the science on the other. Neither the scientist, nor the science can be neutral, though both can be objective. Bromley's distinction is untenable, anyway, since testing the so-called "correspondence" of a theory with reality comes down to reaching intersubjective consensus concerning the adequacy of a model. Consequently, the "objectivity" of a science cannot be separated from the "objectivity" of a scientist. Both kinds of "objectivity" are always simultaneously checked: the objectivity of a theory is a check for the objectivity of the theorist and *vice versa*.

Moreover, recognition of the non-neutrality of objective science prevents scientists from thinking of theories as simply "corresponding" to reality. In this sense, the objectivity of economic theory does not guarantee "truth" (or correspondence between the model and reality), with its connotations of uniqueness and universal validity. Different scientists do not only choose different segments of reality to study, as Bromley acknowledges (Bromley 1991, 221). Their choices at the same time originate from a specific perspective, from specific underlying value ideas. Consequently, developments within a specific discipline do not automatically result in what Bromley calls a growth of science (Bromley 1991, 221). They can also result in different - objective, but differently non-neutral - disciplinary theories[5].

3 DESCRIPTIVE

Bromley strongly objects to the orthodox inclination to prescribe the policy objective. He spends ample room to demonstrate the (propagandistic) "ideology" of conventional economics. Part of this ideology is (allocative or productive) efficiency as an 'objective truth rule' (Bromley 1991, 12). By objective truth rule Bromley refers to the twin ideas that economic objectivity implies allocative efficiency and that this efficiency consequently is, at least according to economists, the correct thing to strive for, both for the economist and the politician. According to Bromley, the intellectual tradition of economics as a policy science is dominated by the notion that the task of the economist is to indicate what ought to be done in the name of economic efficiency and Pareto optimality (Bromley 1989, 232-235). Conventional economists hold that the proper policy objectives are given by the conceptual foundation of benefit-cost analysis, i.e. welfare economics and the criterion of a potential Pareto improvement. Under this approach there is only one objective, namely to increase net national income. "Efficiency" is interpreted as allocative (or productive) efficiency. Bromley objects that allocative efficiency is neither objective nor necessarily the correct decision-rule for public policy.

With regard to his former judgement, I can only partly agree. I agree that allocative efficiency is not a value-free criterion. Bromley himself analyses, through an overview of the history of economic science, the many normative choices inherent in the concept (Bromley 1991, 207-216). I do not agree, however, that allocative efficiency necessarily contradicts scientific objectivity. The value judgements underlying the concept of allocative efficiency – e.g. the belief in the primacy of

[5] In one passage, where he speaks of 'multiple ways of knowing' and of truth as 'both relative and elusive', Bromley seems to recognise this (Bromley 1993a, 838).

individual preferences and in the Pareto principle (Bromley 1989, 2) – are part of the paradigmatic ideology of welfare economics. Hence, they carry off the consent of all economists converted to this paradigm. Allocative efficiency is indeed part of "objective" science, in the sense that it boasts intersubjective consensus, at least within the community of consenting (orthodox) economists[6].

With regard to Bromley's latter judgement (regarding efficiency as a decision rule for public policy), I fully agree. The problem is, however, that, given the value judgements underlying the orthodox economic paradigm, conventional economics cannot but recommend public authorities on allocative efficiency, since it is the only kind of insights in economic reality it is able to offer. Either public authorities' objective is allocative efficiency and in that case orthodox economists have something to offer. Or their objective differs from allocative efficiency and then they are at loss for words[7]. I will explain further on that one cannot simply separate the values underlying a political objective from the values underlying a paradigm. Policy science is not a technical application of theory science; one and the same theory science cannot be used for whatever political objective. Paradigmatic ideology inevitably switches to propagandistic ideology – without changing its content – as soon as science is used as a policy toolbox.

Since Bromley objects to the idea that economic scientists prescribe political objectives, he wants economists - as policy scientists - to place their theories in the service of the objectives as defined through collective action.

> [T]he objective policy scientist should be the last to denigrate those objectives of the citizenry that do not happen to accord with the economist's view that people should do what is "efficient". After all, if economics is serious about the sanctity and autonomy of the individual then it does seem somewhat inconsistent to disregard the wishes of those affected by collective choice as unscientific and to advocate, instead, the Pareto rule. Simply put, it is logically inconsistent to venerate individual preferences as expressed through volitional choice in markets, but to denigrate and to discount individual preferences as expressed through collective action. The economist as policy scientist is concerned with problem solving and helping to do what is desired by those affected by the particular event under consideration, not with advocating what is said to be right by the postulates of welfare economics (Bromley 1989, 234).

In Bromley's view, it is – as I mentioned already in subsection 1 – empirically observable political objectives that should function as a criterion to evaluate the

[6] Bromley's quotation of Harberger precisely is an illustration of the latter's endeavour to keep the consensus within a community of economists intact. 'About this time, Arnold Harberger, in a self-admitted tract, felt compelled to reassure the timid, and to bolster the irresolute. Fearing that there was potentially corrosive diffidence among applied economists, Harberger offered the "Three Basis postulates for Applied Welfare Economics" [...]. There he noted, with some apparent concern, "In an era when literally thousands of studies involving cost-benefit analysis or other types of applied welfare economics are underway at any given moment, the need for an accepted set of professional standards for this type of study should be obvious. [...]"' (Bromley 1991, 214).

[7] I cannot hold back the following amusing quotation (which at the same time confirms my statement): '[...] when the neo-classicist starts pontificating on proper social policy motivated on Pareto-efficiency grounds I understand that to be related to the drunk searching for his misplaced car keys under the street light, not because he dropped them there, but because that happens to be the place where there is enough light to see' (Bromley 1985, 782).

social and ecological performance of an economy and its institutional change. To conclude, according to Bromley, policy scientists should keep to description, not prescription of policy objectives. Though I agree with Bromley that an ecologically relevant science should describe rather than prescribe, I do not unequivocally agree that political objectives should be the subject matter of such scientific description.

Bromley's proposal to fall back on empirically observable political objectives is problematic in two respects. First, whose political objectives should be taken into consideration? The political objectives a "descriptive" policy scientist looks for can either be those of decision makers (Bromley 1989, 234-236) or of the people affected by a policy (Bromley 1991, 223). In both cases, Bromley acknowledges the inherent normative choice. This choice regards who is deemed the appropriate mouthpiece of political objectives.

Second, can an investigation of political objectives be separated from a search for scientific instruments? Bromley suggests in some passages that political objectives and scientific instruments can be separated.

> [...] in policy science the economist must first ask (or determine) the goals and objectives of those affected by a policy, an activity that requires the greatest possible level of objectivity, and then objectively draw on theory to propose which avenues will maximize the chances of attaining those objectives (Bromley 1991, 223).

A few passages later, however, Bromley admits that it is not always easy to maintain a sharp distinction between policy objectives and policy instruments. Therefore, he recommends the policy analyst

> to become involved in the policy process in a way that will facilitate the dialectic evolution of both policy objectives and policy instruments (Bromley 1991, 227).

The problem manifest in the latter quotation is the lack of transparency with regard to the values underlying both paradigmatic ideologies and political objectives. I, therefore, proposed, in section 4.2 of the previous chapter, to drop the political means/ends dichotomy and to accept that politics is about institutional arrangements *tout court*. In section 1, I proposed to accept that evaluating the social or ecological performance of an economy and of its institutional change is a political, not a scientific matter.

To conclude, I agree with Bromley that economists have a descriptive rather than prescriptive task. Contrary to Bromley, I claim that this task relates to (the social and ecological performance of) the institutional organisation of existing economies, not to political actors' non-transparent and continuously changing set of values.

4 EXPLANATORY

In section 2, I mentioned that Bromley indicates three aspects of scientific objectivity, namely consistency, coherence and correspondence. These aspects are deemed to contribute to "adequate" models of economic reality (Bromley 1991, 8, 54, 57). According to Bromley, the adequacy of the models depends more on the accuracy and complexity with which they "reflect reality", than on the accuracy of their predictions.

> In contrast with much predictive work in which the reality of our assumptions may be less important than the accuracy of our estimates, prescriptive economics demands that our models be an accurate reflection of reality (Bromley 1991, 57)[8].

Theory science aims, according to Bromley, at an accurate abstract representation of what goes on in daily life, while policy science aims at policy recommendations that correspond accurately with what the individuals affected by the policy problem want to achieve. To reach the intended "accuracy" Bromley starts with conceptual analysis (with regard to phenomena such as institutions, property rights, collective choice, and political objectives) (Bromley 1989, 32; 1991, 8, 170).

Bromley's stress is on explanation rather than on prediction. On the one hand, Bromley argues time and again that economists have to look for cause-effect relationships rather than for mere correlation or for symptoms (Bromley 1989, 232; Bromley 1991, 131, 168). To understand or to explain an economy means to know cause-effect relationships. On the other hand, Bromley warns us for the limited predicting ability of (conventional) economics.

> Our models are most rigorous when concerned with incremental change within a constant institutional setup (Bromley 1991, 79).

What it means to look for cause-effect relationships (rather than for mere correlation or for symptoms) is a question that, in my opinion, Bromley does not answer sufficiently. I already mentioned earlier that one can discern in Bromley's writings two domains of economic analysis: the domain of social and ecological performances of institutional arrangements constituting an economy, and the domain of institutional changes. With regard to the former domain, Bromley thinks of cause-effect relationships as relationships between institutions and (social/ecological) outcomes.

> The linkage between institutions, patterns of interaction, and outcomes provides a model of cause and effect (Bromley 1989, 250).

I wonder the accuracy of reading the relationship between institutions and outcomes as a cause-effect relationship. Suppose that we take economic activities as an analytical starting point. Economic activities show at the same time institutional and social/ecological dimensions. Institutions on the one hand and social/ecological performances on the other are dimensions of economic activities, rather than the latter being an effect of the former and the former being a cause of the latter.

With regard to the latter domain, Bromley thinks of changing economic conditions – new scarcities, new technological opportunities, new distributions of income or wealth, or new tastes and preferences (Bromley 1989, 110) - as causes of changing institutional arrangements.

---

[8] In order to make the terminology used in the previous quotation consistent with my terminology, I suggest to replace the term "prescriptive" by the terms "normative" or "non-neutral".

> Just as [...] institutional arrangements will determine the nature and scope of commodity transactions, the economic conditions at any moment will be important in determining the institutional transactions that will occur, and hence the institutional arrangements that will emerge (Bromley 1989, 110).

Note that the meaning of the verb "determine" is ambiguous in the above quotation. In its first meaning the term only refers to the meaning of institutions. Institutions are the regularising aspect of economic activities, of which commodity transactions are a subset. Institutions thus distinguish between (or "determine") those activities that are compatible with the ensemble of rules – i. e. the "nature and scope" of institutionally admitted commodity transactions - and those that are not. In its second meaning the term refers to a (cause-effect?) relationship that extends in time. First in time, we have changing economic conditions, and later in time we get altered institutional arrangements. If we accept that there exists such a "relationship in time" – which is more than mere correlation - between economic conditions and institutional arrangements, is it correct to refer to it as to a cause-effect relationship? In section 4.2 of chapter 7, I explained that, according to Bromley, no existing model of institutional change is able to capture the "rationality" of institutional changes. This suggests that economic conditions can at most retrospectively – in a historic sense (see section 2.3 in chapter 4) - be indicated as "causes" and institutional changes as "effects". Political processes are an interface between both. The event-like character of these processes prevents us from thinking about the "relationship in time" between conditions and changes in regular , i.e. natural-law-like, terms. Economics of institutional change is - should therefore be - at most about explanation, not about prediction[9].

Bromley's stress on explanation rather than prediction (and my argument that economists' description should regard the social or ecological performance of an economy, not political actors' non-transparent and continuously changing objectives) suggests that we should drop the dichotomy between theory science and policy science. In Bromley's view, policy science is an application of theory science. Stated differently, policy science is meant to (descriptively) record political objectives, while theory science is a non-propagandistic toolbox policy scientists make use of to offer suitable policy recommendations. A recognition of the non-neutrality and of the limited predictive capacity of theory science implies, on the contrary, a recognition that the insights provided by theory science can only contribute to a limited range of political objectives, and that these insights cannot simply be transformed into instruments. A particular theory only suits particular political objectives. And particular political objectives ask for a particular theory. The relevance of an economic theory for public policy depends on the compatibility between the value ideas underlying both. Since, moreover, these value ideas can never be completely transparent, economic insights cannot be translated into political instruments as if it were a simple technical matter. For that reason, I

[9] Though the following quotation makes me hesitate whether my interpretation conforms to Bromley's: 'The next step will be to develop general equilibrium models that allow us to explain and assess institutional change such that the circularity of "efficiency" is avoided' (Bromley 1997, 54).

suggested, in section 2.3. of chapter 4, that ecological economics should not aim at providing public authorities with "instruments" in order to allow them to realise their political objectives as efficiently as possible. They should rather aim at providing them with "insights" into actual institutional reasons for the non-realisation of their political objectives. The development of policy "instruments" out of scientific "insights" is a political, not a scientific matter. It rests on a lot of - often implicit - normative, and hence typically political, choices concerning a desirable future, not on a scientific extrapolation of the *status quo*.

5 (IM)PARTIAL

As mentioned in section 2.2.2 of chapter 7, property regimes define the rights and privileges various "owners" of one and the same valuable asset have (and the concomitant duties and non-rights of non-owners). Rights and privileges define economic actors' autonomy. They do not define choice sets yet. Choice sets are sets of actions that economic actors can take given their relative income on the one hand and the costs of the actions on the other. To what extent economic actors can realise their autonomy depends on their (economic) power. In section 1.3 of chapter 3, power was defined as the capacity of Alpha to create voluntarily a new legal relation affecting Beta. Miners have, for instance, economic power if they succeed in buying rights to their future labour power from their mine owners. (Economic) power thus depends on the initial distribution of income and on the magnitude of the costs – transaction costs and costs of the rights to be bought -. Bromley's ecological economics does not supply insights into institutional reasons for the initial distribution of income. It offers insights into institutional reasons for economic actors' autonomy; it does not offer insights into institutional reasons for economic actors' economic power.

Initial distributions of wealth only provide us with a picture of economic power at a given moment in time. Economic actors have, however, an interest in not letting their relative economic power decrease over time. Their relative economic power depends on how distributions of wealth evolve, i.e. of the nature, magnitude and (un)certainty of the benefit streams economic actors' can draw from their valuable assets. I suppose that economic rationality relates to economic actors' interest in not letting their relative economic power decrease. The concrete content of this rationality depends on institutional definitions of benefit streams. Bromley's ecological economics does not provide insights into institutional definitions of benefit streams either.

In section 2.1.2 of chapter 3, I explained, with the help of some examples offered by Bromley, that institutional contexts enforce some preferences and weaken others. I suppose – I am putting out feelers - that it is institutional definitions of benefit streams that define which private preferences are institutionally enforced and which are institutionally weakened. In other words, I suppose that it is institutional definitions of benefit streams that define the actual social and ecological performance of our economies. In order to show the plausibility of my supposition, I will develop the following example. Farmers had, until recently, been institutionally stimulated to augment their production so that their products became at the same time cheaper. The institutional context in which farmers were deemed to produce more and cheaper reflected farmers' presumptive right – their privilege – to pollute, for instance, via the residues of pesticides used or via the overabundance of manure. Recently political preferences, however, changed. These changes urged for institutional transactions resulting in a new institutional context that reflects at the same time farmers duty not to pollute and their duty to produce ever more and ever cheaper. Consider now present farmers. They can at the same time have a preference not to pollute and a preference to pollute. The former preference is stimulated by entitlements expressing farmers' duty not to pollute. The latter preference is stimulated by (a whole set of) entitlements reflecting farmers duty to produce ever more and ever cheaper. The present institutional context thus shows institutional tensions that, until now, enforce farmers' preference to pollute and weaken farmers' preference not to pollute. The ultimate question thus seems to be what institutional reasons exist for the political preference to let farmers produce ever more and ever cheaper. Or, considered from the power perspective, whose relative wealth position is supported by – who draws the largest benefit streams from - the institutional organisation that reflects the political preference in question.

Since Bromley's approach can explain neither momentary nor evolving distributions of income and, hence, of economic power, I evaluate his ecological economics as partially impartial. It is impartial because his analysis of property rights and property regimes allows us to understand – to a certain extent – the relationships between the institutional organisation of an economy and the definition of private interests. It is impartial because it allows us, in other words, to abstract – to a certain degree - from existing private interests. It is not completely impartial because it does not offer insights into institutional definitions of benefit streams and, hence, into institutional reasons for the enforcement of particular preferences, i.e. into institutional reasons for the actual social and ecological performance of our economies.

6 CONCLUSION

In order to explain the nature of Bromley's ecological economics, I had to translate some of the concepts he uses into my terminology. In section 1, I showed that Bromley admits the paradigmatic non-neutrality of ecological economics and that he repudiates its propagandistic non-neutrality. I object that one cannot make a clear distinction between both kinds of non-neutrality. Science's paradigmatic non-neutrality transforms into propagandistic ideology as soon as scientific knowledge is technically used for public policy. Bromley tries to justify the non-neutrality of ecological economics by defending that the values constituting its normative perspective should result from empirical observations. I object – and here I agree with Weber - that non-neutral science cannot and should not be justified thus.

In section 2, I dealt with Bromley's argument that economic science should be objective. Bromley's (residual) logical positivist idea that objectivity implies neutrality causes him to wrestle with the meaning of objectivity. I argue that a recognition of the distinction between objectivity and neutrality on the one hand and an interpretation of objectivity as intersubjective consensus on the other solves much of the problems the concept causes to Bromley. This distinction relieves Bromley from distinguishing between the objectivity of the scientist and of the science. It allows, moreover, to consider a multiplicity of objective, but differently non-neutral sciences. I agree with Bromley that "consistency" and "coherence" contribute to intersubjective consensus and, hence, to objectivity. I consider "correspondence" as a separate aspect rather referring to explanatory than to objective science (see section 4).

In section 3, I commented on Bromley's objections to conventional economists' inclination to prescribe the political motive for institutional change. In order to offset this inclination, he argues that political actors can have several motives and he distinguishes, with the help of economic metaphors, between four types of motives. Though I fully agree that political actors can have several motives for institutional change and that it is not the economist's task to prescribe them, I reject Bromley's classification of motives for two reasons. This classification stems from Bromley's endeavour to define political objectives in a way that respects empirical reality (i.e. from his endeavour to justify his normative perspective scientifically). I object, first, that his endeavour necessarily fails, since it denies the nature of politics. Politics is about institutional arrangements *tout court*, not about objectives on the one hand and means to realise them on the other. Institutional arrangements rather than objectives are the domain of politics. They are momentary reflections of a non-transparent and continuously changing set of values, motives or objectives. I object, second, that economists do not need to define political actors' political motives since ecological economics should provide public policy with insights, not with recommendations.

In section 4, I argued that, though Bromley's stress is on explanation rather than prediction, his keeping on to the (political) means/ends dichotomy brings him on the slippery slope of recommending institutional changes. I argue that economists cannot simply recommend institutional changes, because the values underlying both economic paradigms and political objectives are not transparent and are, consequently, not necessarily compatible with each other. It is economists' task to provide political actors with insights, rather than instruments (or recommendations). Bromley's stress on explanation, not prediction, supports this viewpoint with regard to scientific knowledge related to the social or ecological performance of economies and, even stronger, with regard to scientific knowledge related to reasons for institutional change. The latter knowledge is, indeed, of a historical kind.

In the final section 5, I suggested that, due to his concentration on property rights and property regimes, the insights Bromley offers us into the relationships between the institutional organisation of an economy and the content and distribution of private interests are restricted. Bromley provides us with insights into institutional reasons for economic actors' autonomy, not into institutional reasons for economic actors' actual strategies. Actual strategies depend on economic actors' trial to keep their relative economic power intact. And relative economic power depends on initial and changing distributions of income and, hence, on the institutions defining benefit streams. I assume that it is the latter kind of institutions that are decisive for economic rationality. Since Bromley's ecological economics does not pay attention to these institutions, I evaluate its nature as partially impartial.

CHAPTER 9

CONCLUSIONS

I started this book rather provocatively. My initial thesis was that, for the sake of sustainability, economists should improve their political influence. Economists can improve their political influence in many ways. One way is, for instance, to practise the political skills needed to become a successful political actor in favour of particular economic viewpoints. Another way is to ameliorate the dialogue between economists and citizens and professional politicians, or between economists and scientists from other disciplines. Both ways are valuable. In order to solve the problem of sustainability, we need, indeed, a combination of insights, taken from various natural and social sciences. Economic science cannot provide all necessary insights on its own. In order to ameliorate the political impact of economics, it is, indeed, helpful that economists practise some political skills. In the introductory chapter, I explained, however, that, in this book, I choose neither of these two ways. I am, instead, questioning whether current economic paradigms are well equipped to provide political actors with the economic knowledge they need to tackle the problem of sustainability.

In this book, I did not intend to create a new economic paradigm. My purpose was to develop, in the first part of the book, norms for an ecologically successful economic science. By an "ecologically successful economic science" I mean, to begin with, an economic paradigm that is able to offer us the knowledge needed in order to contribute in a fundamental way to the problem of sustainability. I mean, further, an economic paradigm of which the nature is such that it can have a real political impact. In the second part of this book, I put these norms to the test by comparing them with the theoretical work of David Pearce and Daniel Bromley respectively. Both authors are exemplary economists. They both represent different positions within the field of economic science. Pearce's work is rather in the tradition of environmental economics; Bromley's work is rather in the tradition of ecological economics. This confrontation of the norms developed with the theoretical work of Pearce and Bromley can tell us several things. It can learn us whether these norms are feasible, depending on the extent to which they are already realised in existing economic paradigms. It can learn us, moreover, in which way and to which extent the respective work of Pearce and Bromley can contribute to political solutions for the problem of sustainability.

1 NORMS FOR AN ECOLOGICALLY SUCCESSFUL ECONOMICS

What are the starting points from which to develop norms for an adequate economic paradigm? To begin with, we should define the problem of sustainability (subsection 1.1). We should, further, reflect on the nature of politics (section 1.2). A conceptual analysis of (economic) action tells us that institutions are crucial entities. They are, at the same time, politically defined and conditioning the ecological performance of an economy (subsection 1.3). From these three starting points, we can develop norms for both the *content* and the *nature* of an ecologically successful economics. An ecologically successful economics should offer us *substantive* knowledge concerning *institutional reasons* for the *unmanageability* of the ecological performance of *industrial* economies (subsection 1.4). It should provide political actors with *insights* rather than *instruments*, i.e., with objective, descriptive, explanatory and impartial knowledge (subsection 1.5).

1.1 The Problem of Sustainability

Pezzey recapitulated the general ecological tendencies of our industrial economic history. These general tendencies are growing use of energy, decreasing bio-diversity and growing appeal on the assimilative capacity of ecological systems. Typical for this ecological evolution of our industrial economies is that it gives rise to problems that are often global in space, long-term in time and with an uncertain and possibly irreversible impact on human well-being. In other words, present generations cause problems that, until now, they did not prove to be able to manage reassuringly and that, hence, are left to their descendants. This inability prevents present generations from acting as responsible citizens towards future generations. For responsibility presupposes manageability. This observation of our defective responsibility for the ecological future of our descendants is at odds with our sense for intergenerational justice. I consider this to be the essence of the problem of sustainability. Consequently, with respect to the problem of sustainability, an economic paradigm will provide adequate knowledge on condition that it helps us to take our responsibility again. In other words, an economic paradigm will provide adequate knowledge on condition that it enables present generations to manage the ecological impacts of their own economic actions without loading future generations with uncertain and possibly irreversible, unwanted consequences.

To conclude, I consider the problem of sustainability as a problem of defective responsibility: present generations did, until now, not prove to be able to manage the ecological impacts of present economic actions on future generations. These ecological impacts are of a specific kind: they cause problems that are often global in space, long-term in time, uncertain, possibly irreversible and unwanted according to present standards. I assume, moreover, that these ecological impacts relate to the nature of our industrial economies.

1.2 Politics

We cannot discern in human reality something like an economic or a political sphere just like that. In order to perceive these spheres, we have to construct them. Political theories on the one hand and economic theories on the other are such conceptual constructs. Theories, as conceptual constructs, are never neutral. They are value-laden perspectives on a particular domain of human reality. Consequently, various conceptual constructs with regard to the same domain of human reality can occur at the same time.

From a brief overview of the history of economic theory, I constructed four entries that constitute possible perspectives on the economic sphere: decision units, rationality, products, institutions. The fourth entry can be considered an overarching one. These same entries can also be used to constitute perspectives on the political sphere. Many economists, however, seem to doubt whether the economic and the political sphere should be distinguished from each other. A comparison between the political theory of Buchanan and Arendt tells us that doubts do not arise with respect to the first and the third entry. Economic and political actions are commonly considered to take place in specific (economic or political) "decision units" and to create specific "products", either commodities or (legalised) institutions. Doubts arise concerning the rationality of economic and political action. According to Buchanan, the rationality of political action does not differ from the rationality of economic action. According to Arendt, on the contrary, both economic and political action show their own typical rationality. Economic rationality is conventionally represented in the metaphor of *homo oeconomicus*. The political philosophy of deliberative democracy describes (a normative ideal for) political rationality.

I argue that we should follow Arendt. We should confirm a typical economic as well as a typical political rationality. (This implies that we can and should distinguish between the economic and the political sphere. This does not imply that both spheres can always and easily be separated.) Economic rationality is a concrete version of an economising rationality. Economic actors act autonomously in order to satisfy their private preferences as good as they can. Economising rationality is a kind of instrumental rationality. Abstract *economising* rationality becomes concrete *economic* rationality within a particular institutional context. Political rationality is a matter of creative deliberation between politically free and equal individuals. It aims at defining and redefining the institutions of a human society. It aims, more particularly, at defining and redefining the institutions conditioning autonomous economic action.

We should follow Arendt because a deliberative democracy is better equipped to deal with the problem of sustainability than is Public Choice theory, for two reasons. To start with, a deliberative democracy leaves room for a typically political – i.e., creative and democratic - interpretation of the ideal of "sustainability". It does not reduce the ideal prematurely to the economic ideal of optimal allocation. A deliberative democracy does, further, not straightforwardly resign to political power relationships. It contradicts an interpretation of politics as a bargaining process between vested interests. It tries to offset vested interests by making institutional reasons for them visible.

To conclude, we should distinguish between the political and the economic sphere. This distinction confirms that the economic and the political sphere both have their own typical "products", "decision-units" and "rationality". A comparison between the political theories of both Buchanan and Arendt shows that disagreement concerning the nature of the political and economic sphere relates especially to the "rationality" of economic and political actions. The rationality of the economic sphere is commonly represented in the metaphor of *homo oeconomicus*. Arendt's analysis of political rationality gave rise to the normative ideal of a deliberative democracy. Arendt's interpretation of politics is more fruitful to contribute to the problem of sustainability than is Buchanan's (economic) interpretation of it.

1.3 Institutions

My search for an ecologically successful economics led me up to institutions as crucial entities. I define an institution as a *social rule* (in singular) guiding people's actions and the *folk views* justifying and explaining the rule and its relevance in a particular situation. This definition considers institutions as the symbolic dimension of human actions. This symbolic dimension of human actions is the counterpart of their ecological (or physical or material) dimension. This particular definition, which connects one institution with one social rule, has the advantage that it allows us to distinguish between economic and non-economic institutions, to order institutions in a hierarchy and to classify types of (economic) institutions.

Institutions guide people's actions. They restrict and enable action in a double way. First, one party's restriction corresponds to another party's liberation. Second, institutions define people's degrees of freedom or their autonomy. Institutions make people free by limiting their freedom. Institutions do not simply coerce, they liberate simultaneously.

Bromley distinguishes between conventions and entitlements. Conventions depict self-policed institutions. Entitlements (or laws) are politically recognised and enforced institutions. Institutions as entitlements are thus *political* entities. They come into existence as the often unintended result of intentional interaction. As such, they correspond to Arendt's interpretation of "interaction things" as unpredictable, irreversible and not really "made".

Institutions as entitlements, finally, are "public facts" in the double sense that they result from political interaction and that they hold for all members of a political community. (The latter does, however, not exclude that institutional rights can be assigned to either an individual, a group or to all members of a polity.) I introduced the concept "public fact" to distinguish institutions from "public goods". Public facts are political entities, while public goods are economic entities.

My argument to distinguish between the political and the economic sphere urges me not only to reflect on institutions in general, but also to define *economic* institutions. Depending on the entry used, economic institutions are institutions that define economic decision units, economic rationality or economic products. I follow Bromley in his argument that two kinds of institutions defining economic decision units can be distinguished. The first kind defines an economic decision unit versus another economic decision unit. The second kind defines the internal organisation of an economic decision unit. I follow Schmid in his argument that economic goods consist of both an ecological and an institutional dimension. It is the institutional dimension that defines a thing as either a private or a public economic good. This institutional dimension itself is, what I called previously, a public fact.

I strongly lean on Bromley to discuss the institutions defining economic rationality. From Bromley's reflections on the two examples of a Prisoner's Dilemma and a Prisoner's Dream, we learn two things. First, we learn that the choices economic actors make cannot be equalled to their preferences. Choices are not revealed preferences. They are strategies chosen to satisfy their private preferences as good as they can given the existing institutional organisation of an economy. Different institutional arrangements urge people to choose different strategies in order to satisfy their same private preferences. From this observation, I conclude that the ecological performance of an economy does not only depend on the private preferences individuals hold, but also on the institutional organisation of an economy. Second, we learn that the conventional (neo-classical) interpretation of economic rationality comes down to economising (or simply instrumental) rationality. The conventional interpretation is too abstract to provide us with insights into the ecological performance of an economy. Only within a specific economic context, i.e., within a specific institutional organisation of an economy does abstract *economising* rationality become concrete *economic* rationality.

Embroidering on the two examples offered by Bromley, we still get more insights into the relevance of an institutional analysis of an economy. To start with, we learn to understand institutional arrangements as reflections of *public preferences* for the protection of particular *private choice sets* (and, hence, of particular private preferences). Institutions as public preferences do not simply protect existing private preferences. Between existing private preferences and institutions as reflections of public preferences lie political processes that transform given and/or create possible private preferences. Politics is not simply a matter of bargaining; it is a matter of deliberating and of judging. This interpretation of institutions as reflections of public preferences shows that it makes sense to look for an institutional expression of the public preference for sustainability. We learn, further, that institutional arrangements stimulate some private preferences and temper others. This implies that to understand the ecological performance of an economy in the long run, we do not really need to know the private preferences of separate individuals. It suffices to know an economy's institutional organisation. This is another way to say that an internal relationship exists between the ecological performance of an economy and its institutional organisation. This latter conclusion supports my research question: it shows that it makes sense to look for institutional reasons for (the seemingly unmanageability of) the ecological performance of our industrial economies. The observation, finally, that institutional arrangements can either stimulate or temper either egoistic or altruistic private preferences suggests that it is not necessary for public authorities to adopt a moralising attitude in order to convert egoistic economic actors to ecologically benign behaviour. Public authorities should rather create the institutional conditions for sustainable economic practices.

The distinction I make between the political and the economic sphere clarifies the particular link between both spheres. (Economic) institutions are the entities that condition the ecological performance of economic action. Economic institutions as entitlements are at the same time the "interaction-things" following from political action. This link explains the kind of hierarchy that exists between the political and economic sphere. Politically defined institutions are preconditions for economic actions. They enable economic actions and they restrict them at the same time. This kind of hierarchy is a logical one: politically defined institutions are logically prior to economic actions.

1.4 The Content of an Ecologically Successful Economics

Typical ecological problems gave rise to, what is called, the problem of sustainability: problems that are long-term in time, global in space, uncertain, possibly irreversible and unwanted according to present standards. These problems are typical for **industrial economies**. Until now, we did not prove to be able to manage them so that we do not load the ecological impacts of our industrial economies on future generations any longer. Therefore, I argue that the content of economics should be such that it enables present generations to manage the ecological impacts of their industrial economies again. Or, in other words, the content of economics should be such that it allows present generations to take their responsibility towards future generations.

In order to be able to take our responsibility, we need to know **reasons** for the present unmanageability of the ecological performance of our industrial economies. Only knowledge of reasons will allow us to look for fundamental answers to - rather than fight symptoms of - the problem of sustainability. Without knowledge of reasons, political actions can at most by accident contribute in a fundamental way to solutions for the problem of sustainability.

Our interpretation of the political and the economic sphere shows that institutions are crucial entities. Economic institutions link the political with the economic sphere. On the one hand, economic institutions condition economic actions. On the other hand, economic institutions (as entitlements) are politically defined. Consequently, in order to contribute to political solutions, economics should provide us with knowledge concerning **institutional reasons** for the problem of sustainability. Embroidering on Bromley's reflections on the Prisoner's Dilemma and Prisoner's Dream, our hypothesis that an internal relationship exists between the institutional organisation and the ecological performance of an economy gets confirmed. This implies that it really makes sense to look for *institutional reasons* for the *present unmanageability* of the ecological performance of *industrial economies*.

Knowing institutional reasons for the problem of sustainability implies that we need to know the **institutional whole** of an economy. We cannot be contented with knowledge of separate economic institutions. We need to know the ecological performance of the *ensemble of economic institutions* conditioning a *particular economic action* rather than the ecological performance of a particular economic institution. We need to know the *aggregate* ecological performance of the *ensemble of economic institutions* conditioning the *ensemble of economic actions* within an industrial economy rather than the ecological performance of separate economic actions.

Knowing the institutional whole of an industrial economy can look a task that is too huge and, hence, impossible. Two approaches within the tradition of economic science show us ways in which this task can adopt feasible proportions. First, the idea that the problem of sustainability relates to industrial economies, suggests that it suffices to look for **dominant** institutions. Dominant institutions are institutions that are most pervasive in space and persistent in time. In order to trace dominant institutions, we have to look for order hierarchies. According to Ramazzotti, an order hierarchy is a substantive one. It focuses on the effects of institutional rules. The extension of an institution's effect defines its rank in a particular order hierarchy. A genetic hierarchy, on the contrary, is a formal one. Its concern is not with the content of institutions, i.e. with the direct effects that they exert on their fields of action. It is with the procedures to be followed and with the level of the hierarchy that must deal with specific fields of actions.

Second, next to a hierarchical approach, we can take a classificatory approach. We can aim for a **classification** of economic institutions. We can try to classify various economic institutions according to their respective contribution to the ecological performance of industrial economies.

To recapitulate, **the content of an ecologically successful economics should regard institutional reasons for the present unmanageability of the ecological performance of industrial economies. An adequate economics should provide us with knowledge concerning the particular ecological performance of a classification of dominant institutions.**

1.5 The Nature of an Ecologically Successful Economics

An ecologically successful economics is an economics that is politically influential. Economics is politically influential with respect to the problem of sustainability in case it helps political actors to decide on institutional transformations that make industrial economies more sustainable. Given my interpretation of politics as a deliberative democracy, deciding on desirable institutional transformations is not a matter of technically deriving adequate institutions from scientific knowledge. It is a matter of providing political actors with the knowledge they need to stimulate – rather than replace – political debates concerning a desirable and feasible institutional organisation of a sustainable economy. Scientific **insights** succeed better in this respect than do scientific *instruments*.

Scientific insights are empirical regularities made comprehensible. They are perspectivistic, i.e., value-laden descriptions of human reality. Scientific descriptions aim at **objectivity**. Close reading of Weber's writings suggests that objectivity comes down to intersubjective consent. Logic and mathematics can contribute to such consent. They are, however, neither necessary nor sufficient. Consequently, economic science is not necessarily of a "pure" kind. It can be of a historical kind as well. Objectivity as intersubjective consent cannot guarantee a complete separation between facts and values. Objectivity remains, hence, unavoidably non-neutral.

Economic insights should **explain** past and present relationships between the institutional organisation of an economy and its ecological performance. It should not, as economic instruments implicitly do, *predict* these relationships. For politically created regularities are not necessarily extrapolations of past and present ones. An explanatory economics aims at conceptual constructs of human reality that make more and more regularities comprehensible. It does not merely aim at a logically consistent and mathematically rigorous system of "laws". This suggests that an economics fulfilling the political role of a muse shows more resemblance with historical than with mathematical sciences.

Economic insights should, moreover, aim at *non-neutral* **descriptions** of past and present relationships. Non-neutral descriptions especially foster political debates when the perspective taken is not straightforwardly evident. Economic knowledge should not, as economic instruments unavoidably do, *prescribe* the values to which future relationships should respond.

A politically successful economics should, finally, ameliorate the quality of political interaction. This quality depends on the political freedom and political equality of citizens and professional politicians. In order to ameliorate political freedom, economic knowledge should offer insights into the relationships between the definition and distribution of private interests on the one hand and the institutional context on the other. Such insights enable people to imagine a desirable institutional organisation of society as a precondition for a desirable definition and distribution of private interests. In order to support political equality, economics should inform us on economic sources of unequal political power relationships. Economics should, in one word, be **impartial** rather than *partial*.

To conclude, my specific interpretations of politics, institutions and the problem of sustainability prompt me to propose **four norms for the nature of an ecologically relevant and politically successful economics: objectivity, explanation (rather than prediction), description (rather than prescription) and impartiality**. The metaphor of economics as a political muse (rather than as a toolbox for public policy) recapitulates the intention of these four norms. **Economics should provide political actors with *insights* rather than *instruments*.** Such insights should help political actors to create and recreate an economic order of which they deem the ecological performance dignified both for present and future generations.

2 MUTUALLY TESTING NORMS AND ECONOMIC PARADIGMS

2.1 The Problem of Sustainability

My interpretation of the problem of sustainability – abstract though it is – is not straightforwardly compatible with Pearce's. Pearce's interpretation of the problem of sustainability is thoroughly influenced by his neo-classical way of thinking. The neo-classical perspective prompts Pearce to consider the problem of sustainability as a problem of allocative efficiency. It is true that, in his view, the boundary conditions for the criterion of allocative efficiency can vary. Either Pearce holds on to his ethical starting point that present generations should keep their natural capital constant. In that case, he can be classified as an adherent of the "strong sustainability" criterion. A constant level of natural capital (expressed in physical terms) is then the boundary condition for an efficient allocation of scarce natural resources among both present and future generations.

Or Pearce weakens his "strong sustainability" criterion. For the criterion of a constant level of natural capital is, indeed, difficult to make operational. What does a constant level of natural capital mean? Does it mean that its total physical amount may not change? Or that the physical amount of separate natural resources may not change? Or does it mean that the total economic value of natural capital should remain constant? Or the total economic value of each separate natural resource? And which of all separate natural resources should we take into consideration? Anyhow, Pearce's welfare-economic approach easily tempts him into translating the originally physical meaning of the concept "constant natural capital" into monetary terms. In line with the neo-classical paradigm, such translation relies on people's private preferences for particular natural resources, not on a reasoned consideration of their ecological meaning for present or future human societies. Such translation, based on individuals' private preferences and expressed in monetary terms, transforms the concept "sustainability" from a "strong" into a "weak" version. In case of "weak sustainability", the boundary condition of allocative efficiency is no longer a constant natural capital expressed in physical terms, but the institutional organisation of an economy that conditions individuals' economic preferences. "Weak sustainability" comes then down to the old-fashioned economists' concept of "optimality".

According to Beckerman, weakening the "strong sustainability" criterion into a "weak sustainability" criterion makes the whole idea of sustainability redundant. For "sustainable development" then simply comes down to increasing the (monetary) level of well-being. Since the "weak sustainability" criterion is based on people's

private preferences for natural resources, it has no built-in barriers against ecological tendencies that arise from present generations' private preferences, but that are possibly damaging for future generations. That is the reason why I called Pearce's interpretation of sustainability not straightforwardly compatible with the interpretation I propose.
According to Bromley, the conventional metaphor of sustainability as allocative efficiency, either with strong or weak boundary conditions, fails for another reason. It fails because intergenerational allocative efficiency is impossible. Present generations cannot allocate the right quantity and quality of (natural and man-made) capital to the generations living now and in the future. For the idea of allocative efficiency requires that future generations express their private preferences for particular natural resources. The essential problem of sustainability as a problem of allocative efficiency is that we do not and cannot know what those in the future would wish for us to do. This is not a mere problem of uncertainty or of risk. It is a problem of necessarily lacking information. For that reason, Bromley repudiates an interpretation of "sustainability" as a problem of efficient allocation. This interpretation is, in his view, no more than a scientific fiction.

There is another reason why the metaphor of sustainability as allocative efficiency is misleading. In chapter 4, I argued that economists' interpretation of the concept "allocative efficiency" is ambiguous. At times, it is used as an independent criterion referring to the extent that economic actors succeed in satisfying their private preferences, given their income, given the transaction costs they have to pay and given their bounded rationality. Since economic actors' private preferences are not known, but revealed on markets, bystanders cannot but conclude that the outcome of market processes are Pareto-optimal. The only thing economists can do, not as bystanders but as participants, is extending individuals' bounded rationality, so that these individuals satisfy their private preferences better than before. This independent interpretation of the concept "allocative efficiency" can at most refer to economic actions taking place *within* the existing institutional organisation of an economy. At times, however, the concept is used as a standard with which to evaluate the (ecological or social) performance *of* an economy. I agree with Bromley (see chapter 7) that this interpretation of the concept is not correct, because the meaning of efficiency is dependent on the existing institutional organisation. Since allocative efficiency only gets its concrete meaning *within* an institutional organisation, it cannot be used to evaluate the performance *of* an institutional organisation. In order to evaluate the performance *of* an economy one necessarily relies on an independent criterion other than allocative efficiency. Therefore, because it is our evaluation of the ecological performance *of* industrial economies that gives rise to the idea of sustainability, sustainability cannot be a simple matter of allocative efficiency. Implicitly, sustainability must always refer to another standard as, for instance, Pearce's criterion of a (physically) constant natural capital.

The problem with this "strong sustainability" criterion is – apart from the fact that it is not clear how to make it operational - that, until now and despite economists' and other scientists' recommendations, we did not prove to be able to stop general tendencies of declining natural capital. Despite international political agreements and despite huge technological efforts, CO_2-emissions are, for instance, still rising, total energy use is increasing, and bio-diversity is decreasing.

In line with his institutional approach, Bromley proposes another interpretation of the concept "sustainability". In his view, the problem of sustainability is a problem of a suitable economic order. Prior to the problem of allocative efficiency lies the problem of how to construct an economic order that provides a socially acceptable provisioning program for those living now and in the future. This economic order cannot claim to leave future persons exactly the domain of choice they would select for themselves. This order can at most claim to be a reflection of what *we* deem to be so valuable that it is worth to be left to our descendants. In order to help us clarify what an economic order that is valuable enough to leave it to future generations means, Bromley proposes a Rawlsian veil of ignorance. He concludes – initially at least - that suitable institutional arrangements must be thus that they mean an entitlement of *duty* for the present and *right*, protected by an inalienability rule, for the future, rather than the present situation of *privilege* for the present and *no right* for the future.

Bromley's (initial) institutional conception of sustainability still is very abstract. It leaves room for many interpretations. It is, nevertheless, fundamental in at least one respect. Contrary to the conventional metaphor of (weak) sustainability, it is compatible with my interpretation that the problem of sustainability is a problem of defective responsibility with respect to the ecological impacts of present economic actions on future generations. Restoring our responsibility implies that we aim at making our present ecological problems manageable, so that we do not load future generations with unknown and perhaps unacceptable risks. This is what I consider to be the meaning of present generations having duty and future generations having inalienable right. The fundamental political message implicit in Bromley's initial conception of sustainability is to construct an economic order of which the ecological performance does not cause problems for future generations that are uncertain, possibly irreversible and unacceptable according to our own standards.

Unfortunately, Bromley qualifies his initial interpretation of sustainability. For reasons of efficiency, he deems it, on second consideration, sufficient to protect the right of future generations with a liability rule. This qualification shows that even Bromley is not immune for the ambiguity of the concept "allocative efficiency". As Bromley argued earlier, efficiency cannot be a measure to evaluate and define specific institutions, since it is a particular ensemble of institutions that is a measure for (the concrete meaning of) efficiency.

Bromley's initial conception of sustainability does not necessarily imply a (physically) constant level of natural capital. The idea of a constant level of natural capital suggests that we can define a level that present and future generations are able to manage safely. Even stronger, since, with regard to particular natural resources, we are afraid that we already crossed this safe border, the idea of a constant level of natural capital suggests that we can define and return to an *optimal* level that is just safe for present and future generations. In my view, not only does the suggestion that scientists are able to define optimal levels of natural resources testify of (natural-)scientific *hybris*. The suggestion that politicians are able to manage the ecological performance of economic activities and keep it at optimal levels testifies of even worse (social-)scientific and political arrogance. Bromley's proposal to look for an economic order that provides a socially acceptable provisioning program can be interpreted in a way that is much more attractive than the constant-natural-capital idea. It can be interpreted in a way that respects the nature of our extensive, but nevertheless restricted scientific capacities and in a way that respects and stimulates our creative, democratic freedom.

2.2 Politics

Neither Pearce nor Bromley distinguish clearly between political and economic action. This does, nevertheless, not imply that their interpretation of politics is the same in all respects. Pearce's interpretation of politics resembles more on Buchanan's interpretation of it than on Arendt's. Institutional change comes, in his view, down to adding institutions to the existing set of institutions constituting an economy. In order to define the institutions to add, one should first ask for people's private preferences. For, according to Pearce, political democracy is about respecting and aggregating individuals' private preferences. These private preferences emerge *within* a particular institutional context. They do not emerge from public debates and are, consequently, not fit to express views *on* a desirable institutional organisation. These preferences should, moreover and whenever possible, be expressed in monetary terms. Expression in monetary terms facilitates the aggregation of private preferences. To recapitulate, in Pearce's view, the political definition of institutional change rests on economic calculation.

Bromley's interpretation of politics is more ambiguous than is Pearce's. On the one hand, he refuses to distinguish between economic and political action. This becomes manifest in his classification of institutional transactions (i.e., implicit rights transfers) as a kind of economic activities. On the other hand, he objects to the conventional interpretation of institutional change as a change in function of allocative efficiency. Even stronger, his comments on other trials to grasp the rationality of economic change suggest that his interpretation shows more resemblance with Arendt's interpretation (institutional change as an unpredictable political event) than with Buchanan's.

2.3 The Content of an Ecologically Successful Economics

Both Pearce's and Bromley's scientific endeavour is meant, in a certain sense, to "manage" the ecological performance of our economies. However, the way both consider of this "managing" activity is different. The difference relates to the various ways in which they regard the relationship between an economy and its ecological performance.

Pearce regards this relationship as an external one. This means that he understands an economy as a kind of system with an input and an output of natural resources and of waste. Inputs and outputs can be regulated through institutional adaptations of the economy, i.e. trough adding institutions to or replacing some of the institutions of the existing set of institutions constituting an economy. These adaptations are a matter of trial-and-error, because Pearce's welfare economics cannot explain scientifically the ecological performance of the existing set of institutions constituting an economy itself. According to Pearce, the latter kind of scientific knowledge is impossible. Pearce rejects the idea of an "existence theorem". He considers scientific investigations of the internal relationships between an economy and its ecological performance as a premature undertaking. Pearce is contented with "monitoring" the ecological performance of existing economies. He, therefore, proposes an ecological Input-Output analysis and introduces a Materials Balance Model. Both instruments are meant to record the amounts of natural resources used and of waste produced. Pearce's welfare economics is then considered a toolbox that provides professional politicians with economic instruments – i.e. with institutions such as taxes, subsidies or Command-and-Control measures - to keep the use of resources and the production of waste at a particular (politically decided or scientifically calculated) level. In other words, Pearce's welfare economics is considered a toolbox that provides political actors with recommendations for institutional adaptations. These institutional adaptations are meant to internalise ecological "externalities".

To recapitulate, in Pearce's view, investigating institutional reasons for the ecological performance of our industrial economies is a premature and even unfeasible venture. Rather than providing political actors with institutional reasons for the present unmanageability of the ecological performance of our industrial economies, he provides them with institutional adaptations. According to Pearce, trial-and-error will learn us how to adapt our institutions gradually so that ecological externalities, made explicit in an ecological Input-Output Model or a Materials Balance Model, get finally internalised.

Contrary to Pearce, Bromley regards the relationship between an economy and its ecological environment as an internal one. This internal connection becomes manifest in his treatment of externalities. In order to explain Bromley's line of reasoning, we should first explain the particular subject matter of Bromley's theoretical work.

Bromley concentrates his analysis on property rights as one type of economic institutions and on property regimes. On closer consideration, property regimes prove to be a hierarchical set of property rights referring to a particular valuable asset. It is a particular property regime that defines a particular valuable asset as an economic commodity. Such a property regime connects, at the same time, a hierarchy of "owners", either public authorities, groups or individuals. Property regimes condition the economic autonomy of owners (and non-owners) with regard to the valuable asset in question. Ownership is not a matter of absolute, but of relative control.

Property regimes thus define a "thing", either a physical object or an intangible skill, as an economic commodity. Conventionally, economists distinguish between private and public commodities. A private commodity is a valuable asset to which a private property regime is attached, while a public commodity is a valuable asset to which a public property regime is attached. Bromley's analysis of four types of property regimes – private, common, state and open access – suggests, however, that these types are analytically not sharp. The distinctions between the four types are rather gradual than strict and, consequently, the classification of economic commodities as either public or private results more from convention than from inherent institutional characteristics of the commodity in question. This observation prompts me to argue that, instead of distinguishing between different types of property regimes, it is analytically more precise to investigate what rights related to one and the same valuable asset belong to a particular group, subgroup or to particular individuals. In order to solve particular ecological problems, one should, consequently, not spend too much energy discussing whether a common or a private property regime is more effective. One should rather spend energy discussing the concrete content and the respective owners of the rights that should constitute the property regimes that relate to the ecological problem in question.

Bromley's analysis of externalities is an illustration of this latter statement. Bromley argues that the kind of externalities that occur, and whether these externalities get solved or not (and to what extent) depends on institutional arrangements. Externalities are manifestations of (ecological or social) interdependence or interference. Though all "autonomous" actions interfere ecologically or socially with other "autonomous" actions, not all situations of interference are externalities. Whether ecological interference is considered an externality depends on whether the costs of the interference passed on to the other party are deemed legitimate given existing legal arrangements. The term "externality" is reserved for situations of ecological (or social) interference that burden second parties with legally legitimate costs. Only those situations of interference that are deemed legally legitimate can be considered externalities. Hence, the kind of externalities that will occur depends on existing institutional arrangements.

Whether and to what extent an externality will be solved within a specific economic situation depends on who must pay the (transaction) costs in order to get a solution that is acceptable to all parties, the magnitude of these costs, and whether the injured party is able to pay the costs. Part of the answer to these questions depends on the operational rule with which a specific property right is protected. Entitlements can be protected either by property rules, by liability rules or by inalienability rules. Consequently, whether and to what extent externalities will be solved depends, in its turn, also on existing institutional arrangements.

Bromley's analysis of externalities is illuminating. Nevertheless, I argue that we should make a sharper distinction between an externality and an interference. An externality is a situation of legally legitimate (ecological or social) interference that (momentarily) gives rise to (either real or hypothetical) monetary costs. Within a particular institutional organisation of an economy, externalities get, by definition, resolved at an optimal level. This does however not imply that the ecological or social interference gets resolved at a (politically or socially) acceptable level.

I argue that a more accurate definition of the concept "externality" can set ecological problems sharper. It shows, first, that viewing an interference as an externality implies a translation into economic terms and, in case of a conventional scientific approach, making solutions dependent on the institutional organisation of an economy. This means that one translates a political problem (a problem concerning the institutional organisation of an economy) into an economic one (a problem asking for a "rational" solution from within existing institutional arrangements). Second, it shows that welfare theory cannot offer (objective) policy prescriptions since externalities get, by definition, solved within an economy (on a Pareto-efficient level). The only thing welfare theory can do is either to offer direction to individual economic agents for judging their bargains or to propose government interventions – i.e. institutional changes - that transform Pareto-irrelevant interferences into Pareto-relevant ones, so that the level of interference will shift.

In Bromley's view, ameliorating an economy's ecological performance is about discussing the best possible combination of private and public commodities. Apart from the fact that I question the dichotomy "private" *versus* "public" commodity, I do not fully agree with Bromley. I argue that ameliorating an economy's ecological performance is about discussing which ecological interests we deem private and which we deem public. It is, in other words, about discussing our public or political preferences for the best combination of private and public ecological rights. The former kind of ecological rights are rights that economic actors should transfer explicitly *within* the given institutional organisation of an economy. The latter kind of rights are rights that are legally protected and hold for all members of a political community, independent of their income. They result from implicit rights transfers. I admit that the realisation of both these rights can be met with the help of economic commodities, either "private" or "public". (And private rights are not necessarily met with "private" goods, nor are public rights necessarily met with "public" goods – whatever this may signify.) However, I suppose that these rights are not necessarily met with the help of economic commodities. I suspect that, with regard to some rights, one can imagine a different institutional organisation of an economy in which the rights in question do not get endangered. Consequently, in this alternative economy, these rights do not need private nor public protection (and, hence, neither "private" nor "public" commodities to realise them). In order, however, to imagine such alternative economies, we need more insights into the relationships between an economy and its ecological performance than Bromley's analysis of property rights and property regimes can offer us.

According to my interpretation, the problem of sustainability refers to our defective capability to manage the global, long-term, uncertain and possibly irreversible impacts of a growing use of energy, a declining bio-diversity and an increasing appeal on the assimilative capacity of ecosystems. I argue, in the introductory chapter, that these general ecological tendencies relate to the industrial organisation of our economies. Typical for industrial economies is that production processes become more and more "roundabout" and that the circulation velocity of commodities accelerates. Bromley's analysis of property rights and property regimes cannot explain these developments. Property regimes are sets of institutions defining economic "products". As such they define some boundary conditions of economic actors' autonomous actions. They thus define *possible*, *individual* ecological performances. They do, however, not explain why the *ensemble* of *actual* economic actions shows the pattern mentioned. In order to explain the latter, I suggest that Bromley's analysis should be complemented with an analysis of the institutions defining economic "rationality". In chapter 3, I argue further, based on an elaboration of Bromley's examples of the Prisoner's Dilemma and the Prisoner's Dream, that a particular institutional organisation can stimulate specific private preferences and temper others. Which preferences are stimulated and which are tempered depends, on closer consideration, on the future benefits one can expect from satisfying one or another preference. From this, I conclude that the institutions defining future benefit streams are decisive for understanding (concrete) *economic* - rather than mere *economising* – rationality or, in other words, for a better understanding of the general ecological performance of industrial economies.

To recapitulate, Bromley's analysis of property rights and property regimes makes the hypothesis that an internal relationship exists between the institutional organisation and the ecological performance of an economy more concrete. It illustrates that it makes sense to investigate institutional reasons for the ecological performance of an economy. From Bromley's analysis we learn that property regimes are manifestations of an institutional hierarchy. This hierarchy is of a genetic kind. Bromley's analysis does not inform us on order hierarchies. Consequently, it does not provide us with knowledge concerning the institutions that are dominant within our industrial economies. From his analysis we learn, moreover, that property regimes can explain possible, individual economic actions. They cannot explain the aggregate ecological performance of industrial economies. I suggest that, in order to get this aggregate performance explained, we need an analysis of another type of institutions, namely institutions defining benefit streams. While *property regimes* transform valuable assets into *economic commodities*, *institutions defining benefit streams* transform abstract economising rationality into more concrete *economic rationality*.

2.4 The Nature of an Ecologically Successful Economics

Pearce aims at objectivity, but he does not expect this objectivity to be neutral. Objectivity is, in his view, realised with the help of empirically observable data and a logically consistent and mathematically rigorous system of laws. Pearce has no problem with acknowledging the non-neutrality of the Pareto-criterion and of his (particular) translation of "sustainability" into "sustainable development". He deems this non-neutrality, however, justified. He deems the ideal of "sustainable development" justified, because, according to him, that is what (most) people aim at. He deems the Pareto-criterion justified, because no convincing arguments exist to prefer another value to the value of Pareto-optimality. I do not contest that Pearce's environmental economics is, in a certain sense, objective. I do, however, not agree that the non-neutrality of his environmental economics is justified, for three reasons. First, in order to make the ideal of "sustainable development" operational, Pearce has to make several normative choices that do not necessarily correspond to political actors' choices. Second, the fact that most people aim at "sustainable development" – how can Pearce be so sure of that? - does not yet justify this perspective. Third, whether or not convincing arguments exist to prefer another value to the value of Pareto-optimality is something that should become clear in the course of political deliberations.

Pearce considers his environmental economics as a toolbox for public policy. This interpretation causes Pearce on many occasions to stop acting as a descriptive scientist and to start acting as a prescriptive politician in disguise. Allocative efficiency, for instance, is, according to Pearce, an all-embracing objective of ecological policy and a main standard with which to judge actual politics. This interpretation causes Pearce, moreover, to be rather concerned with prediction than with explanation. Pearce is not interested in explaining the internal relationships between the institutional organisation of an economy and its ecological performance. He is rather interested in monitoring the ecological in- and outputs of an economy, in making an inventory of the monetary values people impute to ecological entities, and in prescribing economic instruments that manage people's behaviour as effective and as efficient as possible. Pearce's environmental economics is rather of an "exact" than of a "historical" kind.

Finally, Pearce's welfare-economic approach is a partial science. It does not offer scientific insights into economic power relationships nor into the relationships between the institutional organisation of an economy and the definition and distribution of private interests. Instead of inviting political actors to abstract from their private interests, it stimulates them to stress the interests they happen to have. Instead of providing political actors with insights that offset existing power relationships, it re-enforces the idea that politics is a bargaining process between various parties with given power and given interests.

I judge Pearce's approach as a manifestation of scientific *hybris*, for several reasons. If we really are prepared to operate at optimal levels, it does not only require from natural scientists continuous efforts to define and redefine what levels of all kinds of possibly relevant natural resources are "optimal" – i.e., maximal and just safe. It also requires that economics is successful enough to manipulate economic actors' individual behaviour and keep the aggregate of separate economic activities below the decided on optimal level. And, last but not least, it requires that political actors are docile enough to take over economists' recommendations. Considering economists' often heard complaints with respect to the latter and considering the ongoing general evolution of growing energy use, of declining bio-diversity and of increasing pollution, this scientific *hybris* seems to be misplaced. At the same time, Pearce's scientific approach is, in a certain sense, too humble. For Bromley's institutional analysis shows that we can gain at least some insights into the internal relationships between an economy and its ecological performance.

Like Pearce, Bromley wrestles with the idea of a non-neutral but objective economics. Bromley agrees that economics should be objective. Objectivity is, in his view, a matter of consistency, coherence and correspondence. At the same time, he recognises that objective economics cannot simply be equalled to neutral economics. Economics is, in his view however, not allowed to be non-neutral in whatever way. Bromley admits paradigmatic non-neutrality and repudiates propagandistic non-neutrality. I object that one cannot make a clear distinction between both kinds of non-neutrality. The paradigmatic non-neutrality of economics transforms into propagandistic non-neutrality as soon as economics is used as a toolbox for public policy. Due to positivist remnants in Bromley's interpretation of objectivity, he feels obliged to distinguish between the objectivity of a science and the objectivity of a scientist. I suggest that an interpretation of objectivity as intersubjective consent would relieve him from this distinction. It would, moreover, prompt him to abandon the criterion of correspondence (a theoretical model as a unique and universal representation of reality) and to allow for a multiplicity of objective, but non-neutral economic paradigms.

Bromley does not want to be a prescriptive scientist. He, therefore, develops a classification of political motives that can help him to describe, rather than prescribe, people's political goals. This classification distinguishes between allocative efficiency, redistribution of income, redistribution of economic opportunity and redistribution of economic advantage. I do not support this classification. It stems from Bromley's endeavour to record given political objectives (i.e. from his endeavour - an endeavour that parallels Pearce's - to justify his normative perspective scientifically). I object, first, that his endeavour necessarily fails, since it denies the nature of politics. Politics is about institutional arrangements *tout court*, not about objectives on the one hand and means to realise them on the other. I object, second, that economists do not need to ask for political actors' motives since economics should provide public policy with insights, not with recommendations.

Unlike Pearce, Bromley stresses explanation rather than prediction. Economics should explain a) the relationships between the institutional organisation of an economy and its ecological (or social) performance and b) institutional change. The former analysis rests, in Bromley's writings, mainly on a conceptual analysis of property rights and property regimes. The latter analysis is of a historical kind: it investigates the effects of changing economic conditions – new scarcities, new technological opportunities, new distributions of income or wealth, or new tastes and preferences – on institutional change. Nevertheless, his keeping on to the (political) means/ends dichotomy brings him on the slippery slope of prediction rather than explanation.

Bromley's analysis concentrates on property rights and property regimes. This analysis offers us insights that contribute to our political freedom. For property regimes, this hierarchical set of property rights defining a valuable asset as an economic commodity, condition the private preferences of economic actors, either as "owners" or as "non-owners". This analysis does, however, not offer us sufficient insights into economic sources of political inequality. Relative economic power depends on initial and changing distributions of income and, hence, on the institutions defining benefit streams. Since Bromley's ecological economics does not pay attention to these institutions, I evaluate it as partially impartial.

3 CONCLUSION

This book explores economic science from the perspective of sustainability. This exploration has been an exciting enterprise for me. It has given me the opportunity to make acquaintance with the exemplary writings of both Pearce and Bromley. I have been impressed by the work of both authors. I have been impressed by Pearce's endeavours to introduce the problem of sustainability within the tradition of neo-classical theory. I have come to the conclusion that Pearce's way of thinking dominates (national and international) ecological politics. I have been even more impressed by Bromley's institutional approach of the problem of sustainability. His writings have confirmed my hypothesis that it makes sense to look for institutional reasons for the present unmanageability of the ecological performance of our industrial economies. His institutional approach has, moreover, corroborated my hypothesis that economics is not necessarily of an exact kind in order to be politically relevant. An institutional economics can certainly be a valuable political muse.

This exploration has convinced me, more in general, of the richness of the tradition of economic science. Further philosophical investigations of the writings of still other exemplary economists will certainly deepen my search for an ecologically successful economics. I am convinced that the problem of sustainability awaits many scientists of various disciplines to take up this challenge.

REFERENCES

Arendt, H. (1958). *The Human Condition*. Chicago/London: The University of Chicago Press.

Arendt, H. (1961). *Between Past and Future*. New York: Viking Press.

Ayres, R. U. (1978). *Resources, Environment and Economics*. New York: Wiley.

Beckerman, W. (1996 [1995]). *Small is Stupid. Blowing the Whistle on the Greens*. London: Duckworth.

Beekman, V. (forthcoming) *A Green Third Way? Philosophical Reflections on Government Intervention in Non-Sustainable Lifestyles*

Bernstein, R. (1986). Rethinking the social and the political. *Graduate Faculty philosophy Journal*, 11 (1), p. 111-130.

Bernstein, R.J. (1989 [1983]). *Beyond Objectivism and Relativism. Science, Hermeneutics, and Praxis*. Philadelphia: University of Pennsylvania Press.

Boulding, K.E. (1966). The Economics of the Coming Spaceship Earth. In: H. Jarrett (ed.), *Environmental Quality in a Growing Economy*, Baltimore: The John Hopkins Press, p. 3-14.

Brennan, G. (1993). The contribution of economics. In: R.E. Goodin & Ph. Pettit (eds.), *A Companion to Contemporary Political Philosophy*, Oxford (UK)/Cambridge (USA): Basil Blackwell, p. 123- 156.

Briassoulis, H. & van der Straaten, J. (eds.) (1999^2). *Tourism and the Environment*. Dordrecht/Boston/London: Kluwer Academic Publishers.

Bromley, D.W. (1976). Economics and Public Decisions: Roles of the State and issues in Economic Evaluation. *Journal of Economic Issues*, 10 (4), p. 811-838.

Bromley, D.W. (1978). Property Rules, Liability Rules, and Environmental Economics. *Journal of Economic Issues*, 12 (1), p. 43-60.

Bromley, D.W. (1985). Resources and Economic Development: An Institutionalist Perspective. *Journal of Economic Issues*, 19 (3), p. 779-796.

Bromley, D.W. (1989). *Economic Interests and Institutions. The Conceptual Foundations of Public Policy*. New York (USA)/Oxford (UK): Basil Blackwell.

Bromley, D.W. (1991). *Environment and Economy. Property Rights and Public Policy*. Cambridge (USA)/ Oxford (UK): Basil Blackwell.

Bromley, D.W. (1993a). Institutional Economics Revisited: Discussion. *American Journal of Agricultural Economics*, 75, p. 837-839.

Bromley, D.W. (1993b). Reconstituting Economic Systems: Institutions in National Economic Development. *Development Policy Review*, 11 (2), p. 131-151.

Bromley, D.W. (1994). Choices without prices without Apologies. *Journal of Environmental Economics and Management*, 26 (2), p. 129-148.

Bromley, D.W. (1995a). Development reconsidered: The African challenge. *Food Policy*, 20 (5), p. 425-438.

Bromley, D.W. (1995b). Property rights and natural resource damage assessments. *Ecological Economics*, 14, p. 129-135.

Bromley, D.W. (1997). Constitutional Political Economy: Property claims in a dynamic World. *Contemporary Economic Policy*, 15, p.43-54.

Bromley, D.W. (1998). Searching for sustainability: The poverty of spontaneous order. *Ecological Economics*, 24, p. 231-240.

Buchanan, J.M. (1986). *Liberty, Market and State. Political Economy in the 1980s*. Wheatsheaf Books.

Cartwright, N., Cat, J., Fleck, L. & Uebel, T.E. (1996). *Otto Neurath: Philosophy between Science and Politics*. Cambridge: Cambridge University Press.

Christensen, P.P. (1989). Historical roots for ecological economics - Biophysical versus allocative approaches. *Ecological Economics*, 1, p. 17-36.

Common, M. (1988). 'Poverty and Progress' revisited. In: D. Collard, D.W. Pearce & D. Ulph (eds.), *Economics, Growth and Sustainable Environments*, New York: St. Martin's Press, p. 15-39.

Commons, J.R. (1968 [1924]). *Legal Foundations of Capitalism*. Madison: University of Wisconsin Press.

Commons, J.R. (1934). *Institutional Economics*. New York: MacMillan.

Daly, H.E. (1996). *Beyond Growth. The Economics of Sustainable Development*. Boston: Beacon Press.

Davis, L.E. & North, D.C. (1970). Institutional change and American economic growth: a first step towards a theory of institutional innovation. *Journal of Economic History*, 30, 131-149.

De Beus, J.W. (1989). *Markt, democratie en vrijheid. Een politiek-economische studie. (Market, democracy and freedom. A political-economic investigation.)* Zwolle (NL): Tjeenk Willink.

De Wilde, R. (1989). De relativiteit van sociaal-wetenschapelijke kennis. (The relativity of social-scientific knowledge.) In: M. Korthals (ed.), *Wetenschapsleer. Filosofisch en maatschappelijk perspectief op de natuur- en sociaal-culturele wetenschappen* (*Theory of science. A philosophical and societal perspective on the natural and social-cultural sciences*), Meppel: Boom, p. 112-133.

Dietz, F.J. & Van der Straaten, J. (1992). Rethinking Environmental Economics: Missing Links between Economic Theory and Environmental Policy. *Journal of Economic Issues*, 26 (1), p. 27-51.

Dietz, F., Hafkamp, W. & van der Straaten, J. (1994). *Basisboek milieu-economie*. Amsterdam/Meppel: Boom.

Dugger, W.M. (1979). Methodological Differences between Institutional and Neoclassical Economics. *Journal of Economic Issues*, 13 (4), p. 899-909.

Dutch Committee for Long-Term Environmental Policy (1994). *The Environment; Towards a Sustainable Future*. Dordrecht: Kluwer Academic Publishers.

Environmental Balance Sheet 1998. [WWW document] http://www.milieubalans.rivm.nl/inl_samen/sheet.html

Faber, M., Manstetten, R. & Petersen, Th. (1997). Homo oeconomicus and homo politicus. Political economy, constitutional interest and ecological interest. *Kyklos*, 50 (4), p. 457-483.

Funtowicz, S.O. & Ravetz, J.R. (1994a). The worth of a songbird: ecological economics as a post-normal science. *Ecological Economics*, 10, p. 197-207.

Funtowicz, S. & Ravetz, J.R. (1994b). Emergent complex systems. *Futures*, 26 (6), p. 568-582.

Goodin, R.E. (1996). *The Theory of Institutional Design*. Cambridge (US) etc.: Cambridge University Press.

Gremmen, B. (1999). The justification of the application of science. In: M. Fehér, O. Kiss & L. Ropolyi (eds.), *Hermeneutics and Science*, Kluwer Academic Publishers, p. 315-323.

Gutmann, A. (1993). Democracy. In: R.E. Goodin & Ph. Pettit (eds.), *A Companion to Contemporary Political Philosophy*, Oxford (UK)/Cambridge (USA): Basil Blackwell, p. 411-430.

Hardin, G. (1968). The Tragedy of the Commons. *Science*, 162, p. 1243-1248.

Jackson, T. (1998). The Unfinished Symphony. An Evolutionary perspective on the Conception of Sustainable Development. (Paper presented to the second Conference of the European Society for Ecological Economics, Geneva, 4th - 7th March 1998)

Hanley, N., Hallett, S. & Moffatt, I. (1990). Why is more notice not taken of economists' prescriptions for the control of pollution? *Environment and Planning* A, 22, p. 1421-1439.

Hemerijck, A.C. (1994). De politiek van de economie. *Beleid & Maatschappij*, ? (5), p. 229-245.

Keynes, J.N. (1917). *The Scope and Method of Political Economy*. London: A.M. Kelley.

Korthals, M. (ed.) (1989). *Wetenschapsleer. Filosofisch en maatschappelijk perspectief op de natuur- en sociaal-culturele wetenschappen* (*Theory of science. A philosophical and societal perspective on the natural and social-cultural sciences*), Meppel: Boom.

Lewis, D. (1986). *Convention: a Philosophical Study*. Oxford: Basil Blackwell.

Martinez-Alier, J. (with Klaus Schlüpmann) (1990 [1987]). *Ecological Economics. Energy, Environment and Society*. Oxford (UK)/ Cambridge (US): Basil Blackwell.

Mulberg, J. (1995). *Social Limits to Economic Theory*. London: Routledge.

Munda, G. (1997). Environmental Economics, Ecological Economics, and the Concept of sustainable Development. *Environmental Values*, 6, p. 213-233.

Neale, W.C. (1987). Institutions. *Journal of Economic Issues*, 21 (3), p. 1177-1206.

Neale, W.C. (1994). Institutions. In: G.M. Hodgson, W.J. Samuels & M.R. Tool (eds.), *The Elgar Companion to Institutional and Evolutionary Economics* A-K, Aldershot: Edward Elgar, p. 402-406.

Nelissen, N., van der Straaten, J. & Klinkers, L. (eds.) (1997). *Classics in Environmental Studies*. Utrecht: International Books.

Nelson, R.H. (1987). The Economics Profession and the making of Public Policy. *Journal of Economic Literature*, 25, p. 49-91.

Neurath, O. (1912). The problem of the pleasure maximum. In: ES, p. 113-122.

Neurath, O. (1913a). The lost wanderers of Descartes and the auxiliary motive. In: PP, p. 1-12.
Neurath, O. (1913b). Über die Stellung des sittlichen Werturteils in der wissenschaftlichen Nationalökonomie. In: GPMS, p. 69-70.
Neurath, O. (1916). On the classification of systems of hypotheses. In: PP, p. 13- 31.
Neurath, O. (1917). Das Begriffsgebäude der Wirtschafslehre und seine Grundlagen. In: GPMS, p. 103-129.
Neurath, O. (1918). Josef Popper-Lynkeus, seine Bedeutung als Zeitgenosse. In: GPMS, p. 131-136.
Neurath, O. (1919a). Utopien. In: GPMS, p. 137-138.
Neurath, O. (1919b). Through war economy to economy in kind. In: ES, p. 123-157.
Neurath, O. (1921). Anti-Spengler. In: ES, p. 158-213.
Neurath, O. (1922). Weltsozialismus. In: GPMS, p. 203-208.
Neurath, O. (1928). Personal life and class struggle. In: ES, p. 249-298.
Neurath, O. (1929). Wissenschaftliche Weltauffassung: der Wiener Kreis [The Scientific Conception of the World: The Vienna Circle]. In: ES, p.299-318.
Neurath, O. 1930). Ways of the scientific world-conception. In: PP, p. 32-47.
Neurath, O. (1930/31). Einheitswissenschaft und Marxismus. In: GPMS, p. 369-370.
Neurath, O. (1931a). Physicalism: the philosophy of the Viennese circle. In: PP, p. 48-51.
Neurath, O. (1931b). Physicalism. In: PP, p. 52-57.
Neurath, O. (1931c). Empirical sociology. The scientific content of history and political economy. In: ES, p. 319-421
Neurath, O. (1931d). Sociology in the framework of physicalism. In: PP, p. 58-90.
Neurath, O. (1932). Protocol statements. In: PP, p. 91-99.
Neurath, O. (1934). Radical Physicalism and the 'real world'. In: PP, p. 100-114.
Neurath, O. (1935a). The unity of science as a task. In: PP, p. 115-120.
Neurath, O. (1935b). Pseudorationalism of falsification. In: PP, 121-131.
Neurath, O. (1936a). Individual sciences, unified science, pseudorationalism. In: PP, p. 132-138.
Neurath, O. (1936b). An international encyclopedia of unified science. In: PP, p. 139-144.
Neurath, O. (1936c). Encyclopedia as 'model'. In: PP, p. 145-158.
Neurath, O. (1936d). Physikalismus und Erkenntnissforschung. In: GPMS, p. 749-757.
Neurath, O. (1936e). Einheitswissenschaft. In: GPMS, p. 761-763.
Neurath, O. (1936f). Soziologische Prognosen. In: GPMS, p. 771-776.
Neurath, O. (1937a). Unified science and its encyclopedia. In: PP, 172-182.
Neurath, O. (1937b). Prognosen und Terminologie in Physik, Biologie, Soziologie. In: GPMS, 787-794.
Neurath, O. (1937c). The concept of 'type' in the light of modern logic. In: PP, p. 183-188.
Neurath, O. (1937d). The new encyclopedia of scientific empiricism. In: PP, p. 189-199.
Neurath, O. (1937e). The departmentalization of unified science. In: PP, p. 200-205.
Neurath, O. (1938). Wissen und Sein. In: GPMS, 833-843.
Neurath, O. (1939). The social sciences and unified science. In: PP, p. 209-212.
Neurath, O. (1941). Universal jargon and terminology. In: PP, p. 213-229.
Neurath, O. (1942). International planning for freedom. In: ES, p. 422-440.
Neurath, O. (1944). Grundlagen der Sozialwissenschaften. In: GPMS, p. 925-978.
Neurath, O. (1945). F.A. Hayek, The Road to Serfdom. In: GPMS, p. 979-981.
Neurath, O. (1946a). The orchestration of the sciences by the encyclopedism of logical empiricism. In: PP, p. 230-242.
Neurath, O. (1946b). Prediction and induction. In: PP, p. 243-246.

ES: M. Neurath & R.S. Cohen (eds.) (1973). *Empiricism and Sociology*. Dordrecht: Reidel.
GPMS: R. Haller & H. Rutte (eds.) (1981). *Otto Neurath: Gesammelte philosophische und methodologische Schriften*. Vienna: Hölder-Pichler-Tempsky.
PP: R.S. Cohen & M. Neurath (eds.) (1983). *Otto Neurath. Philosophical Papers* 1913-1946. Dordrecht: Reidel.

O'Connor, M. (1994). Codependency and indeterminacy: a critique of the theory of production. In: M. O'Connor (ed.), *Is Capitalism Sustainable?* Political Economy and the Politics of Ecology. New York/London: The Guilford Press.

O'Hara, S.U. (1996). Sustaining production: material and institutional considerations. (Paper gepresenteerd op het congres van The International Society for Ecological Economics: Designing Sustainability. Building Partnerships Among Society, Business, and the Environment, Boston, 4-7 Augustus 1996)

O'Neill, J. (1994). Preferences, virtues, and institutions. *Analyse & Kritik*, 16 (2), p. 202-216.

O'Neill, J. (1995). In partial praise of a positivist. The work of Otto Neurath. *Radical Philosophy*, 74, p. 29-38.

Ostrom, E. (ed.) (1982). *Strategies of Political Inquiry*. Beverly Hills/London/New Delhi: Sage Publications.

Pearce, D., Markandya, A. & Barbier, E.B. (1989). *Blueprint for a green economy*. London: Earthscan Publications.

Pearce, D.W. & Turner, R.K. (1990a). *Economics of Natural Resources and the Environment*. New York (etc.): Harvester Wheatsheaf.

Pearce, D., Barbier, W. & Markandya, A. (1990b). *Sustainable Development. Economics and Environment in the Third World*. Aldershot: Edward Elgar

Pearce, D. (1993a). *Economic values and the natural world*. London: Earthscan.

Pearce, D.W. & Warford J.J. (1993b). *World without End. Economics, Environment, and Sustainable Development*. Oxford, etc.: Oxford University Press.

Pearce, D., Turner, R.K. et al. (1993c). *Blueprint 3. Measuring sustainable development*. London: Earthscan.

Pearce, D. & Helm, D. (1993d [1991]). Economic Policy towards the Environment: An Overview. In: D. Helm (ed.), *Economic Policy Towards the Environment*, Oxford (UK)/Cambridge (USA): Blackwell, p. 1-24.

Pearce, D. (1999). *Economics and Environment. Essays on Ecological Economics and Sustainable Development*. Cheltenham Glos (UK): Edward Elgar.

Peeters, J. (1997). Duurzame ontwikkeling: contradicties en alternatieven. (Sustainable Development: Contradictions and Alternatives.) In: *Oikos*, 1 (3), p. 51-79.

Pezzey, J. (1992). Sustainability: An Interdisciplinary Guide. *Environmental Values*, 1, p. 321-362.

Ramazzotti, P. (1999). Institutions, Structures and Systems: a Hierarchical Analysis. (paper presented at the 1999 EAEPE (European Association for Evolutionary Political Economy) Conference on "Integration and Inequality", Prague, 4-7 November 1999.)

Reisch, G.A. (1994). Planning science: Otto Neurath and the International Encyclopedia of Unified Science. *British Journal for the History of Science*, 27, p. 153-175.

Robbins, L. (1984 [1932]). *An Essay on the Nature and Significance of Economic Science*. London/Basingstoke: MacMillan.

Samuels, W.J. (1994a). Law and Economics. In: G.M. Hodgson, W.J. Samuels & M.R. Tool (eds.), *The Elgar Companion to Institutional and Evolutionary Economics L-Z*, Aldershot: Edward Elgar, p. 8-12.

Schmid, A.A. (1987). *Property, Power, & Public Choice. An Inquiry into Law and Economics*. New York: Praeger Publishers.

Schuyt, C.J.M. (1986). *Filosofie van de sociale wetenschappen*. (*Philosophy of the Social Sciences*.) Leiden: Martinus Nijhoff.

Snel, F.G. (1996). *De vertaling van wetenschap. Nederlandse sociologie en praktijk*. (*The translation of science. Dutch sociology and practice*.) (Dissertation, Utrecht University)

Swaney, J.A. (1992). Market Versus Command and Control Environmental Policies. *Journal of Economic Issues*, 26 (2), p. 623-633.

Taylor, J.F.A. (1966). *The Masks of Society*. New York: Appleton-Century-Crofts.

Tiles, M. & Oberdiek, H. (1995). *Living in a Technological Culture*. Human Tools and Human Values. London and New York: Routledge.

Turner, R.K., Pearce, D. & Bateman, I. (1994). *Environmental economics. An elementary introduction*. New York (etc.): Harvester Wheatsheaf.

Van der Straaten, J. (1990). *Zure regen. Economische theorie en het Nederlandse beleid*. Utrecht: Jan van Arkel.

Veblen, Th. (1965 [1899]). *The Theory of the Leisure Class*. New York: MacMillan.

Weber, M. (1949). *The methodology of the social sciences*. (transl. and ed. by E.A. Shils, H.A. Finch) New York: The Free Press. (MSS)

Weber, M. (1968[3]). *Gesammelte Aufsätze zur Wissenschaftslehre*. (ed. by J. Winckelmann) Tübingen: J.C.B. Mohr (Paul Siebeck). (GAW)

World Commission on Environment and Development (1987). *Our Common Future*. Oxford: Oxford University Press.

GPSR Compliance
The European Union's (EU) General Product Safety Regulation (GPSR) is a set of rules that requires consumer products to be safe and our obligations to ensure this.

If you have any concerns about our products, you can contact us on

ProductSafety@springernature.com

In case Publisher is established outside the EU, the EU authorized representative is:

Springer Nature Customer Service Center GmbH
Europaplatz 3
69115 Heidelberg, Germany

www.ingramcontent.com/pod-product-compliance
Lightning Source LLC
LaVergne TN
LVHW011800200926
848484LV00003B/742
9781402001659